Mestizo Modernity

Reframing Media, Technology, and Culture in Latin/o America

Mestizo Modernity

Race, Technology, and the Body in Postrevolutionary Mexico

David S. Dalton

Héctor Fernández L'Hoeste and
Juan Carlos Rodríguez, Series Editors

UNIVERSITY OF FLORIDA PRESS
Gainesville

Copyright 2018 by David S. Dalton
All rights reserved
Published in the United States of America

First cloth printing, 2018
First paperback printing, 2021

26 25 24 23 22 21   6 5 4 3 2 1

Library of Congress Cataloging-in-Publication Data
Names: Dalton, David S., author.
Title: Mestizo modernity : race, technology, and the body in
   postrevolutionary Mexico / David S. Dalton.
Other titles: Reframing Media, Technology, and Culture in Latin/o America.
Description: Gainesville : University of Florida Press, 2018. | Series:
   Reframing media, technology, and culture in latin/o america | Includes
   bibliographical references and index.
Identifiers: LCCN 2017060696 | ISBN 9781683400394 (cloth : alk. paper) |
   ISBN 9781683403104 (pbk.)
Subjects: LCSH: Mestizaje—Mexico. | Race awareness—Mexico—History. |
   Indians of Mexico—Mixed descent.
Classification: LCC F1392.M47 D35 2018 | DDC 305.800972—dc23 LC record available
at https://lccn.loc.gov/2017060696

University of Florida Press
2046 NE Waldo Road
Suite 2100
Gainesville, FL 32609
http://upress.ufl.edu

| UF PRESS |
UNIVERSITY
OF FLORIDA

To Ariadna and the kids

Contents

List of Figures viii
Acknowledgments ix

Introduction: (Re)Constructing the Racialized Body through Technology 1

1. Science and the (Meta)Physical Body: A Critique of Positivism in the Vasconcelian Utopia 31

2. Painting *Mestizaje* in a New Light: Racial, Technological, and Cultural Hybridity in the Murals of Diego Rivera and José Clemente Orozco 59

3. Emilio Fernández, Gabriel Figueroa, and the Race for Mexico's Body: Immunization and Lamarckian Genetics 100

4. Colonizing Resistance: Liminal Imperiality in the Cinema of El Santo and in Carlos Olvera's *Mejicanos en el espacio* 140

Conclusion: The Legacy of the Modernization of the Body Today 177

Notes 191
Works Cited 203
Index 229

Figures

1. *Cortés y la Malinche* 69
2. *La conquista de México: Cortés triunfante* 75
3. *La conquista de México: Retrato del francisco* 78
4. *La conquista de México: El caballo mecánico* 80
5. *Pan-American Unity* 85
6. *Mecanización de la tierra* 87
7. *Vaccination* 91
8. *Historia de la medicina en México: El pueblo en demanda de la salud* 94

Acknowledgments

I like to say that writing a book is a solitary endeavor that requires an entire community. This project would not be what it is today without the insight, suggestions, and guidance of numerous colleagues in the field. First and foremost, I wish to extend my gratitude to Stuart Day, whose friendship and support made this project possible. He was always available to talk through difficult concepts, and his comments on this project were so helpful every step along the way. I appreciate the comments and conversations that I had with Rafael Acosta, Jerry Hoeg, Jill Kuhnheim, Luciano Tosta, and Vicky Unruh; without their insights, this book would not be what it is. The seeds for this book were sown in three seemingly unrelated courses that I took from Doug Weatherford, Dale Pratt, and Nichole Hodges Persley. I greatly appreciate the guidance and mentorship that each of them provided.

I've been very fortunate to work with and get to know scholars of two wonderful academic fields: Mexican studies and studies in the fantastic. The support and comments of these colleagues have been very important to helping this project develop. I would like to take a moment to extend a special thank-you to J. Andrew Brown, Justin Castro, Maricruz Castro Ricalde, Benjamin Cluff, Miguel Ángel Fernández Delgado, Ruben Flores, Rebecca Janzen, Hernán Manuel García, Miguel García, M. Elizabeth Ginway, Rachel Haywood-Ferreira, James Krause, Sara Anne Potter, Brian L. Price, Jacob Rapp, Ignacio M. Sánchez Prado, Alexander P. Shafer, Ezekiel Stear, Stephen Christopher Tobin, and countless others. Without their friendship and advice, this project would be very different.

I have received nothing but support since arriving at the University of North Carolina at Charlotte in July 2016. My colleagues made me feel welcome from day one. I would like to thank my colleagues in the Department of Languages and Culture Studies (particularly those in the Spanish section) and in the Latin American studies program. José Manuel Batista, Anabel Buchenau, Jürgen

Buchenau, Carlos Coria, Michael Doyle, Concepción Godev, Ann Gonzalez, Eric Hoenes, Edward Hopper, Jeffery Killman, Maryrica Ortiz Lottman, Andrea Pitts, Anton Pujol, Mónica Rodríguez-Castro, Shirley Wright, and many others have gone out of their way to make me feel welcome and to support my professional development. I am very happy that I have the opportunity to work with such great colleagues at an institution like UNCC.

I have been fortunate to receive funding from several sources over the course of writing this book. I would like to thank the University of Kansas Center for Latin American and Caribbean Studies (CLACS), which financed research trips to Mexico and Latin America through a Tinker Grant in 2014 and a Graduate Field Research Grant in 2012. Because of CLACS, I was able to look through archives in Mexico City that ended up playing an important role in shaping this project. I would also like to thank the Dean's Office at the University of North Carolina at Charlotte for providing me a grant to cover subvention funds. These moneys have been so helpful in taking care of all the little details associated with publishing an academic book.

It has been an absolute pleasure to work with the University of Florida Press. Juan Carlos Rodríguez and Héctor Fernández L'Hoeste provided excellent feedback (and enthusiasm) from the start. Stephanye Hunter was a wonderful editor who immediately understood the importance and potential of this project. The anonymous readers provided excellent insights that greatly strengthened the project. My interactions with Daniel Duffy, Rachel Doll, and everyone else were quick and professional.

Finally, I need to take a moment to acknowledge the support of all my family members. My parents, my brothers, and my sisters have all been supportive of this project in their own way. I'm especially grateful to my wife, Ariadna, for her support. She and my kids are my inspiration, and this project wouldn't be what it is if not for them.

A section of chapter 1 was previously published as "Science and the (Meta)physical Body: A Critique of Positivism in the Vasconcelian Utopia," in *Revista Canadiense de Estudios Hispánicos* 40, no. 3 (2016): 534–59; it is reprinted with permission from the editor, Rosalía Cornejo-Parriego. A Spanish-language version of a section of chapter 4 was published as "Intenciones enmascaradas en la pantalla plateada: El Santo y el mimetismo imperial," in *Alambique: Revista Académica de Ciencia Ficción y Fantasía* 4, no. 1 (2016): 1–15; it is reprinted with the permission of the editors, Miguel Ángel Fernández Delgado and Juan Carlos Toledano Redondo.

Introduction

(Re)Constructing the Racialized Body through Technology

Constructs of race in Mexico—as in most parts of the world—are nuanced and at times contradictory. Two almost antithetical events that I witnessed while living in northern Mexico illustrate this fact. In Monclova, Coahuila, I saw a man pick up his clothes from a laundromat; upon finding that a worker had broken the plastic clip on his laundry bag's drawstring, he shouted, "Stupid Indian!" ["¡India bruta!"].[1] A few months afterward, some friends in Matehuala, San Luis Potosí, invited me to dinner, where a woman said, "Everyone in Mexico belongs to the same race, so there is no racism like what you have in the United States." ["Todos somos de una sola raza aquí. No hay racismo como en Estados Unidos."] Her statement caught me off guard because it seemed antithetical to the scene I had witnessed in nearby Coahuila. This led me to question how Mexican racial attitudes could disapprove of discrimination on the one hand even as they marginalized indigenous peoples and cultures on the other. These—and many other—experiences sparked my intellectual interest in how state officials and the community at large approach the problematic distinction between indigeneity and *mestizaje*. After a great deal of thought, I have realized that these two episodes highlight the fact that, beyond focusing on physical features, Mexican society associates a person's racial identity with his or her ties to modernity. Throughout this study I look at an array of literary and cultural production that shows that Mexican people become racially and culturally coded as mestizo as they assimilate to the modernity-driven state through the use of technology.

Both of my aforementioned experiences reverberate with the ideological constructs of the "mestizo state," which Joshua Lund describes as a modernity-driven political entity that enunciates itself through the problematic conflation of mixed-race identity with Western-style modernity (*Mestizo* xv).[2] Although she probably would not recognize this, the woman who proclaimed a homogenous race invoked an imaginary in which her country's Amerindians had become mestizo through modernization. The existence of sleek tollways, the North American Free Trade Agreement (NAFTA), and internet cafés attested to the nation's racially hybrid essence. Everyone was mestizo due not to interracial ancestry but to the fact that the state had overcome indigenous "primitivity." The angry laundry customer, however, interpreted a worker's inability to use a relatively simple technology as proof that she was a ("backward") "india." Far from representing irreconcilable worldviews, these two episodes show the ease with which individuals can move between racial categories depending on a given context.[3]

As it is tied to technology, mestizaje moves beyond an inherited, genetic construction and becomes a racialized articulation of Carlos Alonso's "myth of modernity" (19–37). The fact that individuals can attain different racial statuses by moving proficiently through society underscores Michael Omi and Howard Winant's theory of racial formation.[4] These thinkers emphasize the lack of any "essential racial characteristics" as proof that race is a political construct tied to a specific sociohistorical context rather than any genetic reality (4). Certainly, people from different countries and geographical spaces have long had distinctive genetic and phenotypical traits, but race did not emerge as a political category until governments started using phenotype to assign people their economic roles in society (Prashad 1–36). Omi and Winant limit their research to the United States, so the majority of their work exists outside the scope of this book. Nevertheless, their recognition of race as a social formation remains useful when discussing racial identity in any Western country. One key to race formation within postrevolutionary Mexico was the tie between miscegenation and modernity, a fact that both buoys and challenges the observation of John L. Comaroff and Jean Comaroff that one of the principal (albeit flawed) tenets of Western, twentieth-century thought was that ethnicity—and by extension race—would "wither away with the rise of modernity" (1). On the one hand, mestizaje represented the elimination of ethnicity because it resulted from interracial fusion. On the other hand, it became a distinct racial identity that stood in opposition to the indigenous. State officials believed that a prerequisite to modernization was the transformation of Amerindian individuals into mestizos, and they aimed to achieve this end through a process of race formation that used technology to modernize the indigenous body and transform it into a mestizo entity.

Similar to virtually all constructs of race in the Western world, official mestizaje dictated people's economic and societal privileges based on conditions of the body. Two recent studies, Rebecca Janzen's *The National Body in Mexican Literature: Collective Challenges to Biopolitical Control* (2015) and Sara Anne Potter's "Disturbing Muses: Gender, Technology and Resistance in Mexican Avant-Garde Cultures" (2013), emphasize the body's centrality in the postrevolutionary imaginary in very different ways. Potter—whom I discuss at length later on—analyzes how postrevolutionary artists and writers negotiated the body's relationship to a rapidly modernizing nation by depicting (female) bodies fused with technology. For her part, Janzen alludes to the body's central role in constructing a postrevolutionary nation when she argues that Mexican literature often imagines ways in which state power is reflected on the bodies of marginalized (largely indigenous) Mexicans. Both authors focus on literary and cultural production by people who were critical of the state; as such, they do not engage with state-sponsored work that imagined technology as a means for modernizing and assimilating the masses. Janzen, for example, argues that ill, disabled, and injured individuals "reflect the effects of various branches of the state, and allow us to imagine an alternative nonhegemonic collective body that might challenge this state" (4). Janzen's arguments resonate exceptionally well within the parameters of her study of literature that criticized postrevolutionary reforms. Nevertheless, the signification of sick and disabled bodies necessarily changes when these appear in officialist cultural production because these works supported—rather than undermined—postrevolutionary attempts to construct a cohesive nation-state. In officialist art, illness and disability are overcome as individuals (particularly Amerindians and women) cede to the state and allow it to make them whole. Representations of disability become especially prominent in official discourses if we follow the thinking of Susan Antebi (165), who argues that officialist thinkers viewed indigeneity as a form of disability in and of itself. This became especially clear as postrevolutionary thinkers conflated vices like alcoholism, decadence, and immorality with indigenous identities (Antebi 165). Of course, the most "disabling" aspect of indigenous identity was its supposed ties to "primitivity." State officials thus attempted to overcome so-called Amerindian backwardness by modernizing indigenous bodies through eugenics and technology.

It is important to note that postrevolutionary ideals of official mestizaje built on policies that dated back to independence and the Republican period. Guarantees for indigenous rights actually decreased after Mexico gained independence because elites strove to form a national consciousness by eliminating the Amerindian cultures that the Spanish Crown had supported (Lomnitz, *Exits from the Labyrinth* 276). Mestizaje (both cultural and genetic) represented a means through which Amerindians could assimilate to the state, but it also became a tool for erasing indigenous societies. The key functional role of racial hybridity became especially clear in Mexico by the late nineteenth century, when the *científicos*—a group of positivist bureaucrats in the Porfirian administration—began to invoke paradigms of eugenics. Because most people in the country (including elites) were mestizos to some degree, Mexican eugenics rejected the northern European belief that racial miscegenation was necessarily dysgenic. The intellectual and political currents of the Porfiriato predate my study, but the very existence of these debates shows that discourses of race, science, and the body were already mutually constructing each other in an attempt to define the Mexican nation long before the Revolution. One major difference between Porfirian and postrevolutionary constructs of mestizaje was how they conceived technology's role in promoting mixed-race identity. As Rubén Gallo notes, the intellectuals and artists of the Porfiriato viewed the spread of technology as "telltale symptoms of a decadent society" (*Mexican Modernity* 4), while those of the postrevolutionary period began to embrace the effects that it had on society. Thus intellectuals and cultural producers began to imagine ways that they could modernize not only the nation's arts and letters but also the national body and culture. Their belief that indigenous Mexicans would one day come to form a great proletariat led them to aggressively champion strategies for technologizing the Amerindian body.

Postrevolutionary intellectuals may have believed that their country's indigenes had a bright future, but they also claimed that indigenous Mexico could not fulfill its industrial destiny in its present state. Any greatness for Mexican Amerindians and their posterity could come about only through aggressive projects of official mestizaje. It was in large part for this reason that, according to Pedro Ángel Palou, the mestizo became "the subject of the interpellation of every political discourse, in the *person* of the political project of the imminent Revolution" ["habría de convertirse en el sujeto de la interpelación de todos los discursos políticos, en la *persona* del proyecto político de la entonces inminente revolución"] (14). Statist articulations of mestizaje, which were steeped in theories of modernization, required indigenous people to embrace modern culture by fusing their bodies with technology, a process that they could achieve through various means. Some of the state's preferred technologies for modernizing indigenous bodies included industrial agriculture, medical immunization, factory work in urban centers, and education. A person's ability to function in a modern economy served as a prerequisite to mestizo subjectivity. Palou argues that the mestizo myth became a "social fiction," or a narrative that the state promoted in its attempts of domination and political power (20). The state's ultimate goal in proclaiming (official) mestizaje was to foment greater national unity by convincing (and even coercing) its population at large—particularly those individuals who lived in indigenous communities—to identify with and promote mestizo interests and identity.

As postrevolutionary administrations focused on assimilating Amerindians to the state through mestizaje, they implicitly championed the "brown" mestizo (rather than the *criollo*/white mestizo of the nineteenth century) as the principal protagonist of the postrevolutionary order (López-Beltrán and García Deister).[5] In many cases, the state charged recently assimilated Amerindians with exporting the benefits of mestizo culture to the communities from which they came.[6] As Palou argues, "by transforming them [Amerindians] into *mestizos* it [the state] would erase their indigenous nature; by making them inhabitants of the modern city it would redeem them from backwardness" ["Al convertirlo en *mestizo* se le borraría lo indio; al hacerlo habitante de la ciudad moderna se le sacaría del atraso."] (14, emphasis in original). Amerindians would become explicitly mixed-race as they fused their bodies with technology and modernity; as a result, mestizaje functioned in practice as a project of what Guillermo Bonfil Batalla calls "deindianization" (*Mestizo* 41–42). Because mestizaje was a tool for modernizing indigenous individuals and assimilating them to the state, the eradication of indigenous subjectivity that both Palou and Bonfil Batalla discuss did not require physical violence. Rather, indigenous individuals would give up their native identity of their own free will as they integrated their newly modernized bodies into mestizo society. The exact articulation of official mestizaje evolved over the years; nevertheless, the concept remains in the background of Mexican thought to this day.

My focus on how technology interfaced with the postrevolutionary body refines—and at times even reimagines—contemporary theories of hybridity in Latin America. Néstor García Canclini first used the term "hybridity" to explain how Latin America existed in, out of, and alongside modernity in the 1980s and 1990s, but the term proves useful when discussing Mexico's problematic ties to modernity in previous decades as well. For García Canclini, hybridity is a phenomenon that entails the juxtaposition of the "modern" with the folkloric

(2–11). Given the paradoxical relationship between past and present, he views hybridity as largely deconstructivist, especially as it relates to understandings of Latin American modernity. Despite his work's popularity, numerous critics have challenged his theory as a binary articulated from the center to define the rural (Ileana Rodríguez, "Hegemonía y dominio"; Moraña 652). Beyond these observations, we should also note García Canclini's curious decision to ignore mestizaje despite this racial construct's clear evocation of hybridity. The theorist justifies his preference for hybridity because "it includes diverse intercultural mixtures—not only the racial ones to which *mestizaje* tends to be limited" (11n1). Nevertheless, as our present discussion has shown, mestizaje, while clearly a construct of race, was ultimately a strategy for "intercultural mixtures" and even modernity.

The state's practice of transforming indigenous people into mestizos through processes of corporeal hybridity sheds greater light on the problematic relationship between García Canclini's twin notions of modernism and modernization. The theorist defines modernism as "the means by which the elites take charge of the intersection of different historical temporalities and try to elaborate a global project with them" (46).[7] This definition explains statist articulations and representations of postrevolutionary official mestizaje exceptionally well; indeed, García Canclini highlights both the writings of José Vasconcelos and the art of the muralist movement as examples par excellence of this type of modernism (52–54). García Canclini defines modernization as a largely socioeconomic ideal that entails both industrialization and the education of the population at large so that it can participate in modern society. While the critic emphasizes modernism's many failures in bringing about modernization (41–65), we should note that proponents of official mestizaje employed elitist discourses and projects in an attempt to modernize "primitive" indigenes through various forms of hybridity. State actors employed at least three different "hybridities" in their quest to transform indigenous people into "modern" mestizos: technological,[8] racial,[9] and cultural.[10] Upon undergoing any of these forms of hybridization, indigenous people could become coded as racially hybrid and mestizo in a cultural, economic, and even genetic sense. Rather than bring about García Canclini's famous notion of "modernism without modernization" (41), then, postrevolutionary thinkers strove to bring about modernization *through* modernism.

A form of circular logic began to emerge where the state coded hybridized bodies as mestizo, and a mestizo body was by definition hybrid—technologically, racially, culturally, or some combination thereof. Differing forms of hybridity soon became conflated. As Amerindian peoples and bodies underwent technological hybridity, they became marked with modernity and thus racially and culturally hybrid. As such, official discourses held that these people now belonged to the mestizo "majority." In many cases, authors and cultural producers used technologically hybrid subjects to construct, amplify, and impose preferred racial and gender identities from the center to the periphery. Postrevolutionary representations of the racially, technologically, and culturally hybrid body almost always appeared as future-oriented ideals toward which the nation should aspire. Corporeal hybridity and modernity became the founding elements of a distinctly Mexican society that was technologically advanced, racially and culturally mixed, and clearly gendered. Mestizaje thus represented the discursive tool that could overcome perceived indigenous shortcomings and initiate Mexico into the modern world. I distance my theorizations of hybridity from those of a body of scholars who believe "that hybrids make it possible to break free from modernity, condemned for being too Western and one-dimensional" (Gruzinski 18). Postrevolutionary discussions of official mestizaje used differing forms of hybridity to impose a modernity-driven, homogenizing mestizo identity on the masses.

Beyond allowing the nation to reconcile its indigenous past with its goals of industrialization along a European model, official mestizaje also provided a means for the state to resist U.S. and European assertions of cultural and genetic superiority. According to Ana María Alonso, mestizaje became a paradoxical construct for "creat[ing] homogeneity out of heterogeneity, unity out of fragmentation, a strong nation that could withstand the internal menace of its own failures to overcome the injustices of its colonial past and the external menace of US imperialism" (462). Mexican leaders rejected discourses of white supremacy that abounded throughout northern Europe and the United States. By affirming Mexico's mixed-race identity, they instead asserted their own country's economic and genetic potential (Stepan 8). In this way, mestizaje was a resistant construct that recognized an indigenous potential that other Western nations denied. That said, official mestizaje also entailed projects of "internal colonialism" that depended on a pro-mestizo eugenics that scientifically justified racialized distinctions between rich and poor (Lomnitz, *Deep Mexico* 140).[11] Postrevolutionary mestizophilia may have prescribed a means through which Amerindians could assimilate to the modernity-driven state, but the country's mixed-race essence undermined its prestige on the international stage (Lomnitz, *Deep Mexico* 140). Many Western nations—but most particularly the United States—had historically emphasized Mexico's ties to indigeneity in order to justify their incursions into the country. Each chapter in this book discusses different strategies for resisting foreign imperialism alongside problematic cases of internal colonialism. Each artist that I analyze balances this equation differently, but when they are viewed in their entirety, it becomes clear that officialist thinkers believed that state-sanctioned anti-imperialism necessitated the domestication of indigenous Mexico. State officials saw no moral contradiction between their resistance to foreign imperialism and their own projects of internal empire. Indeed, most viewed both endeavors as necessary components of their modernity-driven, mestizo nationalism.

This fact challenges the assumptions of many midcentury Latin American thinkers who asserted that an enlightened Latin America would not turn toward imperialism (Fernández Retamar 46–55). Rather, notions of empire sat at the heart of Mexican (and Latin American) modernity. By the twentieth century, Mexico's colonial experience had produced a Hegelian master/slave relationship where the country's means of self-representation was patterned after those of its imperial oppressor(s) (Hegel 186–95), a fact that was particularly visible with regard to how it engaged both Spain and the United States. As Mexican elites followed this imperial model, they necessarily established internal empires that mirrored those of their own historical colonizers. Silviano Santiago states that, in (particularly Brazilian) mestizaje, "cultural imperialism desires a response of silence, or, once again, that of the emphatic echo serving to strengthen the conqueror's power" (8). Mestizo normativity found itself at an awkward juncture; while hegemonic in its own national space, global powers treated mestizo identity as a distant "echo" of European whiteness. As mixed-race peoples attempted to validate themselves within these Eurocentric constructs of power, they devalued the indigenous components of their racial and cultural heritage. Statist articulations of postrevolutionary mestizo modernity were highly alienating because they revolved around a desire to emulate a historical conqueror who still refused to recognize the worth of mixed-race subjectivities. As postrevolutionary actors sponsored official articulations of mestizaje, they further validated and institutionalized the racial and gender divisions that had existed since the earliest days of the Conquest. By basing modernity on a historical construct that subjugated both Amerindians and women, the new regime explicitly favored Europe over the indigenous and the masculine over the feminine.

The "Textual Revolution": Lettered Discourse and Officialist Art

The postrevolutionary state's focus on constructing a patriarchal, mestizo society reflected the changing social realities that emerged in the wake of the Revolution. As Thomas B. Irving notes, it was during these years that the masses began to "assume social and political power" (ix). Aníbal Quijano emphasizes the fact that these "masses" were primarily indigenous when he asserts that the Revolution had catalyzed a "road of social decolonization through revolutionary process" (564).[12] Rather than cater to the demands of a newly conscious political demographic, however, government leaders attempted to transform the indigenous majority into mestizos whose "modern" interests would mirror their own. Regarding this practice, Bonfil Batalla states, "It is a curious democracy that does not recognize the existence of the people themselves, but, rather sets itself the task of creating them" ("Problem" 31). Statist nation-building prerogatives aimed to "modernize" Amerindians by initiating them into the technologically advanced world as newly mestizo workers (Taylor and Yúdice 311). Given this fact, Roger Bartra argues that, following the Revolution, "it was no longer enough to evoke the cosmogonic and transhistorical myths of the eternal archetype of the savage, rough Mexican. . . . A parallel myth had to be devised about the man immersed in the *historical* whirlpool that the Mexican Revolution unleashed" (*Cage* 113, emphasis in original). This new myth would play a crucial role in nation-building as it allowed—and even coerced—Amerindians to enter the modern mainstream. As the state put this ideal into action, it necessarily exalted *mexicanidad*, mestizophilia, and heteronormativity as the building blocks of national greatness.[13]

Government officials carefully regulated how this new national myth was disseminated and theorized to ensure that it would support statist nation-building projects. As they did this, they contributed to what Horacio Legrás calls the "textuality" (rather than the historicity) of the Revolution (*Culture and Revolution* 3–5). People's visceral reactions to the recent conflict came more from the images that the state produced for their consumption—often with careful choreographies—than from actual historical moments. This textuality appeared across numerous media, but one of the principal figures to textualize the (post)revolutionary period—particularly in its immediate aftermath—was the *letrado*: a figure whom Ángel Rama defines as a (generally European/criollo male) writer who uses his privileged position as an intellectual to contribute to Latin American politics (1). It was no small irony that a popular social movement that had begun in rural Mexico would end up being defined and theorized from the nation's center with only minimal contributions from the periphery. As Legrás observes, the act of theorizing the Revolution from Mexico City led the diverse elements that had constituted the conflict to "coalesce into a single *representation*" (*Culture and Revolution* 5, emphasis mine), but in reality, these groups remained as diverse (and divided) as ever. Officialist letrados and cultural producers devised numerous strategies through which Amerindian individuals could assimilate to the state, but they never fully exorcised the nation of its indigenous roots. The explicit focus on assimilating Amerindians through mestizaje thus forced state officials to expand their focus beyond the literate elite in Mexico City and engage the nation as a whole through art, radio,[14] and film.[15]

State-appointed artists tended to reach a larger audience than did Mexican writers; through their work it became possible to engage even the illiterate with racially charged representations of cultural nationalism. That said, to paraphrase Rama, "letters provided the guiding thread that . . . could imbue a potentially chaotic diversity with chaotic meaning" (24). Lettered ideals influenced official ideologies, which in turn found their way into state-sponsored, artistic representations of mexicanidad. As such, attempts to establish order required the state to negotiate its articulation of both race and modernity. Mexican letrados (and elites) had failed to dodge the Revolution in part because they had not converted the indigenous masses to their cause. Part of this failure came from elitist policies that ignored the needs of the majority, but it also emerged due to the fact that there was no single coherent lettered ideology. Ignacio M. Sánchez Prado shows that Mexico's lettered community remained divided even after the Revolution when he makes the almost paradoxical observation that literature played a principal role in institutionalizing the Revolution on the one hand (*Naciones* 1) while lettered thinkers enjoyed a great deal of autonomy from statist supervision on the other (*Naciones* 16). State-sponsored artists provided two major advantages over writers: they could reach wide swaths of the illiterate masses that even the best writers could not, and their work was easier to control and censor. This is not to say that state-sponsored artists served as amorphous mouthpieces for the postrevolutionary state; the chapters of this book show that officialist artists held surprisingly diverse perceptions about mexicanidad. Mexican cultural producers belonged to differing ideological camps, and, similar to the nation's writers, they often expressed oppositional ideals.

State-sponsored art became a highly contested medium for discussing and questioning notions of mexicanidad. The idea of funding nationalist art came from José Vasconcelos, perhaps the most important letrado of the revolutionary and postrevolutionary epochs. Beyond commissioning artists to paint representations of mestizo nationalism on the nation's walls, he also initiated the cultural missions, which sent mestizo teachers and medics (called Apostles of Culture) to the largely indigenous rural parts of the country (Díaz Arciniega 46–47). Both the cultural missions and the muralist movement recognized intricate ties among technology, the body, and modernity; however, perhaps because this was never explicitly theorized, each artist and thinker portrayed the relationship differently. Some state-sponsored artists and letrados championed an *hispanista* form of mestizaje, while others employed an *indigenista* approach. Indigenistas favored a "brown" mestizaje that problematically exalted essentialistic aspects of Amerindian culture even as it attempted to coerce indigenous assimilation to the state.[16] Hispanistas, however, preferred a culturally (and perhaps phenotypically) "white" mestizo. The state funded these oppositional representations of racial and technological hybridity in large part because government leaders themselves had yet to fully adopt a racial paradigm. Legrás argues convincingly that *indigenismo* held greater sway in postrevolutionary Mexico "as a social rather than cultural" movement (*Culture and Revolution* 53), but he also notes that it did not fully defeat *hispanismo* in literary and cultural production until the 1950s. Both hispanistas and indigenistas generally agreed that the state had to incorporate indigenous Mexico through mestizaje, but they differed on how (and to what degree) they should acknowledge the country's indigenous heritage. Despite their differences, both movements framed the process of incorporating the Amerindian as a strategy for "redeeming" the nation and improving its culture and quality of life. Mestizaje—whether hispanista or indigenista—thus provided a strategy for culturally and genetically homogenizing the populace. As writers and artists defined and taught the ways in which the Amerindian could assimilate to modernity, they played an essential role in negotiating race in society.

Postrevolutionary projects evolved over the years, but racialized understandings of modernity remained important to governing strategies across time. The focus of the Partido Nacional Revolucionario (PNR) during the 1920s and 1930s was to consolidate power (Bruno-Jofré and Martínez Valle 47–49; Gillingham 176), while the goal became industrialization and the full-scale institutionalization of the Revolution with the advent of the Partido Revolucionario Institucional (PRI) in 1946 (Gillingham 177).[17] Officialist cultural production remained a staple across numerous presidencies because state-funded (and regulated) art reflected the changing objectives of the government. Most criticism has followed the lead of Octavio Paz (*Labyrinth of Solitude* 231–37), who asserts that the prestige of official—and even lettered—discourses fell dramatically following the massacre of Tlatelolco on October 2, 1968 (Franco, *Decline and Fall* 195–99; Avelar 12–13). Tlatelolco was certainly not a singular occurrence, but it, along with other cases of state violence from the decade, unmasked the postrevolutionary state's oppressive nature. Those who had praised the "Mexican Miracle" ["Milagro mexicano"]—a period of impressive industrial growth from approximately 1940 to 1970 (Carmona et al. 19)—now had to acknowledge the very real existence of state overreach. Under these new circumstances, literary movements like la Onda used the written word to undermine official doctrines and resist statist propaganda. Nevertheless, the state continued to trumpet official mestizaje as a core element of national identity and Mexican modernity.[18]

The technologized body existed beyond any single worldview and instead became a trope through which cultural producers—and consumers—could imagine the country's racial identity and its ties to modernity. Differing articulations of mestizaje emerged over the years that corresponded with the civilizing projects of individual administrations. That said, state attempts to assimilate the indigenous population through racial and technological hybridity reflected the desire to assert Mexico's place—politically, racially, and technologically—alongside, or even beyond, those of the United States and Western Europe.[19] Nationalism, mestizaje, and modernity became key ingredients to officialist discourses of mexicanidad. As a result, representations of technological hybridity came from artists and letrados of all political persuasions. Agustín F. Basave Benítez underscores this fact when he argues that "thinkers from the most dissimilar tendencies coincide—and in some cases it is their only common denominator—in their mestizophilia. And it becomes difficult to ignore the idea that this was a preconceived goal when we consider the fact that this ideal was arrived at from the most diverse starting points" ["Pensadores de los más disímiles tendencias coinciden—y en algunos casos es de hecho su único común denominador—en la mestizofilia. Y cuando desde tan diversos puntos de partida se arriba al mismo punto de llegada es imposible desechar la idea de que antes de emprender el camino se tiene una meta preconcebida."] (141). Rubén Gallo adds an interesting corollary to this assertion when he identifies a preoccupation with technology as another idea that united Mexican intellectuals from across the political spectrum (*Mexican Modernity* 4–5). When they are viewed alongside each other, Basave Benítez and Gallo make it clear: the twin ideals of mestizaje and technological modernity sat in the background of most—if not all—articulations of postrevolutionary mexicanidad. The conflation of technological hybridity with mestizaje thus made perfect sense because both ideals signaled national modernity. Whether articulated by a right-wing thinker like Vasconcelos or a leftist like Rivera, the juxtaposition of the body with technology was almost always depicted in a triumphant, nationalistic manner.

Letrados and artists from across the political spectrum asserted the lack of—and resistance to—technological hybridity and modernity as a defining element of indigenous "primitivity." Alfonso Caso, for example, placed four characteristics of indigeneity—language, culture, somatic features, and "group consciousness"—in direct tension with those of mestizo subjectivity (245). Caso certainly did not think that any one of these aforementioned features necessarily indicated Indianness on its own (240–41), but when viewed in their totality, he believed, these traits adequately defined (Mexican) indigeneity. On the opposite end of the ideological spectrum, the anthropologist Manuel Gamio took a "scientific" approach to the question of indigenous Mexico. For him, the ancient inhabitants of the Americas had been destined for cultural greatness on par with that of the Chinese, but the bloody Iberian conquest had destroyed that potential while it existed in embryonic form (*Forjando* 3–4). His work differed from European scientific racism in that he asserted indigenous equality to whites, but he concurred with that intellectual current as he accepted the notion that, in its present form, Amerindian culture lacked the scientific and philosophical grandeur of Western society. Indigenous Mexico was in dire need of a "redemption" that would come as it adopted the mixed-race cultural norms of a "proper" diet, education, and the subsequent eradication of poverty (Gamio, *Forjando* 31–37; see also Brading 79). As his redemptive projects demonstrate, although Gamio opposed European sciences that attributed genetic inferiority to the Amerindian, he, too, traced these people's "backwardness" to conditions of the body.

Gamio and Caso disagreed in many ways, but both coincided in their belief that the state could "cure" indigenous peoples and bodies of their primitivity by fusing them with modern technologies. Susan Antebi argues that programs to physically change the Amerindian body had eugenic overtones, particularly as they aimed to "eradicate racial characteristics and disabilities" (164). This was particularly visible in the cases of education and hygiene, two projects that took on a eugenic nature in Mexico due to the prevalence of Lamarckian genetics, which held that physical changes to the body modified "the organic structure of living things" (Chevalier de Lamarck). Lamarckism differed from Mendelianism—the genetic paradigm of choice within the United States and northern Europe—which rigidly separated distinctions of genotype and learned behavior (Stepan 22–32). Nevertheless, Lamarckism enjoyed a great deal of prestige not only in Latin America but also in European countries like France and Italy (Stepan 2–3). Both of these competing paradigms were rigorously scientific, but they led officials in different countries to conceive of and implement eugenics in antithetical ways.[20] Eugenics ultimately refers to attempts to control human heredity by ensuring that only "desirable" genes remain within the population. The focus on reproduction inherent to Mendelianism led North American and northern European countries to sterilize "dysgenic" people in an attempt to strengthen the gene pool (Paul 1–4). The adoption of Lamarckism in Mexico, however, suggested that state officials could transform Amerindians into mestizos by physically altering their bodies and transforming them into eugenic specimens (Antebi 166–67; Stepan 15; Suárez y López Guazo, "Evolucionismo" 25). Viewed in this light, the Mexican brand of eugenics held that people whose bodies had been technologically modified would become mestizo; furthermore, they would pass their newly found genetic modernity to their offspring. Lamarckism informed Mexican and Latin American science at least into the 1940s (Stepan 65), but as I show in chapter 3, it lingered in the national imaginary until at least the 1950s.

Eugenics, Technological Hybridity, Cyborg Subjectivity, and Mestizo Modernity

Lamarckian thought proved especially useful in Mexico, whose ties to mestizaje signaled it as irredeemably dysgenic in European circles. As the state modernized Amerindian people, it not only "redeemed" those whose bodies it changed, but it also "improved" their genotype, thus ensuring a racially "desirable" progeny. North American and northern European eugenicists constantly criticized eugenic projects within Latin America that focused primarily on hygiene, charging that such endeavors in no way modified the national genome (Trounson 236; see also Wiggam 292). Nevertheless, Mexico's approach to genetics allowed the state to "improve" its current genome, even as it kept an eye toward the future generations whose genotype it was improving. Gamio alludes to the futurity of Mexican eugenics when he states,

We should keep in mind that mestizaje is good for Mexico not only from the ethnic point of view, but principally to establish a more advanced type of culture than the unsatisfactory one that the majority of the population currently endures. While mestizaje can be achieved by valuing education and other means, this assignment will be carried out sooner if racial hybridization is intensified. This is because racial mixing will automatically bring with it an effective cultural progress as the result of the elimination or substitution of our nation's backward indigenous characteristics. (*Hacia* 27)

[Debe tenerse en cuenta que el mestizaje conviene a México no sólo desde el punto de vista étnico, sino principalmente para poder establecer un tipo de cultura más avanzado que el poco satisfactorio que hoy presenta la mayoría de la población, y si bien esto puede conseguirse valiéndose de la educación y otros medios, esta tarea se consumará más pronto si se intensifica el mestizaje, pues éste traerá consigo automáticamente un efectivo progreso cultural, como resultado de la eliminación o substitución de las características retrasadas de tipo indígena.]

The anthropologist's words exemplify Kelley R. Swarthout's observation that the assimilation of indigenous Mexico represented a "patriotic act" (15). Of course, the patriotism that Swarthout refers to was more precisely a form of mestizo nationalism that aimed to "redeem" "primitive" cultures by assimilating them to the modernized state. This strategy implicitly favored European over native cultures even as it invoked eugenic paradigms that differed with those articulated in (particularly northern) Europe. By focusing their eugenic efforts on educating and changing—rather than sterilizing—indigenous bodies, Mexican eugenicists could literally transform Amerindians into mestizos.[21]

Even within the framework of Lamarckism, the simple act of sharing technology with the indigenous population was not enough. State actors had to devote a great deal of time and energy to make sure that these advancements did not fall on deaf ears. The philosopher and aesthetic theorist Samuel Ramos noted this fact when he stated,

Men who in Mexico have tried to solve the problem of civilizing the Indians have believed it possible to adapt them to modern technology, with the idea that it is universal and that any man in possession of his rational faculties can utilize it. They fail to see that to *understand* modern technology is not sufficient reason for adopting it; that it is essential, also, to have the same spirit as that of the men who created it. (*Profile* 119–20, emphasis in original)

Here Ramos refers specifically to failed attempts to take technology, particularly in the form of industrial agriculture, to rural areas. He believed that the state could not modernize indigenous Mexico without instilling a national (mestizo) character, and that this would come about through an education consisting of officialist, pro-mestizo propaganda. Art played a key role in making this indigenous "spirit" more receptive to the technological advances of mestizo society (Villoro 222). Juxtapositions of the body with technology occurred both in the cultural missions with their focus on education and hygiene and through artistic representations of mexicanidad. Art and state hygiene projects synergetically reinforced one another as they asserted the modernizing potential of technology on the body and of the technologized body on society.

Physical changes to the body took on a cultural dimension as they reframed the indigenous experience; as technology altered indigenous bodies, it produced physical changes that, according to Lamarckian paradigms, amended the genome. Given this fact, technological hybridity produced genetic hybridity and thus mestizo subjectivity. Upon entering mestizo modernity, technologically enhanced people and their offspring would be ready to undertake modern activities like industrial agriculture and factory work. Official projects to reconfigure indigenous racial identity through technology allude to theories that Donna Haraway would enunciate a half century later when she asserted that cyborg identities have a strong bearing on performative traits like race, gender, and social class (157). Cyborg imagery is especially visible if we follow the lead of Chris Hables Gray, who rather expansively defines the term as any (generally human) body that "has been technologically modified in any significant way, from an implanted pacemaker to a vaccination that reprogrammed [its] immune system" (*Cyborg Citizen* 2).[22] Obvious problems arise with such an all-encompassing definition; if everyone is already a cyborg, then the figure loses much of its appeal in questioning (post) human being. That said, this more inclusive definition of cyborg identity proves useful in untangling the intimate relationships between race, gender, technology, and the body in postrevolutionary Mexico. As we understand cyborg identity to be a condition that results from the fusion of the body with technology (in its myriad forms), we can use the specialized vocabulary of that theoretical tradition to describe how technology and the body interfaced with one another and informed the reigning constructs of race and gender throughout the postrevolutionary era.

Until very recently, few critics had used cyborg theory to analyze postrevolutionary Mexican cultural production.[23] Sara Anne Potter's "Disturbing Muses: Gender, Technology and Resistance in Mexican Avant-Garde Cultures" stands out for this reason; her groundbreaking study was the first to use posthumanism as a guiding thread to discuss postrevolutionary society across time and space in Mexico. The general thrust of her argument is quite different from my own because she focuses almost exclusively on the cyborg body's ability to challenge—rather than buoy—patriarchal norms and ideals. As she states, "with so much attention paid to the construction of *lo mexicano*, that is, of an idealized and therefore impossible male mestizo subject, it is striking when a female body . . . becomes interwoven with the emerging rhythms and technologies" of Mexico City (vii). Potter implicitly places cyborg subjectivity in conversation with officialist constructs of mestizo modernity, but she does not discuss how the indigenous body interfaces with technology here. Rather, she provides a fascinating discussion of female (generally mestiza) "technified muses" whose ties to technology help them to deviate from—rather than conform to—officialist ideals of gender.

Potter's silence on the topic of race reflects the fact that the artists that she engages were less concerned with assimilating the Amerindian than they were with negotiating the country's relationship with the modern city. One of her most crucial observations is that postrevolutionary writers remained stuck in paradigms of nineteenth-century *modernismo* until the *estridentistas*—a new generation of avant-garde authors and artists—began to negotiate the relationship among art, technology, and the national (female) body (2–3). Inspired in part by (particularly Italian) futurism, these cultural producers placed a strong emphasis on technological advancement. Unlike state-sponsored cultural producers, the estridentistas did not concern themselves with nation-building. Indeed, Lynda Klich asserts that they "sought to challenge the prevailing decorative or folkloric nationalist aesthetics developing in official endeavors" (303), while Odile Cisneros asserts that they "construct[ed] a vision of the city peculiarly divorced from the realities of post-revolutionary Mexico" (Cisneros 207; see also Zaramella 3–5). Viewed in this light, it is especially interesting that the estridentistas turned to the technologized body in their attempts to undermine official discourses: by the 1920s, modern Mexico defined itself to a great deal through its relationship with technology. The fact that the technologized body appeared in such distinct contexts suggests that Potter and I have identified two parallel but oppositional articulations of cyborg subjectivity that appeared in postrevolutionary Mexico. Officialist cultural production invoked technological hybridity as a means for modernizing the indigenous body and assimilating it to the state, while the avant-garde "technified muses" of the estridentistas and their successors challenged Mexican constructs of gender and modernity, though they generally ignored race.[24]

Neither Potter nor I would claim that Mexican artists consciously produced cyborg discourses; the term did not even exist during the first half of the twentieth century. The concept entered the scientific lexicon in the 1960s, when Manfred E. Clynes and Nathan S. Kline theorized the "cybernetic organism" (cyborg) as a means for achieving space travel (29–31), and Haraway did not theorize its resistant potential until the 1980s. Nevertheless, long before the North American and European academies imagined a subversive cyborg body, Mexican artists were using it to imagine ways to negotiate how race and gender would interface with modernity. The role of the technologized body in modern society played out in spectacular fashion with regard to official projects of race formation. Many of the technologies that the state inscribed on indigenous bodies were common in urban Mexico and throughout the Western world, but they had not yet reached the predominantly indigenous rural populations. As state actors infused indigenous bodies with these technologies, they extended technological privilege to Amerindians and initiated them into the modern state. It is for this reason that postrevolutionary artists and letrados of diverse political persuasions viewed technological hybridity as a key component of Mexican modernity. Lettered discourses and officialist cultural production thus aided in redefining the nation's "authentic" racial identity by providing strategies for Amerindians to become mestizos. Literary and cultural production ultimately transformed Mexicans of all races into cyborg actors as official discourses interfaced with the national mind and reprogrammed indigenous (and mestizo) Mexico's relationship both with itself and with the state. Artistic representations of cultural nationalism—which proclaimed the incipient modernization of the indigenous body through its fusion with technology—came to function as Foucauldian "technologies of the Self."

For Foucault, "technologies of the self" are various stimuli and symbols that "permit individuals to effect by their own means, *or with the help of oth-*

ers, a certain number of operations on their own bodies and souls, thoughts, conduct, and way of being, so as to transform themselves in order to attain a certain state of happiness, purity, wisdom, *perfection*, or immortality" ("Technologies" 146, emphases mine). The state funded mestizophilic artwork with the express intent of teaching its population (and particularly its indigenous citizens) how to "perfect" itself and achieve modernization through mestizo identity and subjectivity. As such, it employed a complex system of symbols to manipulate indigenous agency and coerce assimilation to the mestizo order. Viewed in this light, indigenous—and even mestizo—minds became cyborg entities whose subjectivity came to reflect the racially charged imaginaries that the population at large consumed on a daily basis. Andy Clark and David Chalmers view the mind, and by extension subject formation, as the cyborg result of "active externalism, based on the active role of the environment in driving cognitive processes" (*Supersizing* 220). Roger Bartra enters in direct dialogue with the aforementioned thinkers and states that a person's environment produces "a complex, prosthetic cultural and technological system that substitutes functions that we cannot do or that we do slowly and inadequately. This system, along with the brain, constitutes the basis of consciousness" ["Lo que encontramos es más bien un complejo sistema cultural y tecnológico de prótesis que sustituyen funciones que no podemos hacer o que hacemos lenta e inadecuadamente. Este sistema, junto con el cerebro, constituye la base de la conciencia."] (*Cerebro y libertad*). Thus the mind itself is a cyborg entity in that it is the conjugation of the body, particularly the brain, and external symbols that intertwine to form individual subjectivity.

As the postrevolutionary state inundated the population with mestizophilic and indigenista discourses of cultural nationalism, it demarcated the divisions between Amerindian and mestizo by signaling the former as an identity of the past and the latter as the way of the future. Bartra finishes his book *Cerebro y libertad* by stating that, at this moment, cyborgs "are simply humans with implants that appear to have no power over the body" ["Los cyborgs de hoy . . . son simplemente humanos con implantes que no parecen tener ningún poder sobre el cuerpo."] (*Cerebro y libertad*). This conclusion does an injustice to his own thinking, at least within the context of postrevolutionary Mexico. Because cultural nationalism produced official discourses that coerced Amerindians (and women of all races) to acquiesce to the highly patriarchal and Eurocentric demands of official mestizaje, it appears that postrevolutionary official discourses functioned as prostheses that *did* change people's cognitive processes, and thus their relationships with the Self. Viewed in this light, contemporary prostheses gain power over the technologically hybrid (cyborg) human body as they force the brain to internalize and negotiate new symbolic meanings. Discourses of cultural nationalism conditioned postrevolutionary indigenous Mexicans to internalize biopolitical divisions that marginalized their cultures and ways of knowing. Thus official discourses represented oppressive technologies that coercively informed and constructed state power.

As officialist thinkers undertook processes of race formation through technological hybridity, they validated biopolitical ideals that favored mestizo society over the indigenous. The state distanced itself from its revolutionary values as it adopted worldviews that barred those indigenous people who refused to assimilate from popular citizenship, but at the same time it ironically placed itself alongside the modern, Western democracies that it hoped to emulate. Foucault traces the emergence of biopolitics to nineteenth-century Europe, when state power became associated with the ability to preserve—rather than take—human life ("Birth of Biopolitics" 202–7). Beyond its air of apparent benevolence, the biopolitical state has an oppressive underbelly; in their defense of life, state officials almost always favor one segment of the population (mestizos in this case) over another (Amerindians in Mexico). Claudio Lomnitz traces biopolitics back further than Foucault and posits colonial Mexico as one of the earliest biopolitical—or at least protobiopolitical—societies (*Death* 80–96). Thus it should come as no surprise that the postrevolutionary state would justify and articulate the traumatic process of modernization in biopolitical terms. One of the state's principal tenets was that indigenous people should abandon their heritage for mestizo culture because this would improve the quality of life of everyone in the country. Despite this assertion, modernization could never represent a universal good because it was never intended for indigenous communities. Within this discursive framework, Mexico's Amerindians by definition remained on the periphery until they assimilated to the mestizo order. Gareth Williams explains the coercive underbelly of postrevolutionary biopolitics as he argues that "modernity in Mexico was orchestrated by a total state that strived at all times to suppress the duality of state and society" (12). Williams's words explain the postrevolutionary state's constant endeavors to construct a mestizo national body that it could forcefully assimilate; as it did this it suppressed the voices of those indigenous actors who did not uphold officialist values and doctrines.

In many ways, the postrevolutionary state began to code Amerindian bodies and lives as "bare" and even subhuman. Here it is useful to turn to Giorgio Agamben, who problematically argues that biopolitical states divide their populations into two groups: *bios*, those people who live full, "good" lives; and *zoê*, those people whose bare lives do not even register as human (10–14). One of Agamben's most problematic assertions is that the zoê live beyond the protection of the law and can therefore become "homines sacri" who can be killed with impunity during times of crisis. Given that postrevolutionary biopolitical paradigms rarely (if ever) reached this extreme at an institutional level, Agamben's theories apply only partially to this time period.[25] That said, I concur with Janzen, who argues that Agamben can help us to elucidate the state's relation with the national body. As she argues, "biopower, for Agamben, focuses on the bodies of marginalized people, which in the traditional philosophical understanding were bare life, zoê, that could be transformed into good life" (10). The state's attempts to assimilate indigenous actors revealed its desire to transform a perceived zoê into bios. In order to justify the marginalization of contemporary Amerindians without undermining the value of the mestizo "majority" that they hoped to foment, state-sponsored artists—particularly indigenistas—reified the pre-Columbian past. Mestizo Mexicans thus became the official heirs of pre-Columbian greatness, while contemporary Amerindians were problematically coded as backward and in need of saving. Because it conflated mixed-race identity with modernity, the state had to invent strategies that would allow present-day Amerindians to achieve mestizaje. For this very reason, officialist thinkers and cultural producers turned to technological hybridity as a strategy for creating mestizos in previously indigenous communities.

The key role of the technologized body in creating and enforcing biopolitical divides within postrevolutionary Mexico sits in direct opposition to Haraway's assertion that "the cyborg is not subject to Foucault's biopolitics; the cyborg simulates politics, a much more potent field of operations" (163).[26] Despite Haraway's assertions to the contrary, the technologically hybrid, cyborg subject of postrevolutionary Mexico by definition interfaced with and informed the biopolitical state. The allure of technological hybridity was its ability to modify the reigning biopolitical paradigms; however, the result was not an elimination of biopolitics but the installation of a new one. Cyborg identity often afforded greater privilege to previously marginalized individuals and communities; at other times, this fusion with technology simply amplified a person's position in existing hierarchies of power. This oppressive potential for cyborg identity grates against the grain of Haraway's thought. In her first discussions of cyborg identity in 1985, Haraway focused on the figure's liminal status as a hybrid entity articulated from the threshold of human, animal, and machine (151–52).[27] Given its ambiguity, the cyborg became the perfect metaphor for questioning the boundaries of race, class, and gender (155–61). This led her to assert a highly liberatory potential latent to the figure as it resisted gendered (and racialized) structures of power. The majority of the criticism has since challenged her optimism; Clynes dismisses her arguments when he states that cyborg identity—such as that attained when a person rides a bicycle—does not change a person's "essential identity" (Gray, "Interview" 49). Jennifer González asserts that "despite the potentially progressive implications of a cyborg subject position, the cyborg is not necessarily more likely to exist free of the social constraints which apply to humans and machines already" (61; see also Anne Balsamo 155).

The critiques mentioned above are well taken; simple tool use—or even the fusion of the body with technology—does not (generally) change a person's sex or gender, and in the U.S. context from which she writes, it rarely (if ever) amends racial identity. However, given the greater slippage between racial categories in Mexico, it appears that, in that context, technological hybridity actually could (and did) interface with and amend how society read people's racial identity. That technologized bodies would interface with the body politics of Latin American countries differently from how they do with those of Europe and North America buoys J. Andrew Brown's observation that current cyborg theories "often fail to transcend the North American and European contexts in which they are articulated" (*Cyborgs* 2). As we adapt theorizations of posthuman identity to the Mexican context, it appears that technological modifications of the body redraw the reigning body politics, and, perhaps more interestingly, leave new paradigms of equally rigid racial and gender performativity in their stead. When Judith Butler developed the term "performativity," she did so focusing specifically on the extent to which interpellations of the sexed body produce constructs of gender and sexuality, which in turn shape the agency of individuals within society. Her observations about gender hold true for other social constructs of corporeal agency—particularly those of race—as well. Haraway wrote her "Cyborg Manifesto" a few years before Butler would publish *Gender Trouble*, and her assertion that cyborg entities break down performative interpellations of the body suggests a special, resistant element to the articulation of the technologically hybrid body. Cyborg identity does not automatically denaturalize or subvert interpellations of the body, but it does trouble the reigning body politics—particularly those of gender and race—as it becomes a new body within the system. This forces society to negotiate what privileges and responsibilities cyborg entities should receive, which shows that cyborg identity can be either liberatory or oppressive. As the technologized body reconfigures the reigning body politics, previously subaltern bodies can become more legible and receive greater privilege. This is rarely due to a more just body politics, but rather to the superimposition of a new type of body onto the system.

Cyborg discourses within postrevolutionary Mexico both elucidate and challenge the ways in which U.S. scholars have historically tied the figure to mixed-race identity. The Chicana scholar Chela Sandoval, for example, attempts to rhetorically deracialize the cyborg by viewing it as "a differential form of oppositional consciousness, as utilized and theorized by a racially diverse U.S. coalition of women of color" (410). Even as she deracializes the figure, she also highlights its ties to hybridity and even mestizaje (408–9, 410–12). Her rhetorical strategy proves useful in maneuvering beyond the black/white racial binary that continued in the U.S. imaginary until at least the end of the twentieth century (Daniel 36), but it is impossible to articulate mestizaje free from constructs of race. This is especially the case in Sandoval's work because her figure takes on a resistant nature only as she places it in direct opposition to Western white male hegemony. She provides excellent theorizations of how U.S. women of color can resist, but her uncritical treatment of mestizaje as a discourse of inclusion seems inappropriate in the Mexican context. Part of Sandoval's treatment of mestizaje comes from the fact that she inherits the intellectual tradition of Gloria Anzaldúa, whose *Borderlands: The New Mestiza* reconfigured Vasconcelos's "cosmic race" and posited a "mestiza" as the champion of her own racially hybrid (and diverse) U.S. Southwest (77–91).[28] Given the back-and-forth dialogue between Sandoval and Haraway, as well as Anzaldúa's prominent role in the background of both women's writing, it becomes clear that the Chicano/a movement greatly informed theories of cyborg identity. This suggests that Vasconcelos specifically—and, by extension, the postrevolutionary ideology of official mestizaje generally—lies in the background of cyborg theory. Viewed in this light, our knowledge of how projects of official mestizaje would play out in Mexico proves invaluable in tempering some of cyborg theory's inherent optimism.

Unlike Sandoval, postrevolutionary letrados and state officials viewed mestizaje as a clear racial category that they could use to eugenically modernize and "improve" indigenous Mexico. That it could achieve racial hybridity by technologizing Amerindian bodies suggests that the liberatory potential of cyborg identity depends on differing subjects' points of view. From an officialist standpoint, changes to the reigning body politics became liberatory as they protected the state from both transnational (particularly U.S.) white supremacy and indigenous "backwardness." That said, it is difficult to view the paternalistic goal of "redeeming the Indian" as liberatory when viewed from the indigenous subject position. State projects employed a rhetoric of domination in order to coerce Amerindians—as well as women, workers, and children (T. Benjamin 479)—to conform to the patriarchal norms of official mestizaje. The postrevolutionary state's ambiguous, anticolonial, yet colonizing articulation of technological and genetic hybridities calls to mind the assertions of Gill Kirkup, who states that the cyborg's "usefulness for cultural deconstruction of gender [and race] has become apparent, but its usefulness as a tool for material changes is yet to be proved" (5). Within postrevolutionary Mexico, the cyborg body truly did foment "material change," albeit in the opposite sense. As the state took advantage of the technologized body's potential to undermine previous, Porfirian constructs of race and gender, it inscribed a new one that was equally oppressive.

Racial and technological hybridity proved especially problematic because both were coded specifically as the illegitimate progeny of oppressive systems of domination. Racial hybridity invoked the mythic union of Hernán Cortés with la Malinche, a violent relationship that many thinkers have cited as the source of the nation's painful constructs of race, gender, and ethnicity.[29] In a similar vein, Haraway posits cyborg identity as "the illegitimate offspring of militarism and patriarchal capitalism, not to mention state socialism" (151). The technological hybridity of Mexico differs from the cyborg of Haraway's thought in many ways; however, it still results from Westernized notions of modernity, industry, economics, and imperialism. Somewhat ironically, then, postrevolutionary letrados and artists viewed official mestizaje—itself a construct of internal colonialism—as key to resisting Western encroachment in Mexican affairs. For her part, Haraway attempts to move beyond the problems of the cyborg genesis when she says that "illegitimate offspring are often exceedingly unfaithful to their origins" (151), thus positing the figure's resistant qualities despite its oppressive parentage. A similar dynamic emerged within the discourse of official mestizaje, where racially hybrid Mexicans may have been the progeny of an imperial Europe and a "degenerate" indigeneity, but their racial and cultural fusion would create an inclusive, even "cosmic" race (Vasconcelos, *Cosmic Race*).[30] Despite its problematic articulation, most postrevolutionary thinkers viewed mestizaje as an evolutionary improvement to the body. As such, a posthuman reading of this racial discourse sheds further light on how it was understood in postrevolutionary society.

At its core, posthuman theory denaturalizes the primacy of *Homo sapiens* in the world. Because contemporary humans evolved from protohuman ancestors (Cochran and Harpending 1–23), it is only natural that another entity will eventually succeed them. This ultimate transcending of the human may occur through cybernetic fusions between flesh and metal (Naam 233), contact with aliens and other intelligent nonhuman life, or, less spectacularly, through natural selection and evolution. All of these examples of the posthuman appear in postrevolutionary Mexican literary and cultural production, and their ties to racial ideologies are usually quite clear. The most extraordinary facet of posthuman theory is that contemporary *Homo sapiens* are cognizant of the potential to move beyond the human and that they will play an integral role in their own evolution (McIntosh 5–6). State actors in Mexico clearly operated within posthuman paradigms as they engaged in eugenic projects that would racially "improve" the nation and move the race forward. Theorists like Robert Doede signal the defining characteristics of post- and transhumanism as the belief in "perpetual progress, spurning most traditional biological, genetic, religious, and intellectual constraints on progress, and . . . an implicit trust in science and technology to bring unlimited lifespan, intelligence, personal vitality, and freedom" (228).[31] His argument justifies a posthuman reading of the postrevolutionary state's unshakeable faith in both technology and progress, but he also seems to elide the possibility of transcending the human through genetics. This reflects in part his subject position in an academy where Mendelian genetics is the norm. His words take on new value when applied to early and mid-twentieth-century Mexico, where the prevalence of Lamarckian paradigms made it impossible to distinguish physical changes to the body from those to the genotype. The evolution of the national genome sat at the heart of Mexico's attempts to "perfect" its population by fomenting mestizo subjectivity through technological hybridity.

Beyond equating mestizo modernity with the posthuman, many postrevolutionary artists pejoratively ascribed "protohuman" elements to those racial identities that differed from or challenged mestizo normativity. Most representations of the protohuman referred to indigenous Mexico, but as I show in chapter 1, José Vasconcelos used protohuman discourses to critique Anglo-Saxon society as well. Similar to posthumanism, protohumanism juxtaposes contemporary humanity with an Other whose humanity is somehow incommensurable to that seen in present-day society. Whereas posthumanism places humanity alongside that which may come, protohumanism considers those "prehistoric" beings that preceded contemporary societies. The difference may be biological, as in the case of the evolutionary ancestors of *Homo sapiens*, or it may refer to ancient human beings and civilizations whose ways of life are forever hidden due to a lack of written language and historical records (Pratt 15–16). It is problematic to denote pre-Columbian Mexico as prehistoric in chronological terms, but we can still assert a type of discursive protohumanity in that there are no decipherable writings from before the Conquest. For Dale Pratt, protohumans have a culture and language, but they remain Other precisely because we have no legible, firsthand account of their society (17). Pratt's definition suggests that postrevolutionary Mexico ascribed protohuman tendencies to pre-Columbian societies; these representations were generally favorable, but they also signaled indigenous Mexico as irrevocably lost and Other. These ancient civilizations' incommensurability emerged not from an inferiority to modern Mexico, but from a lack of decipherable records from the previous society.

Officialist thinkers contradicted their generally positive affirmation of pre-Columbian cultures when they ascribed protohuman qualities to both the indigenous people of colonial times and even those of contemporary society. In both cases, this Amerindian protohumanity depended on assertions of indigenous illiteracy and passivity in creating national history. That state leaders could discursively associate indigenous people with protohumanity reflects José Rabasa's assertion that, since its inception, mestizo society has systematically withheld indigenous peoples from official history (138–47). Many state-funded murals and films equated contemporary Amerindians with protohumanity by juxtaposing them with a conquered pre-Columbian society. José Clemente Orozco, for example, emphasized the primitivity of colonial Amerindians through clothing—or the lack thereof—and physical features that posited them as cavemen. Chapter 4 shows how the specters of indigenous legend—particularly la Llorona and indigenous mummies—became monstrous articulations of the protohuman. Both of these cases show that, despite generally favorable representations of pre-Columbian societies, postrevolutionary artists and directors viewed indigenous identities and cosmologies as a threat to the mestizo order.

The ultimate goal of officialist literary and cultural production was to impose a new mentality on the inhabitants of Mexico—criollo, mestizo, and indigenous. Officialist works often favored market-based economics, and they necessarily celebrated the incorporation of Amerindians into metropolitan centers and the workforce. Racial identity stemmed not only from interpellations of the body, but also from a person's ability to move within "modern" society. The very act of accepting technological hybridity became a means by which indigenous Mexicans could shed their previous racial identity and conform to the new, mestizo imaginary. At least when viewed through the postrevolutionary government's lens of official mestizaje, a body could not be both indigenous and technologically hybrid. As they accepted technological hybridity, indigenous bodies entered culturally, economically, and even genetically (in a Lamarckian sense) into the mestizo mainstream. Far from liberatory, cyborg discourse often became yet another imperializing force. In the pages that follow, I track numerous representations of cyborg and posthuman imageries in state-sponsored literary and cultural production from the postrevolutionary period and discuss their ramifications on racial identity in Mexico. As I look at Mexican essays, murals, films, theatre, and narratives produced between the 1920s and 1970s, my project shows how official discourses of race and technology evolved over the decades. However, I also emphasize the remarkable fact that Mexican thinkers of numerous stripes constantly returned to the technologized body to articulate their competing versions of mestizo modernity.

Chapter 1, "Science and the (Meta)Physical Body: A Critique of Positivism in the Vasconcelian Utopia," discusses José Vasconcelos's notion of a cosmic race through a posthuman reading of his seminal essay *The Cosmic Race* [*La raza cósmica*] (1925) and his largely forgotten play *Prometeo vencedor* (1916?). Because Vasconcelos and his Ateneo colleagues were all famously antipositivist, they were suspicious of scientific discourses that purported to hold a monopoly on the truth. However, they also lived in a twentieth-century society in which scientific discourse had gained intellectual hegemony. My chapter begins by asserting science as one of many discourses that compose Vasconcelos's philosophy of aesthetic monism, which subordinates human knowledge to an overriding aesthetic imperative. Afterward, I use a close reading of *Prometeo vencedor* to assert the key role of science—especially in the guise of technology—in establishing both a worldwide mestizo society and a spiritual, posthuman superation of the body.

Chapter 2, "Painting *Mestizaje* in a New Light: Racial, Technological, and Cultural Hybridity in the Murals of Diego Rivera and José Clemente Orozco," discusses the tensions inherent to an official project of mestizaje through racial and technological hybridities. The chapter analyzes the state-funded murals of Diego Rivera and José Clemente Orozco, two artists who served as de facto mouthpieces for the state as they trumpeted the postrevolutionary tenets of official mestizaje through their work. My analysis shows that, despite sharing the state's seal of approval, the two men communicated contradictory racial discourses as they disagreed about the proper place of the nation's European and indigenous heritage within the official ideology. This is because, at its core, both men's work was pro-mestizo despite the fact that they conceived mixed-race identity in very different ways. Orozco's understanding of racial and technological hybridity tended toward hispanismo as he constantly validated the result—if not the means—of the Spanish Conquest. Unlike Orozco, Rivera carefully separated European science—which he celebrated—from the cosmology that had permitted the destruction of thousands of indigenous lives. Instead, he posited an essentialistic indigenous spirit that would redeem mestizo Mexico from the conquering nature it had inherited from its European progenitors. This paternalistic understanding of indigeneity led to an indigenista discourse that became the favored paradigm of official mestizaje—at least as represented in state-funded discourses—through the midcentury.

Chapter 3, "Emilio Fernández, Gabriel Figueroa, and the Race for Mexico's Body: Immunization and Lamarckian Genetics," looks at an especially interesting articulation of the posthuman within the indigenista films of Emilio "El Indio" Fernández. Here I identify an attempt to modernize indigenous peasants by exposing their bodies to modern medicine. I view these films in the context of Roberto Esposito's "immunization paradigm," a biopolitical theory that compares the medical process of immunization to the state's role of subject creation. When a people lacks a natural immunity to a vice—improper racial and gender performativity in the case of these films—a new actor, such as the state, must step in and provide an artificial immunity. Using this theoretical framework, I analyze his films *Río Escondido* (1947), *María Candelaria* (1944), *Enamorada* (1946), and *The Torch* (1950). My approach to these films suggests that we read them as allegories for a postrevolutionary society where immunological discourses prescribe appropriate gender and racial performativity for the nation.

Chapter 4, "Colonizing Resistance: Liminal Imperiality in the Cinema of El Santo and in Carlos Olvera's *Mejicanos en el espacio*," discusses two venues that continued to debate the relationship among modernity, technological hybridity, and mestizaje as the postrevolutionary state began to lose credibility. I focus primarily on the Mexploitation cinema of El Santo and Carlos Olvera's novel *Mejicanos en el espacio* (1968). The novel is highly critical of the state, while the movies (somewhat ironically) support mestizo nationalism. The 1955 ban of *lucha libre* from Mexican televisions led to the production of more than three hundred lucha libre films, fifty-two of which starred El Santo. Due in part to a desire to placate the censors, the directors of lucha libre cinema validated statist ideals of mestizaje and modernity. Throughout his cinema, El Santo played an authentically Mexican, mestizo superhero who defended the nation both against the threat of external empire—symbolized by aliens and foreign mad scientists—and from the specters of the indigenous past. Whether fighting foreign or indigenous monsters in a particular movie, El Santo constantly asserted mestizo Mexico's right to colonize its indigenous population even as he decried foreign attempts to meddle in his country's internal affairs. For its part, Olvera's novel deconstructs and ridicules official discourses that justified internal empire. *Mejicanos en el espacio* imagines a twenty-second-century Centroméjico that attempts to assert its modernity by mimicking the imperial behavior of nations like the United States. In the end, the novel suggests that mestizo Mexico's drive for empire actually validates the global hierarchies of power that allow other countries to interfere in its own domestic politics.

Through these chapters, I show that technology played a key role in race formation in Mexico throughout the twentieth century. Beyond adding to our understanding of the texts that they engage, these chapters also elucidate the attitudes and ideologies that inform race relations into the present. As we look at Mexican literary and cultural production, we get a glimpse into how some of the country's brightest minds viewed the role of technology in subject formation. My case studies show how these thinkers invoked various hybridities to reconcile questions of race, gender, culture, and modernity within the nation. Hybridity informs not only Latin American theorists, but also postcolonialists like Homi Bhabha, Gayatri Chakravorty Spivak, Stuart Hall, and Paul Gilroy. *Mestizo Modernity: Race, Technology, and the Body in Postrevolutionary Mexico* adds to current conversations in both fields by focusing on the hybrid body.

Indeed, one of my aims in writing is to show the value of in-depth case studies in showing how posthuman theory can shed light on the ways that the technologically hybrid body interfaces with postcolonial discourses and the state. While I focus primarily on Mexico, my findings shed light on Latin America and the developing world at large. This book also adds to our understanding of twentieth- (and perhaps twenty-first-) century identitary discourses in Mexico, particularly the problematic relationship among race, technology, and modernity.

1

Science and the (Meta)Physical Body

A Critique of Positivism in the Vasconcelian Utopia

No thinker more fully embodies postrevolutionary Mexican racial attitudes than José Vasconcelos, the great proponent of Latin American mestizaje. The philosopher first publicly enunciated his "aesthetic" ideal of racial hybridity in Lima in 1916, and he went on to write numerous texts on the subject that had a great effect throughout the region (Marentes 80). He spent most of the Revolution abroad, but returned to Mexico after President Álvaro Obregón invited him to head the country's education efforts. Vasconcelos founded the Secretariat of Public Education [Secretaría de Educación Pública] (SEP) and served as its first secretary from 1921 to 1924. The government leader explicitly opposed both *indigenismo* and nineteenth-century positivism on philosophical grounds (Skirius, *José Vasconcelos* 21), but his work largely—and perhaps inadvertently—buoyed each of the aforementioned discourses by adding a metaphysical value to mixed-race identity (Sacoto 154–60). It is truly remarkable that his racial theory, which flirted with fascism (Sánchez Prado, "Mestizaje" 390), also reverberated with the thought of such disparate figures as the communist muralists, the leaders of the modernity-driven capitalist state, and even Chicano activists in the southwestern United States (Anzaldúa 77; Stavans 4–6, 11–13). At times Vasconcelos disapproved of how others articulated his ideas (Marentes 60–74); at others he compromised his aesthetic ideals with political pragmatism (Fell, *Águila* 216; Swarthout 119–21).[1]

His seminal essay *The Cosmic Race* [*La raza cósmica*] (1925), which problematically argues for mestizo identity in Mexico, has enjoyed a special place in the Mexican canon because it supposedly captures the essence of the mixed-race dogmas that permeated the postrevolutionary state. Ironically, he published the work while living in exile in Barcelona shortly after resigning from his position with the SEP, so his text was not immediately available within his home country.[2] However, his "language of race" (Lund, *Mestizo* x) had already played a fundamental role in shaping discourses of mexicanidad far beyond the academy. Octavio Paz notes the philosopher's perpetual relevance within Mexican thought when he writes, "The philosophy of Vasconcelos contains fragments that are still alive and fecund, portions that still illuminate and even prophesy" (*Labyrinth of Solitude* 155). Vasconcelos aimed to create a new Mexican and Latin American order through his writing and participation in the government. Despite many studies that cite his as the authoritative voice of early postrevolutionary official mestizaje, his work also had serious breaches with official discourses. Given his prominence in the public sphere, however, his was one of the most influential voices of the Mexican intelligentsia. Prior to writing *The Cosmic Race*, Vasconcelos had already published other texts, most notably the philosophical play *Prometeo vencedor* (1916?), that identified mixed-race identity as a necessary component of progress and modernity. In this chapter I view his essay *The Cosmic Race* and his play *Prometeo vencedor* alongside one another. After situating my argument within the existing scholarship on *The Cosmic Race*, I provide a close reading of his play to show that Vasconcelos viewed science—when subordinated to aesthetics—as key to producing an improved humanity, and even posthumanity. *Prometeo vencedor* may have been "universally ignored" (Legrás, *Culture and Revolution* 100), but it provides fascinating insights into how the author understood race and eugenics.

Vasconcelos's racial theory reduces world history to a narrative in which different races have dominated global politics for a finite period of time before humanity has advanced and a new race has taken over (*Cosmic Race* 9–16). The Mexican thinker's racial theory builds on yet rejects the work of Herbert Spencer, a nineteenth-century English philosopher who believed that all human races had evolved to fit their natural habitats and that, as a result, "the white man excels . . . in moral susceptibility" (25). While Vasconcelos agreed that humanity was in a process of constant progression, he resisted Spencer's notion of European—particularly Anglo-Saxon—moral superiority and instead posited mestizaje as the racial ideal. The Mexican letrado's understanding of an ever-progressing humanity placed his work in direct conversation with the evolutionary paradigms of the day, a fact that suggests that his work warrants a posthuman reading. Because one underlying supposition of posthumanism is that it considers humanity to be an evolutionary phase that was born from protohuman ancestors (Cochran and Harpending 1–23), it is only natural to assume that contemporary humanity will one day sire new posthumanities that will eventually take its place. Vasconcelos's mestizo identity remains in the human—rather than posthuman—sphere, but it still represents a new, perfected articulation of humanity. The thinker sincerely believed that racial hybrids would eventually become the hegemonic race as white criollos interbred with Amerindians and blacks. Despite this mixed heritage, mestizaje would not value all sides of the racial equation equally (Ortega 37–42); Vasconcelos's belief that European hegemony resulted from superior racial practices led him to favor cultural forms that would Europeanize mestizo identity (Garciadiego 179–91). The thinker constantly affirmed that the active role for indigenous subjects in ushering in a utopian humanity would be their sacrifice of both body and culture to the national cause by procreating a mixed-race state. Indeed, Vasconcelos's racially charged ideology called on Mexicans of indigenous and African descent to knowingly and happily "redeem" themselves through a "voluntary extinction" that would occur as they bred with "superior" races and sired a (post)human future (*Cosmic Race* 32).[3]

The thinker's aesthetic justification for mestizaje differed from that championed by the postrevolutionary state, which primarily employed racial hybridity as a discursive tool for incorporating indigenous populations into the workforce. It is for this reason that Betsabé Arreola Martínez argues that Vasconcelos "provided a philosophical, historical, and anthropological dimension to ethnic heterogeneity through the incorporation of indigenous peoples to civilized society by making them mestizos" ["Vasconcelos jug[ó] un papel fundamental al otorgarle una dimensión filosófica, histórica y antropológica de la heterogeneidad étnica, mediante la incorporación de los pueblos indígenas a la vida civilizada haciéndolos mestizos."] (4). Vasconcelos did not want to undertake indigenista projects, and he certainly did not wish to build a capitalist state following the U.S. model. Nevertheless, in fetishizing racial miscegenation, he aligned himself with the utilitarian focus of postrevolutionary official mestizaje. At the same time, official mestizaje came to embrace Vasconcelos's redemptive discourse, thus ascribing a metaphysical, nationalistic value to a movement that had historically enunciated itself in purely utilitarian terms. The two visions of racial hybridity were thus conflated as one functioned in practice and the other as a philosophical and ideological explanation of national character. The final sentence of the introduction to *The Cosmic Race* states, "We in America shall arrive, before any other part of the world, at the creation of a new race fashioned out of the treasures of all the previous ones: The final race, the cosmic race" (40). Far from merely justifying the incorporation of darker-skinned Mexicans into the economy, Vasconcelos viewed racial miscegenation as necessary to redeeming the nation's soul. This spiritual dimension, with its clear allusion to progress, fit naturally within the official discourse of a state that fetishized industrialization and "progress."

The letrado's close association with the modernity-driven, postrevolutionary state meant that his racial philosophy would inevitably interface with scientific discourses. This is especially noteworthy because Vasconcelos's most visible ideological battle was against positivism, a discourse that took hold during the Porfiriato (1876–1910) (Quintanilla 195–200; Zea, *Precursores* 117). For Charles Hale, positivist politics' "principal characteristics were an attack on doctrinaire liberalism, or 'metaphysical politics,' an apology for strong government to counter endemic revolutions and anarchy, and a call for constitutional reform" (27). The quest for objective truths produced institutionalized favoritism toward scientific knowledge. Abelardo Villegas argues that this led to serious hubris and assertions of scientific superiority "that were defended not by the ever-cautious science, but by the scientifists, the positivists" ["que nunca defendió la ciencia siempre cautelosa, sino los cientificistas, los positivistas"] (*Autognosis* 11). For this very reason, positivism was vulnerable to critiques from humanistic and metaphysical viewpoints. As Leopoldo Zea points out, however, positivist thinkers simply ignored those philosophers who challenged their ideas (*Positivismo* 16). This outright rejection of metaphysical knowledge led Vasconcelos and several intellectuals from his generation to form El Ateneo de la Juventud, an organization that advocated humanism over positivism. The members of the organization held very different political and ideological views: some supported Porfirio Díaz, while others supported Venustiano Carranza, Francisco I. Madero, and even Victoriano Huerta (Crespo 71–73).

Rather than politics, then, antipositivism and a distrust of an overemphasis on science served as the binding glue that kept the Ateneo together. According to Vasconcelos, "the relativity of scientific knowledge, invading the sovereign spheres of philosophy, transform[s] principles of logic, morality, taste, and all forms of thought" ["La relatividad del conocimiento científico, invadiendo las soberanas esferas de la filosofía, transformaba los principios lógicos, la moral y el gusto, y todo el pensamiento."] (*Monismo* 3). Science did not represent a threat in and of itself; instead it became problematic only as it attempted to assert itself beyond its proper sphere. The letrado's general acceptance of science despite his antipositivism resulted in part from his reading of the French philosopher Henri Bergson; indeed, Vasconcelos once stated that his readings of the aforementioned thinker led him to believe that "a philosophy is not complete . . . if it ignores the knowledge of its time: in our case, a philosophy that ignores scientific data from the past century is incomplete" ["No es completa una filosofía . . . que hace a un lado el saber particular de su tiempo; en nuestro caso, una filosofía que no tome en cuenta los datos de la ciencia experimental del último siglo."] ("Bergson" 239). Vasconcelos certainly believed that the *científicos* had committed a grave error, and even produced a spiritual plague (*Monismo* 3–5), by exalting science above all other forms of knowledge. Rather than reject science outright, however, Vasconcelos favored "aesthetic monism," a symphony of discourses, all of which were subordinated to a metaphysical paradigm (Romanell 503–8).

As secretary of public education, Vasconcelos implemented programs that upheld this ideal of aesthetic monism by emphasizing both the humanities and the sciences. His opposition to positivist education almost certainly took on a personal dimension; his decision to study law had come about only because positivist forces had removed philosophy from university curricula (Jaén xx). Given his historical antagonism toward positivism and the sciences, many critics have interpreted Vasconcelos's aesthetic monism as a form of antiscience (Foster 66–67; Garrido 76). These studies rigorously show how Vasconcelos challenged scientific paradigms and knowledge throughout his work, and they prove invaluable to understanding his thought. Hale, however, asserts that Vasconcelos "repudiated positivism, except in aspects of his social thought" (259). As such, Vasconcelian politics—at least within Hale's view—would become the postrevolutionary state's newest incarnation of positivism.[4] Hale is right to recognize certain congruencies between Vasconcelian thought and that of his positivist forebears. Joshua Lund, for example, notes that the letrado's racial discourse followed in the *científicos*' footsteps by serving as "an effective articulation of race and time that helps to reconcile the hegemony of the nation with the sovereignty of the state" (*Impure* 108). Vasconcelos's allusions to evolution theory—even in light of his rejection of Darwinism and (especially) Spencerism (*Cosmic Race* 3; Stavans 16–17)—for example, placed him in conversation with the scientific discourses of the day, while his ideal of corporeal "progress" invoked the positivist notion of using science to "improve" society. Clearly, Vasconcelos's antipositivism grew out of the intellectual tradition of his positivist forebears.

Vasconcelos frequently and paradoxically turned to scientific discourse to buoy his antipositivist ideas. This led to "an often unwieldy interdependence of the mystical and the material" within Vasconcelos's writings that makes it especially difficult to place him ideologically (M. G. Miller 29). Jerry Hoeg clears up some of the confusion by referring to science as "an 'over there' within the *Raza cósmica* [*The Cosmic Race*] [and by extension the author's entire oeuvre], an other that must, at some point[,] emerge" (76).[5] Science necessarily sits at the heart of Vasconcelos's writings, but its role is one of catalyzing a metaphysically perfected, utopian (post)humanity. This chapter further develops Hoeg's "over there" by showing how Vasconcelos carefully crafts a utopian philosophy in which science plays a key, supporting role in the aesthetic politics of continued human evolution.[6] My findings differ from those of previous studies on Vasconcelos—like those of Alberto Zum Felde (419-29) and Jaime A. Giordano (545-48)—that emphasize the metaphysical dimension of Vasconcelos's thought but downplay the role of science beyond that of ideational antagonist. Such a posture ignores the fact that science enjoyed a privileged position in Vasconcelos's education campaigns (Sosa Ramos 137-40).[7] The secretary of public education viewed scientific discourse as a necessary component of his metaphysics, and he truly believed that his work would bridge the gap between philosophy and the sciences, thus signaling a "proper," aesthetic path for Mexico, Latin America, and the world (Jaén xix).

The philosopher's primary goal was to place all types of human knowledge—ranging from science to the humanities—in their proper place. He frequently recurred to scientific discourses to give further credence to his mixed-race utopias. For example, *The Cosmic Race* begins with the assertion that geologists now recognize America as the site of Atlantis (7). This (pseudo)scientific argument suggests a forever utopian element, as well as an ancient archeological prestige and culture, in Latin America (Grijalva, "Vasconcelos" 336-37). Here we must amend Paz's assertion that Vasconcelos's "traditionalism did not look to the past for support: it was to be justified in and by the future" (*Labyrinth of Solitude* 154). Instead, we can more precisely state that Vasconcelos justified his vision of Mexico and Latin America through utopian discourses centered both on the region's past grandeur and future potential. According to Ruth Levitas, utopian discourses function as a "method" for facilitating the "imaginary reconstitution of society" (xiv). Her approach allows us to gauge how Vasconcelos used notions of both past and future to create a regional ideal that appealed to readers from all over Latin America. Within his world, eugenic and technological advancements would work hand-in-hand with enlightened, lettered, and officialist philosophies to catalyze a truly "cosmic" race. Once again we see a potential for the reconciliation of scientific and humanistic knowledge, but any attempt at this must recognize the primacy of the metaphysical.

This tension between science and spirit played out dramatically in Vasconcelos's tenure with the SEP. The secretary of public education aimed to provide identical educational opportunities to all Mexican children regardless of race, so he opposed teaching indigenous children in their native languages (Fuentes 124). Nevertheless, certain (neo)positivists, particularly Manuel Gamio, undertook indigenista initiatives that aimed to incorporate Mexican Amerindians into the state by tailoring education to this population's needs. Faced with this reality, Vasconcelos compromised his mixed-race aesthetics and authorized indigenista policies "because he feared that the SEP would lose its mandate for indigenous education to the 'scientists' in the Department of Anthropology" (Swarthout 119). This resulted in two oppositional government ministries with mandates to assimilate the indigenous population. The SEP advocated a cleansing of the spirit, while Gamio's Department of Anthropology favored science and secularism (Swarthout 120; Fell, *Águila* 221).[8] The disagreement between the Secretaries of Education and Anthropology probably cost the country a great deal of resources and direction as it attempted to assimilate its Amerindians. Furthermore, the at times contradictory government agencies sent mixed messages regarding the means and reasons for assimilation. Gamio and Vasconcelos positioned science differently in their writing due to how they viewed positivistic discourse. As Ignacio M. Sánchez Prado argues, "for Gamio, a true heir of positivism, the task of developing the nation fell to science, and mestizaje referred simply . . . to the integration of the Indian to national life through the instruments of modern anthropology" ["Para Gamio, buen heredero del positivismo, correspondía a la ciencia el desarrollo de la nación, y el mestizaje se refería simplemente . . . a la integración del indio a la vida nacional por medio de los instrumentos de la antropología moderna."] ("Mestizaje" 386). Vasconcelos, however, viewed mixed-race identity as "a historic promise constructed upon the validation of mestizaje as central to contemporary politics and culture" ["una promesa histórica construida de la validación del mestizaje como eje político cultural"] (Sánchez Prado, "Mestizaje" 387). Thus the philosopher emphasized the metaphysical, utopian value of mixed-race identity, while the anthropologist sought only to use science to objectively modernize the state.

Despite Vasconcelos's focus on the spirit, we should not dismiss his racial thought as wholly unscientific. The author clearly wished to engage with positivistic discourses—albeit from a humanist perspective—in order to reframe the knowledge that these produced. This was most obvious regarding eugenics, which was an accepted paradigm within European—particularly British, German, and North American—circles long before Vasconcelos would ever put the pen to the page (Stepan 8). Many contemporary historians, intellectuals, and critics severely criticize the scientific racism of the early twentieth century, but few would label it as pseudoscience; instead, they generally cite more recent scientific advances that have disproven older paradigms (Stepan 5). Vasconcelos upheld certain aspects of white-supremacist eugenics, but he dissented from such worldviews as he posited a history of racial progress to inscribe mestizaje, rather than whiteness, as the eugenic ideal (M. G. Miller 34–35). Sánchez Prado warns against taking *The Cosmic Race* literally, saying instead that the thinker utilized the genre of the "utopian essay" ["ensayo utópico"] to posit mestizaje as a political strategy to articulate Latin American diversity—and unity—that serves as a precursor to transculturation, heterogeneity, and even hybridity ("Mestizaje" 382–83; see also Sobrevilla 21–23; and Klor de Alva 254–58). The strange fusion of scientific and utopian discourse created a unique eugenics that, in Rebecca Janzen's words, "outlines an esoteric and mystical vision of a better corporeal future for Mexico" (5). The critic's assertion rings especially true as we consider the triumphant imagery that Vasconcelos associated with racial miscegenation; he clearly posited that mestizo eugenics would transform Mexico (and the world) by spiritually improving the population.

Vasconcelos's thought fits within the current of early twentieth-century Latin Americanism that struggled to imagine ways for the region to maintain its autonomy in the face of a politically and economically aggressive United States.[9] José Enrique Rodó, one of the founders of the movement, "admired" North American (read: New World Anglo-Saxon) pragmatism's ability to revolutionize and modernize the United States (51), but he also asserted that the country's utilitarianism had left it morally bankrupt (46–50). Rodó prescribed inward meditation and reading the classics—particularly the works of the Greco-Roman tradition—as the best way to resist Yankee materialism (9–30). Rodó's work heavily influenced that of Vasconcelos (Crespo 97–99); indeed, both believed that U.S. imperialism posed an existential threat to Latin American (and

Mexican) society.[10] Nevertheless, Juan Carlos Grijalva notes that Vasconcelos moved beyond Rodó by heading an intellectual effort to reconcile his nation with its racial past ("Introducción" 9). Vasconcelos's play *Prometeo vencedor* is one of the earliest examples of his Latin Americanism; it exalts the classics by creating a futuristic world steeped in Greek mythology, but it also builds on and contributes to Mexican discourses of mestizaje that Rodó largely ignored. Thus the literary work invokes Latin Americanist ideas with a distinctly Mexican flavor. Claude Fell decries the play's overall low quality ("Ideario" 550), but the work provides fascinating insights into the writer's thought.

Given *Prometeo vencedor*'s intricate nature and deep intratextual ties to *The Cosmic Race*, it is surprising that the academy has largely forgotten it. Both texts represent different periods in Vasconcelos's life and career.[11] The essay came out shortly after his tenure with the SEP, and it preceded his failed presidential run by only four years; however, the writer published his play before embarking on his career in the public sector.[12] Rather than emphasize mestizaje as a political strategy as in *The Cosmic Race*, this earlier text couches mixed-race identity primarily in aesthetic terms. This shift in focus allows for fresh perspectives regarding the role Vasconcelos imagined for science in bringing about a spiritual, utopian rebirth of humanity. The Mexican philosopher's emphasis on a future utopia leads Silvia Spitta to argue that *The Cosmic Race* "today reads more like science fiction than the American and mestizo manifesto Vasconcelos proposed to write" (334). She would probably say the same about *Prometeo vencedor*, where (imagined) actors utilize futuristic technologies to embody mixed-race, eugenically improved protagonists. Vasconcelos's use of the utopian ideal means his work differs from most science fiction, where dystopia is generally the norm. The playwright shows no fatal flaws in mestizo society; instead, he emphasizes the harmonious nature of his fetishized mixed-race world order. Within this society, eugenic and technological advancements have worked hand-in-hand with enlightened, lettered philosophies to catalyze a truly "cosmic" (or celestial) race. Once again we see a potential for the reconciliation of scientific and humanistic knowledge, but any attempt at this must recognize the ultimate supremacy of the metaphysical.

Posthuman Presences in *Prometeo vencedor*

Vasconcelos dedicates the majority of his three-act play to three principal characters: Prometheus [Prometeo], Satan [Satanás], and a philosopher who is later reincarnated as Saturnino. María Sten categorizes the work as "more philosophical than dramatic" ["más filosófica que dramática"] (42), a fact that rings particularly true given that the play was never staged. A brief plot summary will facilitate the discussion of its treatment of race and scientific discourse. The first act begins when Satan finds Prometheus sitting between Popocatépetl and Ixtaccihuatl, the two famous volcanoes that separate Mexico City and Puebla. After a long conversation, a recently deceased Latin American philosopher appears on his journey to the afterlife; he proclaims that the people of Latin America will resolve their problems by embracing racial hybridity. The second act shows a renaissance that takes place one thousand years after the first act. Racial hybridity has spread throughout the world, and the philosopher has been reincarnated as Saturnino. He proclaims that humanity will finally transcend the body by refraining from reproduction. Outside of a few "ugly women" ["mujeres feas"], everyone adopts Saturnino's philosophy. The final act takes place years later; Satan, Prometheus, and Saturnino reunite in the Himalayas. The aging philosopher, now a hermit, is one of only three human beings left on earth. He awaits a signal from the other two—who live in America and Africa—via a contraption of bells on strings. After no message arrives, he concludes that the human spirit has progressed beyond the physical plane, and he dies. As soon as the philosopher falls to the ground, a "stupid" man dressed in a kangaroo skin enters the stage, stating that he is the child of the "ugly" women who refused to renounce reproduction. They had established a secret community and used a synthetic mist to evade the high-tech devices that Saturnino had used to search the globe for human life.

This text alludes to the privileged position that Vasconcelos ascribed to drama, and particularly the theatre, in promoting conversations of mexicanidad after—and perhaps even during—the Revolution (Ortiz Bullé Goyri 75–78).[13] The author may not have intended for this particular work to ever make its way to the national stage, but he clearly viewed the theatre as an effective medium for discussing the merits of mestizo identity. Ana María Introna argues that three of Vasconcelos's principal concerns in writing this play were to end European imperialism in Latin America, to signal ancient Greece and India as new historical models for the region to follow, and, perhaps most important, to assert the need for a messianic cultural figure (103–4). To a far greater degree than *The Cosmic Race*, this earlier work explicitly engages posthumanity, science, and technology as natural components of his racial ideal. The narrative is ultimately utopian, but the perfection of humanity occurs only after scientific and technological advances. Ironically, the fact that *Prometeo vencedor* has yet to find its way to the stage reflects its treatment of technology; given the inventions that the playwright imagines—and certain elements, like the sudden materialization of bodies on the stage—the play would have been technically infeasible to stage when it was written. For this reason, Sarah J. Townsend refers to it as a "closet drama," or a playscript that is "unsuitable for any actually existing stage" (45). Vasconcelos may not have intended to stage the play, but his use of a playscript signals that his audience should stage the events of *Prometeo vencedor* in their own minds. As such, theories of performance provide useful insights to the work.

Similar to *The Cosmic Race*, the entire play is an allegory for the whole of human history; the prologue—which is a narrative essay that is not even implicitly performed—tells of an animalian protohumanity that is doomed to roam the earth and acquiesce to those in power until Prometheus arrives and unlocks the secrets of fire, an act that emancipates protohumanity and allows it to become fully human. This beginning resonates especially soundly within posthuman thought because it deemphasizes the supposed exceptionalism of *Homo sapiens* within world history. Here humanity represents the current evolutionary stage of a specific species at a given point in time, and the possibility of evolving beyond this identity clearly exists. The thinker differs from scientific—although not necessarily positivist or Spencerist—understandings of human evolution in that he ascribes a metaphysical quality to human progression. He makes this especially clear as his protohumans' redemption occurs after a renegade deity—rather than a (proto)human intellectual or scientist—shares the knowledge of fire with humanity's ancestors. This fact deconstructs any rigid understandings of the physical and metaphysical realms as both are shown interacting to forge a single humanity—and later posthumanity—together. Within this framework racial "improvements" will not produce a "cosmic" posthumanity per se; instead, they represent ever-improving articulations of humanity that will eventually lead to the superation of the body and the creation of a posthuman spirituality.

The fact that Vasconcelos turns traditional religious antagonists—particularly Satan, but also Prometheus—into his play's protagonists alludes to the revolutionary nature of his redemptive, racial ideology. Just as these characters subvert their respective gods' notions of the status quo, the play's advocacy of racial hybridity grates against global discourses of white supremacy and Mexican and Latin American marginalization. The juxtaposition of these representatives of traditionally unpositivistic ways of knowing with scientific, posthuman discourses is key to uncovering the nuances in Vasconcelos's ideology. Rather than view science and metaphysics as distinctive, incommensurate ways of knowing, Vasconcelos attempts to reconcile both. Prometheus's power comes not from his desire to defy Zeus per se, but from his act of sharing scientific knowledge with—and thus beautifying—a damned protohumanity. Science has become a means for intelligent bodies to undergo metaphysical changes that advance them first from the protohuman stage to humanity, and later through humanity and into posthumanity. Science loses its supposed objectivity as it becomes a key player in the playwright's ideologically charged discussion of human history and aesthetic eugenics. Both (anti)deistic protagonists have very different styles, but they depend on one another throughout. Satan seeks Prometheus because both have stood against their respective deities (Zeus and Jehovah [Jehová]): Satan has constantly signaled the metaphysical shortcomings of any and all deities, while Prometheus has disobeyed a direct command. They have different motives, but Satan believes that they should work together to defend humanity from its oppressors. By overcoming Jehovah and Zeus, Satan and Prometheus nod toward a racial discourse that is both anti-Semitic—Satan has defeated the Jewish god—and even anti-European.[14] Certainly, people from Europe—particularly the Greeks—have made valuable contributions to society, but Vasconcelos signals that humanity has moved beyond Europe and into a mixed-race domain.

Despite their love of justice, both Prometheus and Satan unconsciously perpetuate racist ideologies through their racially charged worldviews and conversations. This is particularly true regarding the treatment of the Amerindian population of the Americas. We see an allusion to the role of indigenous Mexico in Vasconcelian thought in the negative space of the first act of this play. Satan and Prometheus discuss religious figures from the Greek, Jewish, and Christian traditions, but at no time do they mention Quetzalcóatl, Huitzilophochtli, Coatlicue, or any other Amerindian deities. Pre-Columbian religious history apparently does not merit discussion despite the fact that the duo is currently in Mexico. The ramifications of this fact are telling: if Satan has spent his entire life undermining unjust religious orders without ever confronting an indigenous deity, then Amerindians must have less to offer contemporary humanity than do their European counterparts. Furthermore, indigenous traditions cannot constitute Mexican (or Latin American) history; the nation is culturally European and racially/genetically hybrid.[15] Unlike the indigenista artists and intellectuals who reified the indigenous past but viewed the contemporary Amerindian as an obstacle to progress (a phenomenon I discuss in greater detail in the chapters that follow), Vasconcelos simply erases the history of his country's native population, or—as in the case of *The Cosmic Race*—he subordinates it to Europe by affirming ancient America as the site of Atlantis. Throughout the entire first act of *Prometeo vencedor*, the reader awaits any mention of indigenous Mexico, but the closest that we ever come is when the recently deceased Latin American philosopher proclaims his doctrine of racial mixing. Of course, this man focuses on mestizaje—and not on indigenous or Afro-Mexican identities—so even this allusion is only roundabout.

The philosopher's entrance is especially noteworthy, and it constitutes one of the more unperformable aspects of the play. According to the stage directions, several vibrations interrupt Prometheus and Satan as they speak, and then a man slowly appears out of thin air (40). This entrance imbues the philosopher with a supernatural aura that would be difficult to reproduce on a physical stage, especially in the early twentieth century (Townsend 56–57). The deceased philosopher has much in common with Vasconcelos; both the playwright and this character plan to problematically subordinate all races to the "Spanish mold" (Vasconcelos, *Prometeo* 41). The philosopher and Saturnino are fictitious representations of the person that Vasconcelos wished to become, and the philosopher's juxtaposition alongside Prometheus and Satan imbues him with a messianic glow. Unlike these other protagonists, who represent the fallen angels of their respective religious traditions, the philosopher—and his reincarnated form as Saturnino—is a redemptive combination of the Socratic philosopher and the Christological savior. Saturnino's reincarnation (or resurrection) is perhaps the greatest similarity between himself and Jesus, yet his resurrected form is that of a classical Greek philosopher who also has ties to Latin American mestizaje and even Hinduism. The character's salvatory potential comes out especially clearly as we compare him to Prometheus—another figure from ancient Greece—who showed protohumanity the light (literally) through his introduction of fire. The philosopher outdoes Prometheus as he aesthetically perfects the humanity that Prometheus catalyzed. Later, reincarnated as Saturnino, this same soul brings about the superation of the body by initiating a truly posthuman, and even postcorporeal, consciousness. Prometheus may have redeemed the protohuman, but it is Saturnino who completes the process by bringing about a spiritual posthumanity.

The deceased philosopher expresses his redemptive racial theory in the form of a classical Greek dialectic as he fields and responds to questions from both Prometheus and Satan. Prometheus soon recognizes this man as a kindred spirit, but the ever-critical Satan doubts the potential of Latin America to redeem the world as he points out the region's social problems and dictatorships (41). The philosopher agrees that Latin America faces many obstacles, but he also reiterates his conviction that the region's diversity—coupled with its love of liberty—will usher in humanity's salvation (41–42). By the play's end, we realize that the final redemption of "humanity" comes through its erasure and the superation of the body. Vasconcelos's assertion that humanity must overcome its body suggests that critics should view his work from a posthuman perspective. The writer's goal is to take humanity beyond current articulations of itself and bring about something new, even if that means the end of the human race as currently constituted. That Satan cannot dissuade the philosopher—and indeed the fact that he ultimately converts to Saturnino's cause—suggests that mestizaje will redeem not only Mexico and Latin America, but also the world at large. The discursive punch of this segment is especially powerful; Satan has defeated Jehovah, humbled Christ, and been a thorn in the side of all those who hold power—religious, political, philosophical, or otherwise—for millennia. Yet even he cannot find any unresolvable faults with the philosopher's notion of mestizaje, or, later, with Saturnino's goal of transcending the body. Viewed in its totality, Satan's endorsement of racial hybridity becomes one of Vasconcelos's strongest arguments for his racial ideal. The play's ending in the Himalayas both metaphorically expresses mestizaje's global reach and nods toward the Hindu mysticism that greatly influenced the playwright's thought (Jaén xxi). Satan cannot disagree with the philosopher's vision as he sees it carried out to this postorganismal extreme; racial hybridity seems to have transcended the carnal desires that have historically led to imperialism, war, and reproduction.

The way in which Vasconcelos's (imagined) actors embody mestizo subjects on the (imagined) stage elucidates some of the more confusing aspects of the thinker's cosmic race that no criticism has fully reconciled or explained. For example, *The Cosmic Race* posits four historical racial moments, and mestizaje appears as a new, fifth race (37–38). Nevertheless, most scholars of Mexico and Latin America identify mestizaje as Vasconcelos's fetishized "cosmic race." This association makes sense; the thinker discusses his fifth race's aesthetic favorability moments before asserting that the cosmic race will be born in America, and there is a clear relationship between the cosmic race and racial hybridity. However, in the prologue of his essay, Vasconcelos claims to have named his text *The Cosmic Race* because he lacked a better term for this fetishized entity (3). This suggests that the final race exists beyond mestizaje—which was a term that existed long before he wrote the essay. Racial hybridity, then, is a necessary step toward achieving a sixth race that will succeed even mestizaje. This interpretation seems especially appropriate in *Prometeo vencedor*, where Saturnino attempts to create his "celestial race"—an obvious synonym for cosmic race—by ending the process of human reproduction (77).

The cosmic/celestial race as represented in *Prometeo vencedor* has no body; rather it is the posthuman entity that emerges as mixed-race people transcend their corporeal nature through sexual renunciation. The play shows mestizaje as a great genetic and spiritual improvement to humanity, but racial hybridity ultimately remains within the human sphere. The second act shows an established mestizo society that has spread across the globe. According to Townsend, Vasconcelos recognized that the transitionary period—or "political stage" in which letrados would impose mestizaje upon the masses—could be "messy," so he decided to take his (reading) audience well into the future, long after the resolution of any conflicts (57). The result is an emphasis on the superior humanity that has come about through an aestheticized eugenics. Unlike the first and third acts, which take place in mountainous regions, this section of the play is set in a prairie with a purple sky and numerous marble benches. Townsend asserts that this domestication of outdoor space is especially noteworthy because Mexican thinkers often equated Amerindians with nature (58). As such, the place of indigenous society was to be domesticated and incorporated into a classical, Greco-Roman world that upheld Vasconcelian aesthetics.

This scene represents a singular moment in Vasconcelos's writing because it is here that he gives his fifth race a body. The most interesting aspect of this representation is its surprisingly heavy focus on gender and sexuality. Countless *ninfas* populate the stage, calling attention to their beauty by emphasizing their claims to whiteness. Townsend asserts that due to this scene, "readers of *La raza cósmica* [*The Cosmic Race*] can spare themselves the trouble of proving that *mestizaje* is really a code word for whitening" (59). However, the text complicates her assertion as the ninfas seductively invite Prometheus to frolic with them in the following manner:

> We are white like the cleanest marble, and when we let our hair loose it looks like a ray of sunlight bathes our backs. Our lips are red wounds where life burns with the angst of hot embers. . . .
>
> Others are white, with a bluish tint, whiter than that of the most inciting blonde; within our lips lays the passion that creates infernos [*infiernos*: "hells"] and a liquor that incites but does not quench. Each strand of hair on our head is like a voluptuous serpent.
>
> The sun has tanned others of us with its golden rays, and we have the strength to feed long passions.

> [Somos blancas como el más limpio mármol, y al soltar los cabellos parece que un lampo de sol nos baña la espalda. Son nuestros labios rojas heridas donde la vida arde con ansiedades de brasa. . . .
>
> Otras somos blancas, con tinte azulado, más blanco que el de la rubia y más incitante; en nuestros labios hay la pasión que crea los infiernos y un licor que turba y no sacia. Las madejas de nuestros cabellos son como serpientes voluptuosas.
>
> A otras nos ha bruñido el sol con sus rayos de oro, y abrigamos la potencia fina y profunda que alimenta las pasiones largas.] (47)

This is hardly the discourse of a purely "whitened" society; the ninfas celebrate their racial complexion(s), which endow them with a seductive, mixed-race exoticism. Janzen observes that mestizaje "was a fantasy of national unity and mythologized deep divisions of race, culture, and politics in Mexico" (5), and she correctly points out that any form of Mexican mestizaje would by necessity require the Amerindian to disappear. Vasconcelos's representation of the ninfas, however, emphasizes the fact that nonwhite actors from Mexico would also leave their mark on future generations as they helped to perfect the national genome through aesthetic eugenics. These seductive characters represent a new racial conjugation that would set them apart from twentieth-century people, and particularly women, of any race. This is especially obvious with the bluish women, who—beyond clear ties to *modernista* discourse—serve as metaphors for the aesthetic possibilities of racial mixing.

The focus on female sexuality is telling here; the playwright represents his mestizas by appealing to ancient Greek mythology, which held ninfas to be minor gods. While not yet "cosmic," they bear the incremental physical and genetic improvements that are necessary for transcending the body. The ninfas are neither quasi-divine, posthuman subjects nor twentieth-century humans, although their genealogy ties them more closely to humanity than to the utopic posthumanity of Saturnino's "celestial race." Unlike the half-gods of Greek mythology, Vasconcelos's ninfas' "superior" physical bodies result not from a divine sire, but from the synergetic, interracial fusion of inferior progenitors. Their humanity rings clear through their sexuality, which is a highly embodied act that Saturnino aims to overcome. The ninfas' articulation of an advanced humanity underscores the fact that Vasconcelos views beauty, education, and interracial sexual union as components of the same eugenic equation. After pursuing these aforementioned ideals for a millennium, his fictitious society has transcended almost all barriers to human progress. This play, then, advocates a very literal racial hybridity rather than simple whitening. Of course, the fact that everything must fit within European intellectual and cultural traditions suggests a degree of cultural—but certainly not phenotypic—whitening that was inherent to the Mexican brand of official mestizaje in general.

The ninfas' seductive quality is especially interesting when juxtaposed with Saturnino, who descends from a plane and enters the stage to further the aesthetic perfection of humanity. *Mestizaje* and interracial sexual unity are necessary to human development in Vasconcelos's mind, but Saturnino's work underscores the fact that the mestizo age—like every racial era within Vasconcelian thought—is transitory. Janzen argues that one key aspect of Vasconcelian mestizaje was that "marginalized people's bodies w[ould] no longer procreate" (5), which is an argument that most scholars of Vasconcelos would accept. This play sheds new light on Vasconcelian aesthetics; here it becomes clear that, at some point in the distant future, the mestizo peoples of the world will have to make another great eugenic leap forward by also renouncing reproduction and transcending the human body. Racial miscegenation remains key to Vasconcelos's plan; as his play emphasizes throughout, humanity's ability to move beyond the physical has come about only due to the aesthetic eugenics that have existed for over one thousand years. The ninfas thus come to represent both the allure and the vices of mestizo identity. Their proactive eroticism emphasizes the inherently sexual nature of mixed-race eugenics, which in turn focuses their identity on their bodies. These women's hypersexuality casts them as aesthetically "superior" to their ancestors of all races, but this superiority paradoxically comes as heterosexual males—who must now resist their sexual urges—objectify their "exotic" beauty. The ninfas never attain true subjectivity;

despite their great desirability, they do not engage in meaningful discussions, and for the most part they remain in the chorus in the background. Somewhat paradoxically, then, these women's status as objects signals them as the crown jewels of the thousand-year-old mestizo project while their seductive qualities position them as serious threats.

As long as the ninfas are objects without agency, Saturnino can neutralize their subversive potential by instilling values of celibacy in his male disciples. The true danger to his utopia emerges when women become active subjects who deliberately reject the interests of the mestizo patriarchy. The playwright emphasizes this through the "ugly women," who, unlike the ninfas, are not supposed to win the affection of a heterosexual, male audience. Their ugliness makes them indifferent to Saturnino's aesthetics and leads them to resist his philosophies outright. As the first act ends, they enter the stage and argue with the philosopher, telling him that they wish to bear children, but Saturnino retorts that they will never find any man willing to procreate with them. Vasconcelos almost certainly includes this back-and-forth in an attempt to add some humor to his playscript, but this conversation's comedic effect attests to a cultural referent that objectifies female voices. This male chauvinism takes on a racial dimension as it draws attention to these women's apparent ugliness, a trait that Vasconcelos racialized throughout his oeuvre. In *The Cosmic Race* he states, "The world is thus full of ugliness because of our vices, our prejudices, and our misery" (31). Most critics concur that Vasconcelos refers specifically to uneducated Amerindians in this quote. Indeed, Amerindians had less access to national schools than did their mestizo counterparts (Spitta 334; Marentes 96). The fact that the state could educate such ugliness away also suggested that ugliness was performative in nature. As such, a robust education would be able to modify indigenous performativity and incorporate Amerindians into the body politic.

Studies that focus on Vasconcelos's aim to incorporate indigenous Mexicans into the state show us a great deal about postrevolutionary Mexico, but I concur with Sánchez Prado when he argues that "despite its problematic articulation of race and its flirtation with fascism, *The Cosmic Race* provided a way for theorizing resistance to the colonizations that have afflicted the continent. This is precisely what gets lost when mestizaje is identified as a simple articulation of the liberal Mexican and Latin American state" ["Esta fue la función que, a pesar de su problemática articulación de la raza y de sus coqueteos con el fascismo, *La raza cósmica* jugó en el siglo XX: una forma de teorizar la resistencia a las colonizaciones que han aquejado la historia del continente. Este sentido preciso es el que se pierde cuando se identifica el mestizaje como simple articulación del estado liberal mexicano y latino-americano."] ("Mestizaje" 390–91). Vasconcelos's admittedly paternalistic dream of incorporating his nation's indigenes sprang from his desire for Mexican self-determination and modernization through a homegrown path. My reading of *Prometeo vencedor* extends Sánchez Prado's observations by showing how race colored Vasconcelos's anti-imperialism. Similar to what we see in the letrado's seminal essay, ugliness results from a lack of education and a break from the "Spanish mold." But the playwright codes the "ugly women" as Anglo-Saxon by signaling their ties to Australia—a fact that contradicts many studies that argue that Vasconcelos saw (only) the indigenous and black components of pre-mestizo society as "ugly." Not only do these women disassociate themselves from mestizaje, but they also favor the less refined British—rather than Spanish—European tradition.

The ugly women's racial coding is not overly surprising when we recognize that Vasconcelos believed that Anglo-Saxons and Latins (Iberians) had conflicting racial missions (*Cosmic Race* 21; Zea, "Vasconcelos" 30; De Beer 275). The philosopher viewed Anglo-Saxon imperialism—whether British, North American, or even Australian—as a threat to Latin American mestizaje on par with that of the region's indigenous cultures (Scarano 143–46). As such, he emphasizes the threatening aspects of these women throughout. Because he never expected to stage the play, Vasconcelos turns to aspects like his characters' speech to signal them as hideous and other. Vasconcelos argues that indigenous "ugliness" comes from a lack of knowledge in *The Cosmic Race*; in *Prometeo vencedor* he ties the Anglo-Saxon women's ugliness to their ignorance of—and their refusal to acquiesce to—classical authority. The women show no respect for Saturnino's metaphysics and instead opt for a pragmatic ideal that exalts childbirth and motherhood. In response to Saturnino, who has told them that they are too ugly to seduce any men, they reply, "We will find centaurs!" ["¡Buscaremos centauros!"] (68). Their invocation of a human/animal hybrid in response to Saturnino's doctrine of celibacy underscores that these women do not rationally articulate their decision; instead, they turn to basic animal desires—at least within the framework of the play—that inform their understandings of happiness. Their shortsightedness betrays a lack of cultural refinement that makes them unable to accept, or even understand, Saturnino's teachings. Their refusal to bring about an immaterial (post)humanity underscores how these Anglo-Saxons' lack of education speaks to a deeper, spiritual deficit vis-à-vis their mixed-race counterparts.

The confrontation between Saturnino and the "feas" in *Prometeo vencedor* plays Rodó's dichotomy of classical spiritualism and Anglo-Saxon utilitarianism out in dialectic space. The women certainly frustrate Saturnino's plans to move humanity beyond the body, but they do so in a way that validates Saturnino's thought and not their own. Similar to the uneducated Amerindians of *The Cosmic Race*, these women are ugly due to their (performative) ignorance. Their gender, coupled with their ties to Anglo-Saxon whiteness—rather than Iberian mestizaje—is the driving force behind their opposition to Saturnino's aesthetic utopia. Throughout his life, Vasconcelos perceived Anglo-Saxon ambivalence regarding—and resistance to—racial hybridity as a great injustice (Vasconcelos, "Race Problem" 98–99; Stavans 26–28; Jaén xix). Indeed, anti-mestizo ideologies within the United States threatened racially mixed countries like Mexico. Vasconcelos's attempts to philosophically subvert the suppositions that justified his country's continued marginalization should challenge twenty-first-century scholars to reevaluate his work now that nearly a century has passed since he wrote both *Prometeo vencedor* and *The Cosmic Race*. Clearly, he stood at the fore of anti-imperialist projects that opposed U.S. incursions into Latin American politics and territories. One key way for him to do this was by theorizing, and validating, an authentically Mexican (and Latin American) identity that could pose as a counterweight to U.S. hegemony; of course, his invocation of mestizaje also reflected colonial structures of race that validated internal empire and the marginalization of non-Western peoples and cultures (Handelsman 35–36). What the thinker viewed as liberatory, then, posed serious threats to black and indigenous people from Mexico and throughout Latin America.

The Role of Technology in the Vasconcelian Utopia

Vasconcelos's racial elitism held that state-sponsored intellectuals had the obligation to head eugenic programs to "improve" the national body and soul (Crespo 102–3). The problems with such a belief come through, ironically, in his depiction of Saturnino, an "enlightened" individual and imperial figure who imposes his spiritual ideals on the entire world. The reincarnated philosopher uses technology to monitor and facilitate the spread of his doctrine across the globe. If we define science as positivism—or even the Kuhnian notion of organizing observations into paradigms—then it receives no mention in the play. This lack of any reference to the hard sciences, however, does not preclude Vasconcelos from theorizing the role of technology—one of the most obvious fruits of science for the average person—in his mestizo utopia. Villegas argues that Vasconcelos "postulates science as a path to salvation, as the means for reviving the entire universe" ["postula [la ciencia] como tránsito de salvación, como la revivencia del universo entero"] (*Filosofía* 83). Vasconcelos used the term "science" to mean knowledge of all sorts, and he viewed aesthetics as the greatest of the sciences (Villegas, *Filosofía* 83). As such, the playwright believed that the physical sciences would ultimately become an aesthetic tool whose laws adhered to—and even revived—Westernized standards of beauty. Thus the end goal of science, far from producing "objective" fact, was the imposition of a supposedly self-evidently greater (post)humanity.

When Prometheus and Satan arrive at Saturnino's Himalayan home at the beginning of the third act, they find him surrounded by strange apparatuses that signal his technical sophistication (70). The philosopher later explains that he and his disciples used specialized gadgets to determine that there were no more living humans on the planet. The implication here is that, if he had found people somewhere, both he and his disciples would have approached them and preached the gospel of self-renunciation and abnegation. Technology, then, becomes a tool that helps letrado figures to impose their ideology on the masses. It aids Saturnino in imposing his posthuman superation of the body on the world by seeking out those people who either oppose or have not yet heard his ideas. Technology and science are not the end goal of Saturnino's world; rather, they represent the means through which the philosopher can catalyze a glorious posthumanity. Saturnino has not abandoned his aesthetic and political ideals for science; instead, he has incorporated this discourse into his message. He never reifies positivism, but he does rely on technological advances to impose his (post)human identity on the globe.

Saturnino's coercive doctrine of corporeal superation underscores one of the central tenets to the playwright's thought, at least as represented in *Prometeo vencedor*: to ensure redemptive—rather than random—evolution, letrado figures like Saturnino (or Vasconcelos himself) must advocate eugenics. Although Vasconcelos distances his eugenics from positivist, and even scientific, discourses by emphasizing aesthetics rather than biology (*Cosmic Race* 36–37), any manipulation of the human genome necessarily has biological repercussions. Science exists in the letrado's thought as a method and discourse of power that can aesthetically shape human heredity and create a utopic, posthuman existence. This is especially true in *Prometeo vencedor*, where Saturnino utilizes science and technology for coercion and surveillance. Vasconcelos advocates racial miscegenation as the primary vehicle for his success, but he recognizes that it will be difficult to govern people's sexuality without the help of ultramodern, science-fiction-esque devices that track human activities throughout the world. Science still remains in the background of his play as another "over there," but the emphasis on both technology and (forced) racial hybridity pulls the playwright's thoughts on science into focus far more convincingly than does his essay. As metaphysics becomes the favored way of knowing, mestizo science improves beyond even that of imperializing forces. The first major—and probably unperformable—mestizo use of technology occurs during the second act when Saturnino arrives on the stage in his airplane. Given that the first airplanes successfully flew in 1903, less than two decades before Vasconcelos would publish his play, this grand entrance represents the pinnacle of world technology. The "ugly women" do not enter on any comparable machine, so we can also assume that Saturnino's entrance places him ahead of Anglo-Saxon culture both philosophically and technologically/scientifically. This racialization of technological privilege reflects Vasconcelos's view—which the postrevolutionary state would later adopt (Lund, *Mestizo* xi)—of mixed-race identity as the key to Mexican, and even world, modernity. People of other races remain on the margin, both technologically and aesthetically, as Saturnino proclaims the means through which he can advance the collective human consciousness beyond even mestizaje. At this point it becomes clear that primitive people—coded as Anglo-Saxons in this case—are not privy to the same technologies as Saturnino and his disciples are.

When Saturnino's contraption of bells and strings confirms that the hermit is the last living human, Saturnino joyfully proclaims that the souls of the former humanity "will celebrate their definitive divorce from the physical world, to leave, now free, for the eternal spaces" ["va[n] a celebrar su divorcio definitivo del mundo físico, para irse, ya libre, a los espacios eternos"] (79). The cosmic/celestial race Saturnino creates at the end of *Prometeo vencedor* reflects the platonic influences that inform his apocalyptic rejection of the body.[16] Indeed, Luis Garrido asserts three levels of existence in Vasconcelian thought: atom, organism, and consciousness (75). In transcending the body, Saturnino and his disciples have graduated to the consciousness stage, and in this way they become divine. At the same time, this speech also places the cosmic/celestial race within the posthuman sphere. Certainly, the thinker does not frame this entity in such terms because posthumanism was not yet an academic discipline when he wrote this closet drama. Saturnino's invocation of liberty and eternity emphasizes the fact that the apocalyptic shift to the consciousness stage of existence transcends and moves beyond the human sphere. The ties between Vasconcelos's cosmic race and posthumanism become even more obvious as we consider the role of technology in facilitating Saturnino's aesthetic project. The philosopher could not have brought about this spiritual posthumanity without the aid of his inventions.

The appearance of the "stupid" Australian shortly after Saturnino's death poses serious questions to my reading by suggesting that even a technologically advanced society may be incapable of fully overcoming the body. When he first arrives on the stage, the Australian explains how his mother evaded Saturnino's coercive teachings when he states,

> Our mothers managed to seduce a few of the men that Saturnino deceived and took them to live in hiding in the jungles of Australia: the ugliest, most remote region of the world. There they founded a country that they surrounded with an artificial mist that made it invisible to Saturnino's spectacles and apparatuses.... The men constantly said that it was terrible, that they felt disgusted, and that they wanted to return to Saturnino; but our renegade mothers seemed happy.
>
> [Nuestras madres lograron seducir a unos cuantos de los que éste [Saturnino] engañaba y con ellos se fueron a vivir ocultamente, a la región más fea y apartada del mundo; por las selvas del interior de la Australia. Allí fundaron un país y lo rodearon de una especie de niebla artificial que lo hacía invisible a los anteojos y aparatos de Saturnino.... Los hombres decían a menudo que aquello era horrible y se sentían asqueados, añoraban a Saturnino; pero todas las renegadas se mostraban felices.] (83)

The philosopher's inability to convert the Australians to his cause provides one of the most tantalizing puzzles of the entire work, especially given Brian L. Price's observation that Vasconcelos was skeptical of literature that glorified failure as "a central component of the national narrative" (10). Price bases his argument on Vasconcelos's *Breve historia de México* (1956), which was published approximately forty years after *Prometeo vencedor*. It is certainly possible that the author's views on failure shifted in the four decades following his completion of the play. Nevertheless, it would seem that, rather than view the conclusion of *Prometeo vencedor* as Saturnino's failure, we may gain further insight into Vasconcelos's thought if we view this ending as the triumphal moment when mestizo society achieves its full potential and leaves the Anglo-Saxon world behind.

There are two possible explanations for Saturnino's remarkable failure, both with their accompanying significance. On the one hand, perhaps the Australian is correct in asserting that these women's ability to conjure a mist truly did shield them from Saturnino's devices, thus allowing the matriarchal society to grow under his nose. On the other hand, perhaps the philosopher king's machines detected this Australian civilization but did not register its inhabitants as human. The first explanation evokes the highly gendered division of nature (feminine) and technology (masculine) that persisted even within the academy at least until Donna Haraway proclaimed cyborg feminism in the 1980s. If the "ugly women" have the ability to circumvent technology, then they represent a subversive threat by virtue of their gender. The latter possibility suggests that technology can (and did) distinguish the human from the nonhuman, which would in turn imbue science with the interpellatory role of designating bodies as either savable or lost to perdition. Given Vasconcelos's focus on the metaphysical rather than the technical, both factors probably contribute to the Australian society's successful seclusion.

One key to this Australian matriarchy is the women's ability to use their ties to nature to undermine Saturnino's technology. We have already seen that the supposedly feminine values of motherhood—rather than what he views as the "masculine" trait of sexual self-gratification—pose the greatest obstacle to Saturnino's doctrine of self-resignation and the end of procreation. This fact suggests that Vasconcelos viewed femininity as essentialistically incommensurable with the masculine experience, despite the fact that he favored a more liberated femininity than did most Mexican men of his time (Franco, *Plotting Women* 103). Within this argument, the fissures between these oppositionally gendered modes of experiencing humanity allow the "ugly women" to outwit technology by evoking nature. Saturnino's machines are incapable of seeing through the feminine mists because they are programmed to operate only within the patriarchy; as such, feminine nature becomes a blind spot. Just as these women's "innate" (read: natural) maternal instincts lead them to challenge Saturnino's philosophy of the body, their association with the elements undermines his ability to coerce them through technology. Viewed in this light, Saturnino's "tragic" failure would have been fully avoidable if he had contained these women. The play emphasizes this point by highlighting the fact that Saturnino converts everyone except for the "ugly women" to his cause. What is more, these female antagonists become subversive only when they reject Saturnino's teachings and seek a different path for humanity.

Saturnino's focus on the renunciation of the body exposes certain gender- and race-based suppositions that informed how Vasconcelos conceived of the cultural missions and other state-sponsored projects of coerced mestizaje. In both the play and in real life, "enlightened" letrados depend(ed) on the support of women. As secretary of public education, Vasconcelos worked to convince indigenous women to procreate with men of European descent, be they criollo or mestizo. Because he viewed race both culturally and genetically, his demand on (particularly indigenous) women was that they raise children qualitatively different from themselves. This parallels Saturnino's requirements of the "mujeres feas" in that they must ensure the demise of their own culture by accepting his aesthetics. This predictably leads to resistance that threatens his ability to carry out his posthuman project. The "mujeres feas" become subversive figures as Saturnino fails to convert them to his cause—a fact that they emphasize as they effectively kidnap their masculine mates and carry them off to Australia. This narrative supports an imaginary in which seductive, lustful women disregard the supposed wisdom of patriarchal figures like Saturnino and instead harm society by forcing men to give in to their sexual urges against their better judgment. Even when these so-called masculine victims realize the error of their ways, they cannot return to Saturnino's fold. At this point, they are stuck in a matriarchal, Amazonian society from which there is no escape. The greatest tragedy of the ugly women's seductions, at least within the discourse of the play, is that they reproduce children with tenuous ties to humanity.

The Australians' successful seclusion may also testify against their humanity. The play's conclusion posits an evolutionary fork in the road of the *Homo sapiens* species. Saturnino and his disciples transcend their bodies and achieve a posthuman, disembodied consciousness, while the Australian character's caveman condition suggests that he has de-evolved toward protohumanity.[17] Writing on the philosopher's thought as represented in *The Cosmic Race*, Mónica E. Scarano argues that "the racial intermixing now begun in Spanish

America would give way—in Vasconcelos's utopia—to another, more complete mestizaje: the cultural, true palingenesis of the discouraged Latin spirits before the powerful expansionary movements of the Anglo-Saxon world" ["La intermixión racial ya iniciada en Hispanoamérica daría lugar—en la utopía de Vasconcelos—a otro mestizaje más complejo: el cultural, verdadera palingenesia para los desalentados espíritus latinos, frente al poderoso movimiento expansivo anglosajón."] (142). By the play's third act, the dichotomy of mestizaje and Anglo-Saxon racial "purity" has reached a breaking point after persisting for over one thousand years. The world has reached a final judgment where humanity has been either transfigured as it embarks on a new, posthuman path or condemned to revert to protohumanity. Beyond simply representing an inferior articulation of humanity, the Australians have now de-evolved to the point that neither Prometheus nor Satan recognizes any human traces in them. Thus, the play concludes with the ultimate redemption of the mestizo world and the equally dramatic condemnation of what remains of the decadent, postimperial Anglo-Saxon race.

Technology has served as an arbiter in bringing about this final judgment. It has found those human beings who still needed to hear Saturnino's ideas of corporeal superation while at the same time ignoring those hominids living in Australia because they are no longer savable, or even human. If we view the play through this lens, we see not only a harsh criticism against Anglo-Saxon imperialism (be it British, U.S., or even Australian) but also technology becoming the successor to previous deities like Jehovah and Zeus—although the indigenous gods are still generally ignored. Prometheus and Satan have overcome each of the aforementioned deities, but neither one feels the need to subvert science or technology. Instead, both generally agree with the verdict of Australian inhumanity. This is especially odd given that Prometheus sacrificed so much to redeem protohumanity and Satan has spent his entire life challenging and subverting unjust creeds. Rather than affirm Australian humanity, Satan and Prometheus decide that they must once again return to earth to facilitate human evolution. This time, however, Satan—who has been converted to Saturnino's ideologies—will play more than just a satirical role; he will now strive to lead this degenerate protohumanity back to the aesthetic identity that Saturnino and the philosopher have shown him. If there is any hope, it stems from the fact that, like the protohumans of the prologue, this latter incarnation will once again progress toward a disembodied, posthuman communion. Perhaps even Satan and Prometheus will find redemption this time around.

Conclusion

This chapter has filled a void in the criticism on José Vasconcelos by utilizing posthuman theory to show that the writer imagined a scientific discourse that adhered to strict metaphysical guidelines. Equally informative, my reading of his racial theories corroborates and further explains the triumphant discourse he associated with ongoing human evolution and progression. *Mestizaje* certainly functioned as a political strategy for the philosopher, but he also saw it as the most perfect articulation of humanity heretofore created. In the end, Vasconcelos's great contribution to Mexican thought was not his opposition to positivism or even his imagination of a utopian cosmic race. Instead, his work is especially useful when viewed as a mythos that justified the new brand of postrevolutionary nationalism. The thinker's privileged position allowed him to become one of the nation's most prominent letrados, a condition that granted him an unparalleled platform from which to enunciate his version of Mexican nationalism. This in turn brought his aesthetic justification for mestizo subjectivity to the fore in the nation's politics, philosophy, literature, and cultural production. The thinker's utopian drive, and his work to modernize Mexico by transforming its citizens into a triumphant fifth race is still felt today nearly a century later.

Whether he was a hero or villain, Prometheus or Satan, Vasconcelos's prominence allowed him to largely define the terms for race relations in postrevolutionary Mexico. Significantly, his was not the decisive voice regarding the final (official) interpretation of his aesthetics. Even prior to his self-imposed exile from 1924 to 1929, different factions of Mexican society had incorporated his mixed-race ideal into leftist movements through muralism, and following his exit, the capitalist state continued to allude to his notion of a cosmic race through music, radio, film, and many other media (Velázquez and Vaughan 95–118; Hayes 243–58; Hershfield, "Screening" 259–78). One of the most understudied aspects of these at times contradictory discourses is that, despite serious ideological rifts, almost all these official representations of mestizaje imagined the juxtaposition of the Mexican body with technology at some level. It is doubtful that Vasconcelos catalyzed this focus on technology and the body with his obscure closet drama, but he clearly tapped into a hidden part of the collective revolutionary and postrevolutionary psyche as he imagined Saturnino's science-fiction-esque utopia. Vasconcelos was a pioneer in positioning mestizaje as an evolutionary advancement; however, his focus on the written word made it difficult for him to reach the illiterate masses. Toward this end, the thinker commissioned numerous artists to paint nationalist murals on the nation's walls. In the following chapter, I discuss the art of the indigenista Diego Rivera and the more hispanista José Clemente Orozco. These men's art exemplified the tensions inherent to a statist policy of official mestizaje that attempted to negotiate both its European and indigenous heritage through racial and technological hybridity.

2

Painting *Mestizaje* in a New Light

Racial, Technological, and Cultural Hybridity
in the Murals of Diego Rivera and José Clemente Orozco

Ironically, one of José Vasconcelos's most long-lasting contributions to post-revolutionary debates of mexicanidad—particularly regarding proper race and gender performativity—did not come from his writing.[1] Rather, it stemmed from his decision as secretary of public education in 1921 to have artists paint representations of mexicanidad on the nation's walls.[2] By making this move, Vasconcelos signaled that discussions of national identity would extend beyond the realm of the letrado and into that of visual art.[3] The Secretariat of Public Education [Secretaría de Educación Pública] (SEP) aggressively supported murals until the 1960s, and it continues to do so to a lesser extent into the present. No muralists achieved greater fame during this period than Diego Rivera, José Clemente Orozco, and David Alfaro Siqueiros. Also known as the "Big Three," these men continue to occupy a special place in Mexico's artistic and cultural history to this day.[4] Each member of the Big Three ascribed to some version of the global and Mexican left; indeed, as Héctor Jaimes argues, Marxism was the theoretical glue that reconciled their at times contradictory works (15, 52). Unlike their communist counterparts from the Soviet Bloc who viewed racial discrimination as a mask for the true reason for imperialism (that of economic exploitation), the Big Three believed that racism could be the purpose for exploitation in and of itself. As such, their art asserted that Mexico would have to recognize and face its racial heritage if it hoped to regenerate and develop economically.

The government's decision to privilege muralism probably resulted from the fact that the movement grew out of artistic tendencies that had aesthetically challenged the Porfiriato even prior to the Revolution. The seeds of the twentieth-century muralist movement were sown in 1910, when Porfirio Díaz celebrated the centenary of independence with an exhibit of contemporary Spanish art (Feria and Lince Campillo). Ironically, Diego Rivera—a young, respected painter who had traveled to Europe on a Porfirian scholarship (Hamill 41–44)—was the showcased artist of the event (Wolfe, *Diego Rivera* 60–61). In reaction to Díaz's Eurocentric aesthetic, Gerardo Murillo—also known as Dr. Atl—held his own exhibit. Along with many of his pupils from the Ateneo de la Juventud, including Orozco and Siqueiros (Azuela, *Arte y poder* 41–43; Lynch 367–70), he showcased an event that emphasized "authentically Mexican" art forms by celebrating local (indigenous) traditions and styles (Helm, *Modern Mexican Painters* 1–21; Rochfort 15–20).[5] Dr. Atl's event lacked murals not because he was not interested in the medium, but because he did not have access to public walls. Nevertheless, his exhibit helped establish how the national art would contribute to discussions of mexicanidad because the painters who joined him made a conscious decision to include indigenous cultural forms in their work. In the following years, the muralists would assert Mexico's potential by painting harsh landscapes, endemic cacti and plants, and indigenous peoples on the nation's walls.[6]

Although the muralists received state moneys, they were not mere reproducers of official ideologies. Rather, they contributed to discussions about the nature of a national identity through mestizaje, and their influence rivaled—and perhaps even eclipsed—that of their lettered peers. Vasconcelos concurred with their exaltation of racial miscegenation, but he lamented the leftist nature of their art (Swarthout 121), and this was probably in large part because he knew that these artists reached a much larger audience than he ever would.[7] Despite his misgivings, however, Vasconcelos generally respected the muralists' freedom of expression (Rochfort 33; Reed 10–11).[8] The same cannot be said of his successor José Manuel Puig Casauranc, who served as secretary of public education during the Plutarco Elías Calles administration that withheld federal moneys from those who criticized the regime (Azuela, "Machete" 85). Siqueiros and Orozco lost their contracts after refusing to temper their political discourse. The former opted for self-exile (Azuela, "Machete" 85–86), while the latter could not find mural work in Mexico for a year and a half (Azuela, *Arte y poder* 69). Rivera chose to placate state officials by tempering his criticism (Azuela, *Arte y poder* 71–73; Azuela, "Machete" 85); even so, government leaders remained uncomfortable with his insistence on employing Marxist imagery (Richardson 52–53).[9] Thus Rivera, too, eventually traveled to the United States to avoid censorship (Romera Velasco 426). The varying ways in which the Big Three navigated the change in administration after Vasconcelos resigned from the SEP underscored the ideological and aesthetic competition that would later form among them. Their differences extended to representations of mexicanidad, where they imagined often-incompatible versions of mestizo nationalism (Indych-López, "Mural Gambits" 387; Grenier 246). The muralists exalted statist ideals of racial hybridity and modernity, but each painter articulated these values in his own way. Differing articulations of mestizaje were especially poignant in the art of Orozco and Rivera. Orozco favored an hispanista paradigm "that minimized any validation of Indianness" (Greeley, "Witnessing" 267), while Rivera glorified an indigenista "brown mestizo" whose defining trait was an indigenous spirit.

Whether hispanista or indigenista, the muralists strove to produce a culturally hybrid aesthetic that would promote mestizaje by fusing the latest styles of European art—cubism, symbolism, and expressionism—with techniques and colors used in pre-Columbian murals (Rochfort 24–26; Jaimes 18; Tibol, *Diego Rivera* 15–20). As Henry Favre observes, "for these painters, there could be no revolutionary art without revolutionary techniques. Not only did the Big Three rediscover the fresco and the encaustic medium, but they also invented new procedures, employed new materials, used new instruments, and recurred to new colorants" ["No puede haber arte revolucionario sin técnicas revolucionarias para estos pintores, quienes no sólo redescubren el fresco y la encáustica, sino que también inventan nuevos procedimientos, emplean nuevos materiales, utilizan nuevos instrumentos, recurren a nuevos colorantes."] (80). Rivera's experience in Europe played a key role in his artistic development (Cabello 1460; Arquin 56–143). He spent the Revolution and the first years of the postrevolutionary period in Spain and France; while he was there Vasconcelos sent him to Italy. The secretary of public education intended for him to facilitate exchanges between the Mexican School of Fine Arts and the Italian art scene (Bargellini 92), but Rivera primarily hoped to learn the fresco style. The artist's time in Italy greatly affected his subsequent works; his first Mexican murals were so aesthetically European that Vasconcelos sent him to southern Mexico so that he could learn to incorporate indigenous forms into his state-funded murals (Belej 254–55; Gallardo Muñoz 82–83). The artist took the lesson to heart, and at one point, he made the embarrassing decision of using "cactus juice . . . instead of water to dissolve the [paint] pigments" (Traba 19). He ruined the mural in question, but this act attested to his commitment to culturally hybrid, experimental art. This incident also underscores the prominence of indigenous cultures in the muralist movement; indeed, indigenous Mexico's proper role in society represented one of the principal polemics that the artists attempted to resolve.

The muralists' disagreements on the proper articulation of official mestizaje were most evident regarding their oppositional treatment of the technologized body. The academy has not yet made this observation in large part because most critics have not connected the artists' mestizophilia to their representations of technology.[10] This surprising oversight is perhaps in part due to the fact that Orozco and Rivera engaged technology more in their U.S. work (Dartmouth, Pomona, Detroit Institute of Arts, etc.), while their treatises on racial hybridity tended to appear in Mexico (Indych-López, "Mural Gambits" 287). Nevertheless, we can more correctly identify each artist's overriding approach to modernity by identifying connections among their works across international boundaries. As we do this, we can come to see how Rivera and Orozco adapted their art to the distinct sociopolitical contexts where they worked. The artists tailored their work to the expectations of local audiences by accentuating elements that would resonate with the lived experience in a given country. Mexico and the United States provided different opportunities and limits for artistic expression, and the muralists adapted their discussions of the twin values of modernity and mestizaje to each national context accordingly. U.S. audiences were sensitive to representations of sexuality, while the Mexican state opposed works that undermined its authority.[11] Given these conditions, it should come as no surprise that the muralists' art took on distinct personalities depending on where it was painted.[12] That said, rather than omit mestizaje from their U.S. work—or technology from their Mexican work—the artists simply tended to emphasize one or the other depending on the country where they painted a specific mural.

The muralists enjoyed their prestige abroad, but they were most interested in producing a national art that was legible to all Mexicans. As they tackled and theorized controversial political issues at home, they became the newest purveyors of statist doctrines. Unlike their lettered predecessors, they engaged not only the national elite, but also the population at large—especially the illiterate (Monsiváis, "Diego Rivera" 118–21; Sánchez-López 69). There was a certain bookish nature to their art, particularly when they painted series that told cohesive narratives about Mexican and world history. Orozco once famously stated, "Good murals . . . are really painted Bibles and the masses need them as much as spoken Bibles. Many people cannot read books: in Mexico there are a great deal" (quoted in Echavarría 8). Silvia Spitta and Lois Parkinson Zamora note a similar sentiment in the work of Rivera, who "considered himself a modern-day *tlacuilo*, a direct heir of the indigenous priest/painters who represented the collective wisdom of their people" (198). Both artists supplemented their art with written commentary in the form of interpretation and autobiography, an act that tied their artwork explicitly to lettered traditions and writing. That said, the artists agreed that visual culture—particularly muralism—was the most effective means for inculcating "proper" interpretations of national identity in the masses.[13] The interplay between written and visual culture was especially clear in the works of Orozco, whose comic strip in the revolutionary newspaper *La Vanguardia* staunchly supported Venustiano Carranza (Rochfort 20); from this medium, the distinction between art and literature became especially porous. Nevertheless, the muralists were categorically different from letrados like Vasconcelos, because the central medium of their work was visual art and not the written word. The muralists certainly contributed to intellectual discussions about the nature of mestizaje, but their art was first and foremost a tool for teaching Amerindians that they could—and indeed should—assimilate to mestizo culture and society through technological hybridity.

As the muralists depicted technology in their murals, they entered into dialogue with European notions of futurism, a literary and artistic movement that stormed onto the world stage with Filippo Tommaso Marinetti's flamboyant *Futurist Manifesto* in Italy in 1909. This document called for a violent rupture with the past and an emphasis on technological development. Marinetti's manifesto reached Mexico that same year when Amado Nervo responded with his own article, "Nueva escuela literaria." The Mexican writer criticized many of Marinetti's ideas (930–31), but he lauded the Italian's raw enthusiasm, asserting that, with some direction, the futurist movement could become a powerful force in advancing European (and perhaps Mexican) letters. Despite Nervo's tepid endorsement, futurism would not truly take root in Mexican thought until 1921, when Manuel Maples Arce proclaimed the arrival of the estridentista movement by plastering his manifesto *Actual No. 1* on the walls of Mexico City. By this time, futurism had found especially fertile ground not only in Italy but also in Russia. As Tatiana Flores notes (*Revolutionary Avant-Gardes* 22), after suffering devastating wars that had crippled their societies, economies, and political orders, these three countries now attempted to rebuild through aggressive programs of industrialization and technological advancement.[14] Not surprisingly, Italian futurists became associated with Mussolini and fascism (Gallo, "Maples Arce" 313–14), while those from Russia forged strong, if tense, relationships with the Bolshevik Party (Ransome). Estridentista artists and poets lacked the discipline of the futurist movements in Europe (Gallo, "Maples Arce" 310); nevertheless, they ultimately came to conflate technological advancement with socialist ideals (Affron 5).

The estridentista movement lasted only a few years and produced a scant corpus of literary achievements, but it left behind a rich tradition that would influence the nation's written and visual culture for years to come. Sara Anne Potter, for example, treats the movement as the genesis for a technophilic (and at times ambivalent, or even technophobic), avant-garde tradition that has persisted in Mexican arts and letters into the twenty-first century. The ties between estridentista poetry and art became especially clear in 1923, when Maples Arce gave a controversial speech at the official unveiling of *Creation*, Rivera's first Mexican mural (Flores, "Murales Estridentes" 110–11). Several muralists—particularly Jean Charlot, Fernando Leal, Fermín Revueltas, and even Rivera—had clear ties to *estridentismo* and futurism (Flores, *Revolutionary Avante-Gardes* 48–88; Flores, "Murales Estridentes" 113–23). Rivera's ties to futurism were imperfect; the artist publicly claimed to view futurism as an aesthetic that had failed the international working classes. Rather than suggest that activist artists abandon styles like futurism, however, he argued that they should follow the example of the Soviet Union, a nation that had taken the most important bourgeois technological advancements "and adapt[ed] [them] to the needs and special conditions of the new proletarian regime" (53). Even as Rivera distanced himself from (Italian) futurism, then, these words aligned him with that movement's Russian articulation. This fact signals the need for a mild revision of Gallo's excellent argument against an overriding narrative—popularized by Octavio Paz ("Antivíspera" 103)—that posits a historical direct cross-pollination between Russian futurists and the estridentistas ("Maples Arce" 319–22). Gallo is almost certainly correct that Mexico's *writers* did not dialogue with Russian futurists, but its *painters* clearly did. As they engaged with the Russian futurists, artists like Rivera came to the natural conclusion that the parallel projects of redeeming Mexico's indigenous masses, executing programs of technological innovation, and promoting the proletarian revolution were actually different articulations of the same goal. This focus led them to emphasize race and racial hybridity in their work despite the fact that their peers in literature did not.

Of course, the focus on nationalist ideals and racial hybridity was not limited to those muralists who aligned their work with futurism. Despite the fact that no critics associate Orozco with that movement, for example, he clearly engaged with nationalistic ideals of mestizo modernity. Indeed, Orozco differed from the futurist cause less in subject matter than in style and tenor. Similar to Rivera, he viewed technological development as part and parcel to Mexican modernity, but unlike his counterparts, he approached these advances with a decided ambivalence. Given Orozco's affiliation with proworker—but antipeasant (read: indigenous)—unions (Anreus 40), it should come as no surprise that the painter did not necessarily equate technological advancement with social progress. Rather, technology served as the mechanism that allowed the state to continue to oppress people of all races even after they assimilated to the state and became mestizo workers. The artist did not suggest that Amerindians would better themselves as they joined a technologically advanced society; rather, he suggested that by doing this they could better interface with the state and demand greater legal rights. Given the artist's disenchanted relationship with technological advancement, technological hybridity could not represent the same utopian ideals in his work that it did for Rivera. Nevertheless, the artist clearly dialogued with the underlying assumptions of futurism as he asserted technological competency as a key (albeit problematic) component of his hispanista ideal.

One of the most common (and overlooked) means through which Orozco and Rivera dialogued with futurist ideas came through their depictions of indigenous primitivity, which they achieved by accentuating nude indigenous bodies in their murals. This strategy draws to mind Giorgio Agamben's notion of "bare life" (10–14); as Agamben notes, biopolitical states constantly kill despite the fact that they base their legitimacy on their ability to preserve life. The theorist argues that this happens because society divides humanity into two groups: bios and zoê (9). Where bios denotes a fully human existence, the zoê consists of those people who live on the periphery as a dehumanized mass. When states of exception arise, society codes the zoê as homo sacer subjects: beings who "may be killed and yet not sacrificed"—or murdered—because their lives lack the intrinsic value to merit protection under the law (12). Orozco and Rivera carried out their work under precisely the sort of exceptional conditions that could potentially give rise to violent distinctions between an indigenous zoê and a mestizo bios: the specter of the devastating Revolution sat figuratively—and at times literally—in the background of their work. Mestizaje represented an ideal that both men believed could reconcile the nation with itself. But because they imagined the role that the nation's indigenous heritage would play in a modern, postrevolutionary society in radically different ways, their depictions of Amerindian nudity led to very different representations of bare life.

Rivera's nudes asserted a cultural—and even technological—gap between Amerindian and mestizo societies while at the same time exalting an essentialistic indigenous purity that would counterbalance the cold exactness of Western modernity (Yáñez 98; Rodríguez Prampolini 176). His indigenista murals remained mestizophilic as they proclaimed that Mexico should fuse the spiritual strength of its indigenous population with the technical might it had inherited from Europe. Rivera's works often erred on the side of paternalism as they glorified certain aspects of the supposedly bare indigenous experience, but they implicitly decried the violence that these people had faced at the hands of mestizo and criollo oppressors. For Orozco, indigenous nakedness served as a metaphor for a technologically bare existence that kept indigenous Mexico forever on the periphery. His art fits more cleanly in an Agambian paradigm as it equates indigeneity with zoê and homo sacer subjectivities. Indeed, as he juxtaposed bare indigenous bodies with radiant depictions of the Spanish conquerors, Orozco tapped into—and even created—an imaginary in which indigenous protohumanity and European hypermodernity had always coexisted. He did not necessarily condone the violence of the Conquest, but he viewed it as an inevitable event that would continue to play out in Mexico until the indigenous population adopted European technology and assimilated to the mestizo state.

My reading of these artists challenges a conventional wisdom that largely views Mexican muralism as indigenista[15] despite the fact that, of the Big Three, only Rivera truly fit that mold.[16] Warren Carter has lamented that the current criticism's oversimplification of Mexican muralism largely ignores "the political differences between the [Big] [T]hree, and between them and the postrevolutionary government that patronized them" (287). A greater focus on the disagreements between the movement's main protagonists attests to the lively conversations that emerged in postrevolutionary visual culture. The state's decision to canonize the apparently contradictory racial ideals of Orozco and Rivera reveals that there was no forgone conclusion about how to conceive mestizo nationalism. Public walls became a site from which state officials could nationalistically discuss the fine points of postrevolutionary mestizaje and—

perhaps more importantly—construct a collective memory that they could manipulate as they produced a supposedly autochthonous nation (Mandel 38–41, 50–52). The state allowed the muralists to disseminate antithetical views on racial, technological, and cultural hybridity so long as they buttressed the mestizo imaginaries upon which postrevolutionary ideals depended.[17] This led to a paradoxical relationship between the muralists in which they mutually constructed a nationalist ideal of official mestizaje even as they articulated it in incompatible ways. Because the state could fabricate a national mythos through mestizaje along either indigenista or hispanista lines, however, the breaches regarding the exact nature of hybridity—whether racial, technological, or both—in Rivera and Orozco's art did not overly concern government patrons. Rather, state officials lauded the modernity-driven, pro-mestizo ideals that these men's art invoked.

Race and Modernity in Orozco's Murals

Orozco's art charged that Amerindian ways of knowing were antithetical to modern society, but it also suggested certain steps that indigenous Mexicans could take to join the technologically advanced twentieth century. The tension inherent to his treatment of race made Orozco the most difficult of the Big Three to place ideologically (Neumeyer 121). Most critics agree that his association with the left—and particularly with the Sindicato Siqueiros—had more to do with his desire for employment than with his commitment to global communism (Helm, *Modern Mexican Painters* 71), and his works certainly lacked the leftist edge of Rivera or Siqueiros (Grenier 257).[18] His similarities to Goya led some of his contemporaries to disregard his work as not Mexican enough (Ellis 340), but others saw him as the most artistically experimental and creative of his peers (Helm, *Modern Mexican Painters* 64–66; Francis 61). Stephen Polcari differentiates Orozco's art from that of Rivera and Siqueiros by categorizing it as "psycho-mythic and ritualistic and not politically radical" (39). This claim separates Orozco from his peers, but it risks eliding his ties to postrevolutionary politics altogether. The artist's lack of overt politicism, coupled with his experimental style, allowed him to approach statist articulations of official mestizaje with an intense, problematic nuance that often validated conquering, European worldviews. His murals asserted that national redemption would occur as the native population—pre-Columbian, colonial, and contemporary—assimilated to European modernity and even spirituality. Across his work,

Orozco treated indigenous cultures, cosmologies, and bodies as primitive and premodern while his European characters enjoyed clear ties to modernity and even futurity. Given this fact, the analytical tools of both post- and protohumanism prove especially useful in engaging his work. The juxtaposition of Orozco's Amerindians with his Spaniards made it clear that modern Mexico would have to embrace its European side over the indigenous.

His mural *Cortés y la Malinche* (1926), the first postrevolutionary mural to directly engage the Conquest (Belej 258; Rochfort 44), emphasizes how Mexican society can be redeemed through the imposition of mestizaje through racial and genetic hybridity. Painted on the ceiling of the stairwell of the Colegio de San Ildefonso, the mural cements the myth of Mexico's founding parents within the state's postrevolutionary narrative (Machado 67–68). Now a paradigmatic representation of the mythic union of Hernán Cortés and la Malinche, this mural depicts the naked bodies of Mexico's mythic parents standing atop the corpse of a vanquished pre-Columbian civilization as they celebrate the genesis of a new, mestizo society. Frances Karttunen asserts that la Malinche's physiognomic features depict her as "a veritable Neanderthal" (297), which alludes to an underlying indigenous backwardness and even protohumanity. Orozco's representation of a primitive Malinche implicitly dialogued with the futurist ideal of creating a rupture with the past and imposing the modern over the primitive. The image lacks many futurist elements—it shows no modern machinery, for example—but Orozco implicitly refutes la Malinche's bios by emphasizing her ties to primitivity and the protohuman. She thus becomes homo sacer, a being that the Spanish conquistadores can treat as they see fit. It is a true irony that postrevolutionary society would code a trilingual woman who could move freely among Spanish, Náhuatl, and Mayan cultures as backward while imagining the monolingual Cortés as heroic and futuristic. Nevertheless, Orozco's problematic representation of la Malinche as a cavewoman allows him to sidestep her remarkable intelligence and exalt Cortés as the privileged parent of Mexican mestizaje. The mural alludes to the potential for indigenous individuals to achieve a fully human, modern existence, but this is predicated on accepting Western values. Any assimilation to the state necessarily requires that Amerindians sacrifice their identity and conform to the nationalist, mestizo cause.

This mural highlights several differences between how Orozco and Vasconcelos viewed a proper, hispanista mestizaje. Unlike the secretary of public education, the painter did not shy away from the traumatic effects of the Conquest

Figure 1. *Cortés y la Malinche*. Mural by José Clemente Orozco at San Ildefonso. © Artist Rights Society (ARS), New York/ SOMAAP, Mexico City. Photograph by David S. Dalton.

that continued to linger in the national psyche after more than four hundred years. As Orozco stated in his autobiography, "at any given moment, the Conquest looms more immediate than the forays of Pancho Villa" (107). This assertion explains why the artist returned to the union of Mexico's mythic parents when constructing a postrevolutionary identity. The depictions of the Conquest were, according to Rochfort, "not a simplistic nationalist promotion of a preconceived Mexican national identity, but a reappropriation and reassembly of the nation's past into a usable history" (84; see also Eder 231–37). Within Orozco's thought, the Revolution and the ensuing government were logical extensions of Cortés's arrival to Tenochtitlán. By celebrating the "domestication" of colonial Amerindians, Orozco implicitly validated ongoing postrevolutionary projects of internal empire. Indeed, the muralist justified the state's role in transforming contemporary indigenous people into full participants of mestizo modernity. What is more, he denied the need to engage indigenous cultures on their own terms. In his autobiography, for example, he wrote, "Indigenous races are nothing more but an item more in the Hispanic total, with the categorical rights of any group" (108–9). By signaling Mexico's Amerindians as Hispanic—whether or not they spoke Spanish or personally identified as such—the muralist minimized those cultural values that deviated from Europe's. This belief is especially clear in *Cortés y la Malinche*, where he subordinates indigenous subjectivities to Cortés. This and other murals suggest that corporeal hybridity—both racial and technological—provided the means through which indigenous actors could overcome their performative backwardness and become culturally mestizo. One of the ramifications of such an ideology was the devaluation of indigenous life.

Cortés's unimpeded celebration of the slaughter of indigenous peoples implicitly codes Amerindians as homo sacer subjects whose lives exist beyond the protection of the law. Orozco's biopolitics diverge from those of Agamben in that his mural highlights the potential to transform the indigenous zoê into bios, a process that will occur through genetic, cultural, or both kinds of hybridity. The destructive confrontation between Spain and the native population serves as a painful yet necessary event that facilitates indigenous redemption through mestizaje and modernity. The resulting depiction of the Conquest is both apocalyptic (it destroys the indigenous civilizations of Mexico) and Edenic (it emphasizes the [re]birth of a mestizo Mexico). Orozco emphasizes the biblical proportions of this Mexican genesis through his focus on his protagonists' nude bodies, which parallel those of Adam and Eve (Paz, *Labyrinth of Solitude*

87; Cypess, *Uncivil Wars* 9). Analisa Taylor argues that the couple's shared nakedness attests to the equal footing of the European and the indigenous in Mexican society (832), while David Craven argues that Orozco's representation of the Conquest is "divided but not divisive" because it asserts the humanity of both European and indigenous Mexico (48). Neither critic recognizes the wholly unequal relationship between Cortés and his lover in large part because they ignore the dead, bare indigenous body lying beneath the couple's feet. Rather than serving as an allegory for unification and equality, the extermination of this indigenous man purifies society as a whole. The broken, killed bodies of Orozco's art cannot be redeemed, but those Amerindians who do not die can achieve bios in large part because other indigenous people sacrificed their lives to let Spain "civilize" their territory. Unlike Agamben, who views executions as purifying acts only when carried out against non–homo sacer entities (52), Orozco's art posits the sacrifice of Amerindian lives as a key component to the redemption of the indigenous race as a whole. Homo sacer deaths may do little good for the individual who dies, but they can redeem the community at large by paving the way for a mestizo society predicated on racial and cultural hybridity.

Beyond alluding to the biopolitical ramifications of the mural in question, the presence of this naked cadaver in the frame challenges the scholar of Orozco to reevaluate how the artist conceived male nudity, which most critics have signaled as heroic (Cordero Reiman 106–17; González Mello 53–55; Coffey, "Promethean Labor" 63). *Cortés y la Malinche* shows that Orozco's heroic masculinity is also necessarily European and white. Indigenous male bodies pose a threat to mestizo eugenics because they cannot reproduce genetically mixed offspring with Amerindian women. Within Orozco's biopolitics, the indigenous man's faceless death represents a necessary component of the domestication of Mexican society and the advent of modernity. His disappearance opens a space from which heroic, European males can purify future generations through racial hybridity and modernity. Thus Orozco suggests that vanquished Amerindians must acquiesce to the tutelage of the very people who destroyed their ancient way of life if they wish to enjoy full citizenship. The artist codes Cortés's nude body as heroic as it conquers indigenous bodies—both male and female—and sires a modern, Mexican nation; at the same time, indigenous male lives are clearly expendable.

Because Orozco's conquistadores were necessarily (heroic) men, the redemption of indigenous zoê was clearly gendered. La Malinche's comparative privilege vis-à-vis the anonymous dead man emerges because her body can interface sexually with that of Cortés and reproduce a mixed-race nation. By emphasizing a supposed protohumanity, Orozco asserts that she will never be Cortés's racial equal, but her social status also sits above that of killable indigenous (male) zoê. Orozco's depiction of the female nude has also received little attention from the academic community beyond the fact that its representation is almost always chauvinistic and negative (Coffey, "Angels and Prostitutes" 186–93; Neumeyer 122; Lynch 376–77). Although previous studies provide valuable insight into how Orozco imagines the female form, they tend to ignore how race and gender intertwine in the artist's work to construct Mexican subjectivity. Orozco's representation of female—generally mestiza—prostitutes as a negative outgrowth of postrevolutionary corruption has received a fair amount of attention, particularly in his mural *Catarsis* (1934) (Coffey, "Angel and Prostitutes" 187, 198–200); however, no critic has systematically compared the painter's nude mestizas to his nude indigenous women. Unlike that of her mixed-race counterparts, la Malinche's nudity is depicted in a largely positive light because her sexuality can eugenically redeem indigenous Mexico through interracial breeding. La Malinche's protohumanity and her resulting subhuman status, then, come not from her gender but from her ties to indigeneity. If anything, her gender offsets some of the constraints that her race places on her agency.

The mythic union of Cortés and la Malinche sires a mestizo nation not only through mixed-race progeny, but also by establishing new racial and gender performativities that will govern the mestizo economy and society in the years to come. The fusion of biblical and evolutionary discourses—encapsulated in the couple's evocation of Adam and Eve and la Malinche's visual representation as a cavewoman—validates eugenic understandings of race that favored the culturally and racially hybrid subject over the indigenous. As a result of their European blood, the mixed-race descendants of la Malinche—both literal and figurative—are no longer protohuman or primitive. Beyond representing a genesis story for the mestizo state, Orozco's mural implores contemporary Amerindians to have racially hybrid children. One problematic consequence of this posture is that indigenous parents cannot fully redeem themselves even if they contribute to the national bios through interracial breeding. Mestizo children are coded as eugenic and modern even as their mothers continue to lead comparatively bare lives. Orozco asserts that this is in large part because indigenous Mexico is not as advanced as the

European and mestizo segments of society. Thus, the acceptance of racial, cultural, and (as we shall soon see) technological hybridity necessarily entails favoring the European over the indigenous.

Orozco powerfully communicates the idea of pre-Columbian and indigenous Mexico's modernity deficit to European cultures through *El hombre en llamas*, a series of frescos that he completed at Hospicio Cabañas in Guadalajara from 1936 to 1939. The numerous individual panels show mechanoid conquerors from Spain as they storm across a premodern indigenous countryside. Perhaps the artist's greatest personal achievement, the series includes some of his most mature work (Helm, *Man of Fire* 75–76).[19] Rather than focus on the mythic "birth" of Mexican mestizaje and the accompanying discourses of national "redemption" through racial miscegenation and assimilation to a European worldview, these latter murals emphasize an awesome Spanish hypermodernity. Most critics view these murals as unambiguous critiques of the Conquest particularly and authoritarianism in general (Belej 259; García Barragán 113; Neumeyer 124). Mary K. Coffey argues that it emphasizes "the ideological link between technophilia [and] fascism" ("Angels and Prostitutes" 192), an assertion that implicitly signals the series as a critique of (Italian) futurism. Orozco's dialogue with—and critique of—futurism becomes especially clear as we consider his representation of mechanoid conquerors. Unlike his futurist counterparts, Orozco was pessimistic about technology's ability to liberate the people and mediate conflict (Greeley, "Witnessing" 265). It should thus come as no surprise that the *Hombre en llamas* series lacks the positive representations of technology that futurists tended to include in their work. Rather than inspire awe by depicting sleek skyscrapers or reifying transportation, he repulses his viewers through violent and grotesque depictions of mechanized Spanish conquerors who destroy the poorly equipped inhabitants of pre-Columbian Mexico.

Orozco viewed the Conquest as the tragic (but natural) result of two unevenly developed cultures coming into contact. He did not condone the violence and bloodshed that the event had unleashed, but he also believed that Mexicans of all races should adopt Western technology and ideals if for no reason than to avoid yet another violent rupture like the Conquest or the Revolution. His tongue-in-cheek parody of indigenismo sums his thought up best: "Instead of sending cruel and ambitious captains to the New World, [indigenistas claim that] Spain should have sent a great delegation of ethnologists, anthropologists, archeologists, civil engineers, dentists, veterinarians, physicians, country school-teachers, agronomists, Red Cross nurses, philosophers, philologists, biologists, art critics, mural painters, and historians" (*Autobiography* 109). As Orozco made clear, such fanciful ideas may sound appealing, but they failed to measure up to reality; from a historical perspective, it would have been impossible for these cultures to have interacted in a peaceable way. We should take care not to misinterpret Orozco and claim that he believed that people of European descent were better people than Amerindians or that they were justified in their actions. As Jacquelynn Baas states in a paper on Orozco's murals at Dartmouth College, the conqueror is "no more or less admirable than the brutal society that [they] destroy" (172).[20] Rather than assert that Amerindians should assimilate to European ways of knowing to become a more virtuous society, his murals amorally prescribed assimilation to avoid annihilation.

The conjugation of Orozco's painting with the architecture of the building plays an essential role in communicating the artist's beliefs about racial identity and technology. As Alfred Neumeyer notes, "parallel with the rendition of mechanized life, appears a semi-abstract, geometrized design, enhancing the consonance with the surrounding architecture" (128; see also García Barragán 113; and Traba 23). As a former cathedral, Hospicio Cabañas provided an ideal space for questioning the role of the Crown, the Church, the conquistadores, and the indigenous in Mexican society both past and present. Orozco grounded his depictions of the past in the present; the different figures in the frescos represent archetypes for the racial and gender performativities of their day. This is particularly clear in *La conquista de México: Cortés triunfante*, a panel where a mechanoid Hernán Cortés storms Tenochtitlán. Whereas Cortés simply stands atop a corpse in *Cortés y la Malinche*, here he stabs a body as it lies on the ground. Above him, a similarly mechanoid angel looks him in the eye, as if justifying his actions. The artist once again proclaims indigenous primitivity through bare bodies that blend into the ground; the bare ribs of the grotesque, mutilated corpse cause the dead body to appear more stone than human. This stands in stark contrast to the sleek, metallic conqueror, whose color and body contrast with the nature he subdues. Orozco emphasizes the conquistador's dominance of nature by painting the background space behind his mechanical Cortés in similarly dark tones that almost blend in with his protagonist's armor. The conqueror has manipulated the natural world and reproduced it in his own highly modern, technologized image. Orozco reimagines the Conquest in a way that buoys discourses of mestizo

Figure 2. *La conquista de México: Cortés triunfante*. Mural by José Clemente Orozco at Hospicio Cabañas. © Artist Rights Society (ARS), New York/SOMAAP, Mexico City. Photograph by Jason Dormady.

modernity; notions of race start at the body, but they extend to geography, technological competency, and political power.

Orozco emphasizes his ties to hispanismo and Western modernity more explicitly in this fresco than in *Cortés y la Malinche*. According to Raquel Tibol, this mural shows that "the side with the more sophisticated instruments, apparatuses, and armaments wins the war" "[conquista quien posee los instrumentos, aparatos y armamentos más sofisticados]" (*José Clemente Orozco* 157). Spain's lopsided military proficiency accentuates and even legitimizes Cortés's victory as it emphasizes that violence is prerequisite to Mexico's journey toward modernization. The murals at Hospicio Cabañas seem to assert that Spanish conquerors created a modern nation as they eradicated the protohuman remnants of Mexico. While the mechanoid Cortés's "robot war against flesh and blood men" seems utterly unfair on the one hand (Echavarría 34), the fresco celebrates the conqueror's exaggerated masculinity on the other. The technologically hybrid Cortés asserts himself as the father of a newly modernized Mexico as he places his sword between the legs of the Amerindian who lies at his feet. The dead body appears to be more male than female, but there are no genitalia or visible face, so the figure has certain androgynous qualities. If the dead, indigenous person is male, then this is an act of figurative castration that signals hypermodern, posthuman Europeans as the only appropriate (male) progenitors of Mexican society. If the body is female, then this image refers to a forceful rape that forges a new technologically, racially, and culturally hybrid nation. In either case, Orozco posits lethal and sexual violence as necessary components of modernity.

The key figure in justifying the brutality of the Conquest is not the mechanoid Cortés; rather, it is the technologically hybrid angel. This winged figure's presence underscores a divine alliance between the conquerors and a redemptive Providence that justifies the results—though not the means—of the European invasion of Tenochtitlán. Far from a "luciferian [sic] genius" (Echavarría 30) or even a "God of War" (Tibol, *José Clemente Orozco* 157), this figure shares certain characteristics with Walter Benjamin's angel of progress. The mechanical angel may not take pleasure in the violence surrounding him, but the destruction is a "storm of progress" that he must weather for modernization to occur. It is doubtful that Orozco would have learned of Walter Benjamin's theorization prior to finishing this mural; the German theorist wrote his "Theses on the History of Philosophy" in the late 1930s, but the work was not published until 1947. Benjamin's writings remain useful to a discussion of Orozco's mechanical angel whether or not the muralist knew about them because they both use the figure of an angel to discuss the contradictions and problems associated with modernization. Indeed, as a mechanical being, Orozco's angel embodies progress in ways that Paul Klee's angel (which originally inspired Benjamin) does not. One ironic effect of using Benjamin to discuss Orozco's depiction of history is that the theorist was skeptical of those who used history to justify their rule because modernity and material "progress" come at a hefty human cost (682). The problematic nature of Orozco's mythic retelling of the Conquest becomes clear as the mechanical angel sanctifies the conquered, indigenous dead. Homo sacer deaths become (secularly) sacred as they facilitate the redemption of other indigenous people who ultimately embrace modernity and assimilate to the mestizo bios. The artist may disagree with the acts that put Spain in power, but he uses his mechanical angel of progress to validate the political system that the conquerors would later put in place.

The angel's key role in consecrating the Conquest and ushering in an age of mestizo modernity comes through especially clearly in *La conquista de México: Retrato del francisco*, another panel that takes place after Cortés's triumphal conquest. An austere, domineering priest stands at the center of the image; a bare-bodied Amerindian bows before him while the mechanical angel, now unconscious, lies shackled to the ceiling. The priest's body artistically blocks the lines from the opposing elements of the panel—particularly the peasants and the angel—from converging. Rochfort argues that the mural "express[es] the character of the conquest as one that was simultaneously ruthless and harsh, but charitable and forgiving" (112). The presence of several letters in the frame buoys the critic's claim by suggesting that the priest has taught indigenous Mexicans how to read. If the defining feature of protohumanity is a lack of written language (Pratt 15–16), then—at least from a Eurocentric point of view—the friar has elevated native Mexicans to full-fledged humanity. However, the priest has not eliminated the differing degrees of privilege that persist between people of indigenous and European descent. It is possible that the bowing Amerindian will assimilate to mestizo culture in the future, but any such transition will result in second-class citizenship. The priest's divisive presence in the frame suggests that an interethnic communion will never occur through religion. Spiritual leaders purposefully drive a wedge between people of indigenous and European descent as they imprison the angel of progress and impede him from engaging with the

Figure 3. *La conquista de México: Retrato del francisco*. Mural by José Clemente Orozco at Hospicio Cabañas. © Artist Rights Society (ARS), New York/ SOMAAP, Mexico City. Photograph by Douglas J. Weatherford.

native population. Painted in a recently secularized chapel, this image holds that indigenous actors remain incapable of modernizing not because of an inherent "backwardness" but because the rigid dogmas of Catholicism have blocked the mechanical angel from ushering in a greater modernity. Such an interpretation fits within the thought of critics who view Orozco as anticlerical and even nihilistic (Gámez R. and Quintero 83).

The frescos composing *El hombre en llamas* posit the transformation of the indigenous body into a mestizo entity through racial, cultural, and technological hybridity as a more effective means than religion for exorcising racism and discrimination against Amerindians from society. The artist suggests that technology can succeed in reimaging the national biopolitics where Church officials have failed. He depicts such a process in *La conquista de Mexico: El caballo mecánico* (1938–39), where a robotic protagonist atop a mechanical horse depersonalizes the Conquest and reduces it to a conflict between a technologically advanced, posthuman bios and a protohuman zoê. The horseman storms across a plane of oblique angles that divide the conquerors from the conquered by framing them in spaces with different vanishing points. Because the oblique angles are the result of industrial metal scaffolding that runs across the bottom of the panel, Orozco ties this division to notions of industrialization and modernity. The separation of bodies between separate planes will not last in the long term, however. Rather than allow the indigenous inhabitants to remain hidden on their side of the mural, the conquistador reaches his spear into the adjacent plane, kills the bodies on that side with one arm, and drags the Castilian flag behind him with the other. The indifference toward homo sacer death rings especially clear here because dead bodies are only visible as imprints at obscure angles in the frame. Thus, the image celebrates Spain's mythic hypermodernity as the "proper" blueprint for Mexican modernity.

Of course, Orozco's assertion of an advanced Spain that confronted a primitive indigenous nation did not reflect historical reality; as a medieval kingdom, conquering Spain was hardly a blueprint for modernity (Hassig 7–16). Nevertheless, critics like Echavarría state that these murals depict "the first product of the rising science of the renaissance, which made this conquest possible" (28). This argument ignores the help that Cortés received from local rivals to the Aztecs (Clendinnen 65–66), and it shows the level to which the myth of an eternal Spanish modernity has made its way even into the academy. By imagining a technologically advanced Spanish Conquest,

Figure 4. *La conquista de México: El caballo mecánico*. Mural by José Clemente Orozco at Hospicio Cabañas. © Artist Rights Society (ARS), New York/SOMAAP, Mexico City. Photograph by Douglas J. Weatherford.

the artist prescribed indigenous assimilation to the mestizo state as key to mitigating the racial tensions that permeated postrevolutionary society. *El caballo mecánico* provides perhaps the most intriguing example of a national body reformed through technological hybridity. The horseman's victim is one of many people whose faces are literally imprinted on the metal scaffolding, while their limbs swirl above them in the upper-left-hand corner. Despite their literal brokenness, both the faces and limbs follow trajectories toward a single vanishing point in the center of the plane. The angles and lines of the image attest to an imminent reconstitution of the indigenous body—one in which the Amerindian is fused with a mechanized industry. In the strictest of senses, the broken bodies hidden across the panel are not even dead; they are machines that the conquerors will recondition as modern, industrial workers when indigenous peasants join the national proletariat. Unlike many of the other murals at Hospicio Cabañas, this painting serves as a treatise on indigenous hybridization through technological hybridity; Amerindians can overcome their supposed backwardness and assimilate to the modern state if they modernize and renounce their previous culture(s). The Conquest exists in this mural as the moment that spawned the interchangeable values of racial and technological hybridity, and Orozco asserts that these hybridities remain key components of mexicanidad and official mestizaje in the twentieth century.

Throughout his oeuvre, Orozco constantly affirmed a clear legal distinction between Amerindian and European life, ultimately exalting mestizaje as the ideal toward which the nation should aspire. His preference for European culture and modernity framed his contributions to postrevolutionary thought in decidedly hispanista terms. Whether emphasizing indigenous protohumanity or Spanish hypermodernity, the basic tenet remained the same: the path toward an authentically Mexican modernity included the westernization of indigenous peoples and bodies. The muralist had an excellent position from which to disseminate his ideals; however, his were not the only—or even predominant—ideologies on the subject. Most people associate the muralist movement with indigenismo, an ideology that favored the retention of an indigenous spirit in an otherwise "modern" society. This association has largely resulted from the fact that Diego Rivera, the movement's most vocal protagonist, was an unabashed indigenista. Similar to Orozco, this artist constantly juxtaposed the national body with technology in his work; however, he also pointed out the shortcomings of focusing solely on modernizing the indigenous body by positing the need for an essentially indigenous national soul.

Technological Hybridity and *Mestizaje* in Rivera's Indigenismo

Rivera produced the majority of his art in Mexico and the United States, but he was received very differently in each country. At home, people often viewed him more as an opportunist than as a true communist. At one point, the painter renounced his membership in the Partido Comunista Mexicano because he claimed that he could better serve the leftist cause as an artist (see Sánchez Vázquez 270); the party, however, responded by censuring him and calling him a propagandist for the murderous state (Monsiváis, "Diego Rivera" 124; Hemingway 20). The U.S. art-viewing public, however, viewed Rivera as a true

Mexican Marxist (Hemingway 23–25), a trait that contributed to his controversial aura north of the Río Grande (McKay 125–28).[21] He generally painted for bourgeois patrons in North America, but this was because they were the ones that appreciated and paid for his work (Jaimes 113). Despite the fact that he accepted money from the upper classes, his work remained committed to Marxist principles (Kettenman 44–55; Wolfe, *Fabulous* 317–41; Robert L. Scott 1–4). That said, the artist constantly adapted his political discourse to the space in which he painted; as Claudia W. Ruitenberg observes (212–13), his art would lose its political edge if it did not engage the local community, be it Mexico City or Detroit.[22] Rivera's enduring faith in a Pan-American, utopian future became a common thread across his work in both countries. His U.S. murals emphasized technological sophistication as a key element of the proletarian revolution and the ensuing redemption of humanity.[23] Unlike many of his contemporaries who viewed technological hybridity as a means for modernizing Amerindians and assimilating them to the state, however, Rivera believed that an indigenous spirit would temper modern society and ensure that it did not abuse its technological might.

Rivera saw art as a means for communicating essential ideas to the public, and he viewed himself as the arbiter for what constituted appropriate teachings. He jealously defended his own right to artistic expression, but he did not support the same for others. He famously painted over the murals of Jean Charlot at the Secretaría de Educación Pública, for example, due to their purported low quality (Gallardo Muñoz 85–89). As he established himself as an authoritarian figure within the national art, he ensured that the SEP would favor his nationalistic ideologies over those of his contemporaries (Híjar Serrano 640–41). It is largely due to Rivera's powerful persona that Mexican muralism became so closely identified with indigenismo despite the fact that neither Orozco nor Siqueiros fit cleanly in such a paradigm. The artist was certainly not the first indigenista thinker in Mexico, but as he favored visual over lettered discourses, he reached a larger audience than many of his predecessors (and contemporaries) had, and he thus afforded greater prestige to indigenismo. Rivera's visual style carried over to other forms of cultural production, particularly film—as we shall see in chapter 3—and photography (Comisarenco Mirkin, "Donde caben").

It may seem contradictory that an unabashed indigenista like Rivera also revered science and technology. The artist certainly feared technology's potential for harm; in his *Manifesto for an Independent Revolutionary Art*, he and André Breton noted that "today we see world civilization . . . reeling under the blows of reactionary forces armed with the entire arsenal of modern technology." This quote recognizes that technology could be abused, but the artists ultimately cast the blame at the feet of corrupt leaders who would use the advances of the day in ways that caused harm. Rivera did not believe that Mexico should avoid technology; as his U.S. murals show, science and technology sat at the heart of a healthy modernity. As Sergio Pitol explained, "Rivera believes that the levers that will move the continent will be technology, the machine, industrial development and its inevitable result: the proletariat. This will be provided, of course, by the United States. At the same time, the element that most entices him is the primitive, virgin potential of the indigenous world, whose memory will be key in the creation of his inevitable utopia" ["Las palancas que moverán al continente piensa, serán la tecnología, la máquina, el desarrollo industrial y su consecuencia inevitable: el proletariado; eso lo proporcionará, por supuesto, Estados Unidos. Pero por otra parte, la que más le entusiasma, el potencial virgen, primigenio del mundo indígena, cuya memoria será capital en esa realización de la Utopía que él siente cercana e ineludible."] (188–89; see also Gámez R. and Quintero 84; and Belnap 65). Rivera's art had a distinctive futurist aesthetic; each of the murals that I discuss below juxtaposes technological advancements with a divine figure either from a pre-Columbian religion or from Christianity. These murals both emphasized the redemptive value of technology and reminded his audience that physical modernity had to be tempered by an innocent, indigenous spirituality.

The muralist generally placed his country and the United States in a binary relationship where North American technology—which the artist depicted as Anglo-Saxon—would fuse with Mexican indigeneity. Rivera's U.S. murals took on a resistant tenor as they critiqued dehumanizing technologies and lent credence to the marginalized actors and bodies of the Americas. The mural that best encapsulates his ideal of intercultural give-and-take is *Pan-American Unity*—his final U.S. mural (Ugalde Gómez 436)—which he painted at the City College of San Francisco in 1940. Often viewed as a leftist, anti-Nazi work (Lozano, "From Carnival" 388; Lee 212–15), the mural clearly advocates for mestizaje and inter-American cultural hybridity. The work immediately draws the viewer's focus to the center panel, aptly named "The Plastification of Creative Power of the Northern Mechanism by Union with the Plastic Tradition of the South." This panel shows the Aztec goddess Coatlicue; one side of her body consists of organic flesh, while the other looks like "an industrial stamping press" (Brown, "Cyborgs, Post-Punk" 316). Several critics have built on cyborg theory to discuss the significance of this mechanized goddess's presence in the frame. Chris Hables Gray notes that the fresco deconstructs the binary of goddess and cyborg that Haraway canonized in her "Cyborg Manifesto" (181), while J. Andrew Brown asserts this image as an early example of the ties between the cyborg and the (neo)baroque in Latin America ("Cyborgs, Post-Punk" 318–20). David Lomas avoids a posthuman reading, but he argues that "Aztec belief supplied Rivera with a means of picturing [technology's] Janus-like character, conferring on technology-as-*pharmakon* an unforgettable face" (462). When viewed alongside each other, these critics' works suggest that Rivera's depiction of a technologically hybrid indigenous goddess allows him to engage with constructs of modernity, mestizaje, and indigenismo.

Coatlicue captured the postrevolutionary imagination more than perhaps any other indigenous deity because she paradoxically regenerated society through death and birth (Rodríguez Mortellaro 61–62). Rivera accentuates this deity's ambiguous nature by presenting her as a hybrid entity that deconstructs distinctions both between the organic and the machine and between the mystic and the scientific. The goddess's presence in the mural underscores Rivera's implicit call for the fusion of the spiritual and artistic genius of the South with the mechanical prowess of the North. Beyond facilitating an intercultural union by fusing the supposed strengths of Latin and Anglo-American cultures, "The Plastification" also advocates racial mixing. As modernity is inscribed on Coatlicue's body, she becomes a technologically hybrid, and thus mestizo, subject. Rivera divides his mural into two halves that converge at this central image; one side reifies indigenous cultures, practices, and knowing, while the other celebrates U.S. (Anglo-Saxon) industry and advancement. Technological hybridity becomes a way to fuse two very different cultures and foment intracontinental unity. Rivera places Coatlicue's fleshy face on the mechanistic side of the image, while her robotic face appears on the organic side. The resulting yin-yang imagery emphasizes the need for both spirituality and technological competency to coexist on both sides of the U.S.-Mexican border. Thus, Rivera asserts that both civilizations benefit as they incorporate the other's strengths into a hybrid coexistence. As the image of this technologically hybrid goddess powerfully asserts, healthy societies eschew neither modernity nor spirituality; the potential of combining "European" modernity with "indigenous" spirituality forms the basis of Rivera's triumphant mestizaje.

Painting *Mestizaje* in a New Light   85

Figure 5. *Pan-American Unity*. Mural by Diego Rivera at City College of San Francisco. © Banco de México Diego Rivera Frida Kahlo Museums Trust, Mexico, D.F./Artists Rights Society (ARS), New York. Photograph provided by City College of San Francisco.

The deity's hybrid nature suggests that, while spirituality and technological sophistication are important on their own, it is the conjugation of both that will allow for a truly Pan-American utopia. The mestiza goddess is clearly rooted in discourses of indigenismo, a fact that becomes especially clear as Rivera depicts an indigenous deity rather than Christ as humanity's divine example. The artist necessarily downplayed much of the suffering that indigenous peoples had faced from the imperializing force of the North in his attempts to imagine an intercultural, North/South union (Lee 210), but he never fully diverged from his indigenista, mixed-race ideal. The mural's primary focus is the potential for technology and indigenous spirituality to sire a modern mestizaje, but the work also alludes to the creation of racial hybridity through sexual reproduction. Rivera achieves this through a personal allegory; near the bottom of the frame, at Coatlicue's feet, we see an image of the artist holding the hands of the Hollywood actress Paulette Goddard. A mystical, white "tree of life and love" springs forth from their hands as if symbolizing the creative potential of interracial heterosexual relations between dark-skinned Mexicans and their lighter-skinned North American neighbors (Landau 27–28; Aguilar-Moreno and Cabrera 79). A Mexican girl and an American boy sit next to the couple and learn that they, too, must eventually procreate a mixed-race generation. At this time, Rivera and Goddard truly were having an affair (Landau 28), so beyond communicating a mestizophilic ideal, the painter also flaunted his extramarital adventures to the world and to his and Goddard's respective spouses, Frida Kahlo and Charlie Chaplin.[24]

Rivera furthers this polemical imagery by depicting his wife facing the viewers while he engages in an affair literally behind her back. Ellen G. Landau argues that Rivera's depiction of Kahlo associates her with the mythic figure of *la chingada*, "the personification of a long-suffering Mexico violated and deceived by liars and outsiders" (28), but her interpretation is complicated by the fact that the couple was divorced when Rivera initiated his work in San Francisco. Indeed, they remarried while Rivera was working on the mural, but they did so only under Kahlo's condition that they abstain from sexual relations (Comisarenco Mirkin, "Diosas y madres" 205n10). Even so, Rivera certainly asserts himself as a dominant *macho* as he boasts of his extramarital adventures. Beyond the aforementioned commentary on the artist's personal life, we should also note the eugenic, race-based discourse that underpins this painting. Rivera and Kahlo's marital union would have been coded as appropriately eugenic within postrevolutionary circles because both were mestizo/criollo. Nevertheless, Rivera's relationship with Goddard would have been even more desirable under the same rubric because, as interracial progenitors, any children the couple would have had together would have furthered the project of global mestizaje.

Rivera's flamboyant depiction of his affair with Goddard fits within an imaginary in which Mexico turns the tables on traditional Western powers like the United States and establishes itself as the new great colonizer. Claudio Lomnitz argues that "it is perhaps significant that male members of elite families often

Figure 6. *Mecanización de la tierra*. Mural by Diego Rivera at the Secretaría de Educación Pública, Mexico City. © Banco de México Diego Rivera Frida Kahlo Museums Trust, Mexico, D.F./Artists Rights Society (ARS), New York. By permission of Schalkwijk/Art Resource, NY.

marry blonde wives. The slogan *gringos no, gringas sí*, and the high-status practice of marrying white women is not simply an act of 'whitening,' for whitening could just as easily involve mestizo women marrying white men; it can also be construed as an act of national appropriation of the dearest of European products" (*Exits from the Labyrinth* 279). Rivera's affair with the Hollywood actress also symbolizes—at least as represented in the mural—the virility of the Mexican *macho*, whose seductive skills expedite the process of racial mestizaje. The artist represents himself as an imperializing force as he imagines mestizaje not only as something that Mexican intellectuals and politicians must impose on their own country's Amerindian population but also as an ideal that major cultural figures like himself should insert into the white, Anglo-Saxon societies of North America. Rivera's depiction of his own affair visually defines his ideal balance between indigenous "magic"—embodied by Coatlicue—and the (ostensibly Western) modernity that he symbolizes with technology. Both are key to his utopian goal, but Rivera situates both Goddard and himself in the domain of indigenous mysticism rather than that of technocratic, northern industrialism. In the end, this and other murals by Rivera upheld the notion that technological hybridity could transform Amerindians into mestizos. But the painter also asserted time and again that the modern, mechanical world (and Mexico) could avoid corruption only if it internalized spiritual, and even magical, indigenous values.

One of the Mexican murals that best exemplifies Rivera's personal convictions about the proper nature of an Amerindian-centric modernity is *Mecanización de la tierra* (1926), which he painted at the Secretaría de Educación Pública in Mexico City. This mural shares much in common with the highly regarded series of frescoes that he painted at the Universidad Autónoma de Chapingo in Mexico State around the same time (1926–1927). Beyond masterfully "integrat[ing] painting and architecture" (Lozano, "Bad Government" 136), *Mecanización* also celebrates the successes of land reform during the Calles administration (Tibol, *Diego Rivera* 217). The central image is that of an indigenous woman, "modeled on statues of the Aztec fertility goddess Xilonen" (Coffey, "'All Mexico'" 71), who picks and shucks corn in a field. To her left three revolutionaries—representing the *federales*, the *zapatistas*, and the *villistas* respectively—embrace one another. Behind her, a man tills his field with a tractor while a crop duster flies overhead. According to Elena Jackson Albarrán, this mural depicts a postrevolutionary imaginary where "a feminized landscape reached its full potential only with the intervention of masculinized technology, and only through a violent modification of her flesh" (165). Albarrán's assertion is especially interesting because it suggests that the earth itself became a technologically hybrid, mestizo entity as modern technologies both scarred it and increased its utility. Craven furthers this line of argumentation as he notes a "message about the mediation of nature by society that precludes any unqualified belief in an undisturbed 'natural order'" (52). Clearly, Rivera exalted the human domination of the landscape as a necessary component of modern, mestizo society, yet he also emphasized an indigenista discourse throughout *Mecanización*. The production of food, for example, though now mechanical and industrial, remains in the hands of Amerindians rather than local or foreign corporations. As the woman at the image's center demonstrates, technological advancements have reshaped some aspects of indigenous agriculture, but her manual harvest underscores the retention of certain indigenous traditions and modes of production.

Unlike Samuel Ramos (*Profile* 119–20), who claimed that Mexico would have to impose a European/mestizo spirit on its Amerindians prior to spreading technology throughout the nation, Rivera expected indigenous and mestizo cultures to mutually construct one another. For Rivera, the fusion of the indigenous body with technology could transform Amerindians into mestizos; however, this could not be allowed to undermine the native spirit. The painter emphasizes this fact on the left edge of the mural, where a naked female Amerindian—possibly the Aztec goddess of nature, Tozi—shoots what appear to be roots through the heads of two Catholic priests while an indigenous bystander looks on in awe. This image further validates Albarrán's observation that Rivera viewed technology as masculine (and mestizo) while nature was female and indigenous. The vengeful goddess alludes to a resistant indigenous drive to invoke nature against Eurocentric dogmas, though, significantly, not against Western technology. As the indigenous goddess destroys the Catholic priests, she not only defends pre-Columbian cosmologies (both religious and secular), but she also invalidates the hegemony of the Church within indigenous and even mestizo Mexico. Her violent defense of the indigenous masses transcends theological disagreements and denounces the oppression that the Church has purportedly levied on indigenous Mexico since colonial times. But even as the goddess kills two friars, she allows the indigenous man to survive. With the agents of imperialism removed, this man will soon integrate into a society that is both indigenista and mestizo. Along with the woman at the center, he can now live in a technologically modern nation without fearing the imperial aspirations of a Eurocentric/hispanista elite.

Despite its anticolonial posture, Rivera's indigenista artwork paradoxically assisted state officials in establishing an internal empire that would assimilate Amerindians—often against their will.[25] The artist attempted to sidestep the oppressive elements of official mestizaje by framing modernization as a strategy for extending greater privilege to a segment of society that had long lived on the periphery. Technological hybridity is perhaps less obvious in *Mecanización de la tierra* than it is in *Pan-American Unity*. The clearest example of indigenous ties to technology and modernity in *Mecanización* comes as peasants use tractors and airplanes to work the fields that have traditionally belonged to them. The technologies in this image suggest that Western ways of knowing can benefit indigenous Mexico as they aid in creating a mestizo society built on indigenista values. The validation of a new mestizo race that embraces its indigenous roots is necessary to the reconciliation that occurs between the various revolutionary factions in the right-hand side of this work. Each soldier carries weapons that attest to the mechanization of warfare. At first glance, these images remind the viewer that the destruction of the Revolution occurred precisely because technological advances in modern weaponry had perfected the art of killing. Yet because the postrevolutionary state framed the Revolution as a movement of indigenous emancipation, another reading would suggest that technology played a key role in producing a more egalitarian Mexico; the progress of the Revolution came about only after people of all genders, races, and ethnic groups gained access to (military) technology. Rivera painted *Mecanización* nine years after the passage of the Constitution of 1917 but right at the beginning of the Cristero War (1926–1929). Seeing as the Calles administration had hired him as a de facto "painter of the state" (Hamill 122), Rivera's reconciliatory discourse became especially urgent. Just as the protagonists of the Revolution had come together after the war, so too should the various factions of the new conflict.

Technology's ability to both adapt to and improve life in indigenous communities was a recurring theme across Rivera's work. *Mecanización* posits industrial agriculture and the technologies of modern warfare as the tools that will help indigenous Mexico to grow economically and politically. However, these were not the most prominent purveyors of technological hybridity in the artist's work. That distinction goes to medicine, an entity that could literally save a human being as it was inscribed on the body. The painter's fascination with biology and medicine possibly predated even his love of art (McMeekin 10); one of his first murals to discuss the redemptive role of medicine was *Vaccination* (Detroit, 1932), which depicts a young boy receiving an immunization while surrounded by horses, cattle, and sheep. Many in the United States took offense at the parallels between this mural and the Nativity, but Rivera defended his inclusion of these animals by correctly stating that scientists had used them to develop vaccinations for smallpox (R. L. Scott 3; McMeekin 25). According to Luis H. Toledo-Pereyra, Rivera's knowledge of "science and its accompanying disciplines" is obvious to the well-informed viewer throughout his Detroit

Figure 7. *Vaccination*. Mural by Diego Rivera at Detroit. © Banco de México Diego Rivera Frida Kahlo Museums Trust, Mexico, D.F./Artists Rights Society (ARS), New York. Photograph by Sandra Casanova-Vizcaíno.

works (140; see also McMeekin 9–10; Wolfe, *Fabulous* 307; and Gallo, *Mexican Modernity* 2). However, the heart of the image is the vaccinated child who becomes the new Messiah; clearly the artist posited science as the new doctrine of modernity.

A Foucauldian reading of *Vaccination* uncovers certain socialistic overtones to Rivera's scientific paradise. In "The Birth of Social Medicine," Foucault discusses "Labor Force Medicine," which is an advanced form of "social medicine" that emerged as states started intervening on behalf of the proletariat to protect the moneyed classes (333–36). Labor Force Medicine reflects capitalist self-interest because, according to Foucault, the rich aid the poor only because they depend on a healthy working class to provide them with the amenities they desire. Rivera's ironic religious discourse and his focus on the medicated individual reframes Foucault's views of social medicine by emphasizing the positive effects of vaccination on the medicated individual (whether proletarian or bourgeois) rather than the benefits of a vaccinated workforce for a capitalist society. Rivera suggests a socialist aesthetic, then, where the treatment of an individual is an appropriate end in itself. This triumphal, leftist discourse tempts the viewer to interpret *Vaccination* as a proclamation of technology's ability to bring about an enlightened world free from pain and suffering. However, other panels at this site depict the creation of gas bombs and other frightening technological advances meant to increase human suffering. As Linda Bank Downs argues, Rivera's Detroit murals "continue the themes of the unity of organic and inorganic life and the constructive and destructive uses of technology" (109). Her observation of technology's positive uses suggests a link between Rivera and other postrevolutionary intellectuals and artists—and futurists from Mexico and Europe—who viewed technological advancement as a means for forging a new utopia. But her recognition that technology is often negative here underscores Rivera's cautious approach to modernity in general.

Rivera did not believe that scientific, technological, and medical advancement would always bring about positive results. While necessary to producing vaccinations for smallpox, such advances could also devastate humanity when placed in the wrong hands. This fact underscores the peculiar ties between Rivera's futurism and indigenismo: technology could achieve its utopian potential only if subordinated to a spiritual ideal embodied by a folkloric, indigenous innocence. As a result, it could not come from a rupture with the past; instead, technological progress needed to incorporate the spiritual knowledge of past generations. One of his murals that best juxtaposes indigenous practices with the cold practicality of Western science and medicine is *Historia de la medicina en México: El pueblo en demanda de la salud* (1953), which sits in the Centro Médico Nacional La Raza in Mexico City. Similar to *Pan-American Unity*, an indigenous deity—this time Tlazeoteotl, the Aztec goddess of fertility and hygiene (Cabello 1462)—sits at the center of the image. The deity both separates pre-Columbian and European/Western medical traditions from one another and facilitates a dialogue between them. Many viewers may assert that Rivera's depiction of people undergoing highly advanced treatments aligns him with contemporary medicine. However, as Andrea A. Barquero notes, an Aztec *curandero* on the pre-Columbian side of the mural prepares medical herbs while several doctors on the modern side look at those same plants under a microscope to determine the chemistry behind their medicinal properties (57). Beyond celebrating the advances of modern medicine, then, this mural validates indigenous health care and conceives it as on par with that offered in contemporary society (Smith, "Nacionalismo"). Rivera respectfully depicts the healing tradition of the original inhabitants of the Americas—particularly its focus on treating people as a single, integrated unit rather than compartmentalizing the body into several disconnected, alienated systems (Duarte Sánchez 516).

The caregivers on the indigenous side of the mural focus primarily on childbirth and maladies that they can heal with herbs and traditional knowledge. In the bottom-right corner, Rivera depicts a pre-Columbian statue where a woman gives birth from her haunches; next to this, a woman does the same in the presence of several midwives. Pain exists as a harsh reminder of human frailty, but traditional health practices mediate a person's overall suffering. Medical treatment becomes an intimate practice that brings communities together in their focus on the individual. After a person is healed, she reincorporates into society, where she will presumably return the favor by helping someone else in the future. The overriding premise of this segment is the value of social cohesion. The people who inhabit the pre-Columbian civilization of Rivera's imagination have mastered their surroundings and learned to care for each other in a naturalistic way (Villa Gómez 29–30). Given these pre-Columbian medical practices' strong focus on nature, it would be imprecise to code any patients as technologically hybrid cyborgs; they differ qualitatively from the medical subjects of a Western society that constantly employs synthetic drugs, carefully engineered immunizations, and expensive medical equipment. Rather than depict these differences as weaknesses, however, Rivera emphasizes the many positive elements of pre-Columbian medicine.

On the pre-Columbian side of the image, for example, there is no division—social or artistic—between healers and the afflicted. This alternative approach to health care produces a more organic society than that of the twentieth century. Patients and health practitioners are starkly divided from one another

Figure 8. *Historia de la medicina en México: El pueblo en demanda de la salud*. Mural by Diego Rivera at Hospital La Raza. © Banco de México Diego Rivera Frida Kahlo Museums Trust, Mexico, D.F./Artists Rights Society (ARS), New York. Photograph by David S. Dalton.

on the "modern" side of the image based on their role as either physician, patient, or bureaucrat. In the upper-left corner, a multitude of people attempts to enter a hospital, but a line of bureaucrats blocks them. Those individuals who cannot enter the hospital are coded as indigenous through their phenotype. Access to health care, then, is not based on need but on socioeconomic and racial privilege. Rivera's artwork thus refines certain aspects of Foucault's thought; whereas Foucault argues that "Labor Force Medicine" resulted from self-interest within the capitalist classes, the mural charges that the Mexican state's failure to care for poor, indigenous peoples perpetuates the marginalization of Amerindians in the national economy and society.[26] The dehumanizing effects of modern medicine extend beyond racist and classist systems of discrimination: even when people meet with a medic, they have only depersonalized interactions with health care professionals. In most of the treatments depicted in the image, doctors depend on the readings of machines—rather than one-on-one conversations—to diagnose and treat their patients. This results in a dehumanizing medical culture that treats people as mechanistic bodies rather than as individual beings. The technological hybridity that results from modern medicine in this image does not necessarily produce a eugenic "improvement" of the national body, and in many cases it dehumanizes the treated individual.

We should not confuse Rivera's critique of modern medicine with a wholesale rejection of medical technology or its practitioners. The mural celebrates the many successes of Western medicine, positing them as necessary components of modern society. Although he reifies the traditional health care of indigenous cultures, the muralist shows that these folkloric means of healing are insufficient against the problems of a globalized, industrial world. The indigenous side of the mural, for example, depicts a man covered in blemishes who cannot receive adequate care from traditional healers. Rivera deliberately places this body at the point of contact between the indigenous and the European/mestizo worlds at the center of the mural. The illness, probably smallpox, arrived to the so-called New World as a result of the European invasion. According to Rivera's painting, indigenous practices became obsolete only after people from another part of the world brought diseases that native healers could not treat (Noble, *Born to Die* 58–64). Taken to its logical conclusion, this cynical reading proposes that, while indigenous societies were better off on their own, current conditions require them to assimilate to the modern (Western) state and its accompanying medical order if they wish to weather the effects of colonialism on their bodies and health. The mural hardly signals modern medicine as morally redemptive; instead it posits Western medicine as an imperial commodity that becomes necessary only as European values are imposed from the outside.

Of course, the critique that modern medicine merely fixes problems inherent to Western society ignores the fact that medical advancements are always tied to a specific context in which (generally) well-meaning doctors treat the maladies of the day. It is for this reason that *Historia de la medicina en México* does not criticize medical advancements and technologies per se; instead, it questions the depersonalized nature of modern health care and the resulting segregation of bodies. The oppositional representations of modern medicine in *Vaccination* and *Historia de la medicina en México* spring from the fact that Rivera aimed these works at distinct audiences. While in Detroit, he saw the impressive gains of a fully modern, industrial society; despite his communist sympathies, these examples of the triumph of capitalism amazed him (Lomas 460). His U.S. art certainly championed the exploited proletarian worker (Miner 647–48), but it also validated the market-based, U.S. economic system. Thus, it is not surprising that murals like *Vaccination* heralded medical advancement as the culmination of human endeavors against death and suffering. Furthermore, this earlier mural shows an intimate relationship between doctor and patient; the absence of a heartless bureaucracy that withholds care from some allows Rivera to trumpet medicine's redeeming effect on the messianic child. *Historia de la medicina en México* also portrays medicalized bodies as triumphant beings who have overcome disease. However, modern medicine could not achieve its full redemptive potential until it reached all sectors of society. Clearly, the mestizo state had to learn from the medical history of both sides of its official racial identity. In this way, it would produce a highly modern yet personalized health care system.

Rivera concurred with other officialist thinkers from his time as he centered progress on the national body. Technological hybridity was a means for modernizing bodies and initiating them into the patriarchal order of official mestizaje. That said, his indigenismo emphasized (admittedly essentialist) components of indigenous cultures that he believed the state should include in its articulations of an official mestizo identity. Rivera forcefully argued that the country's rich cultural history meant that a proper Mexican modernity would differ from that of other countries, and his murals suggested that the country would enjoy a truly autochthonous modernity that was Western in its technological prowess yet spiritually indigenous. Regardless of his exaltation of indigenous cultures, Rivera's murals also demonstrated his paternalism. Within his thought, the state served as the final arbiter for what constituted the best interests of the indigenous population. Similar beliefs permeated the works he produced both as the artistic mouthpiece for the state and as an artist for commission in some of the largest cities of the United States. In both cases, Rivera attempted to reconcile his affinity toward indigenous cultures with his interest in technological progress. Both elements formed the basis of his utopian dreams, and together they represented the fusion of Western modernity with indigenous spirituality. Despite its shortcomings, Rivera's indigenismo helped reimagine both the role of indigenous voices in Mexico and the ways through which "native" and "modern" Mexicans could interact.

Conclusion

The muralist movement is perhaps the single most rigorously studied component of postrevolutionary Mexican cultural nationalism. This is in large part due to the powerful personalities of people like José Clemente Orozco, David Alfaro Siqueiros, and especially Diego Rivera. My discussion of the works of Orozco and Rivera has shown that, while both muralists favored mestizaje and a type of autochthonous modernity, they differed on how to achieve this end. Orozco's work coded modernity as a necessarily European construct, and his view of official mestizaje focused primarily on imposing European knowledge, cultural forms, and industry on the nation. This was particularly clear as he depicted pre-Columbian people as bare-life protohumans while at the same time emphasizing Spanish ties to hypermodernity and posthumanity in a way that validated the violent subjugation of indigenous peoples due to their supposed primitivity. Orozco's beliefs stood in stark contrast to those of Rivera, who constantly exalted indigenous peoples and cultures. His work was often paternalistic, but his belief that the indigenous soul should form part of the national character provided new spaces for indigenous bodies and subjectivities. Within Rivera's thought, science and the indigenous spirit would purify one another as they came in contact in Mexico. Technology would physically upgrade the population, while indigenous ways of knowing would keep technological sophistication from corrupting Mexico. Rivera's visual style was adopted into many other media, particularly film and photography. The following chapter discusses the films of Emilio "El Indio"

Fernández and his cinematographer, Gabriel Figueroa, both of whom viewed themselves as the cultural heirs of the muralists—particularly Rivera (Mraz 107–8). As we shall see in the following chapter, these filmmakers positioned the national cinema as the medium through which Mexican audiences—particularly those in rural sectors—could learn and internalize official doctrines in the 1940s and beyond.

3

Emilio Fernández, Gabriel Figueroa, and the Race for Mexico's Body

Immunization and Lamarckian Genetics

An iconic shot from Emilio "El Indio" Fernández's *Río Escondido* (1947) captures the young, idealistic Rosaura Salazar (María Félix) as she steps off a train that has brought her from Mexico City to northern Chihuahua. The cameraman, Gabriel Figueroa, captures her solitary figure in a low-angle, deep-focus shot that frames her between a cactus and large, ominous clouds. She then plunges forward on her journey to Río Escondido, where, as a *maestra rural*, she will challenge institutional *caciquismo* by inculcating modern discourses—particularly the desirability of medical immunizations—in her (indigenous) students. The shot exemplifies why so many critics have identified Fernández and Figueroa as the filmic heirs to the muralists.[1] Numerous critics note that the tandem sat at the fore of a cinematographic movement that built on the muralist aesthetic to differentiate itself from Hollywood through filmic techniques—particularly low-angle shots, curvilinear perspective, big skies, and oblique perspective—that posited the national landscape as a protagonist.[2] The director strove to produce what Benedict Anderson calls an "imagined community" (6) that would validate official mestizaje through indigenista discourse. As "El Indio" once proclaimed, "There is only one Mexico: that which I invented" ["Sólo existe un México: El que yo inventé."] (quoted in Taibo 51).[3] This chapter adds to the scholarship on "El Indio" by arguing that the director uses his films to center social progress on the national body. The protagonists of Fernández's movies initiate Amerindians and women into the modernity-driven state by fusing their bodies with modern medicine, thus transforming them into mestizos through technological hybridity.

Because Fernández received moneys from the government—particularly the Secretariat of Public Education [Secretaría de Educación Pública] (SEP)—most scholars view him as complicit with postrevolutionary doctrines.[4] Dolores Tierney critiques this view when she says that this scholarship "elide[s] what can be seen as obvious contradictions of Fernández's films and Mexican post-Revolutionary society" (*Emilio Fernández* 2–3). Her focus does not preclude mexicanidad from the director's oeuvre (indeed, all of her chapters engage the concept at some level), but it opens a space for nuanced readings that more adequately gauge how his work interfaced with the ideologies of the various presidencies that coincided with his career. "El Indio" was a remarkable director who used film to both challenge and disseminate statist doctrines on the silver screen. He certainly accepted government moneys, but his strong personal and political convictions bled through in his work. On the one hand, his films celebrated an autochthonous national spirit inherent to rural (indigenous) Mexico; on the other hand, he often regurgitated officialist perspectives that placed a "backward" rural periphery in tension with a modern and industrialized center (Tuñón, "Ritos"). By separating "El Indio" from the role of mouthpiece for the government, my study detects common discourses of mexicanidad not only in films like *María Candelaria* (1943) and *Río Escondido*, but also in U.S. productions like *The Torch* (1950) that he filmed without financial aid from the Mexican government.[5]

Fernández's work frequently alludes to ways in which medicine can "modernize" primitive (generally indigenous, "deviant" female, or both kinds of) bodies. Viewed in this light, his films largely conform to Rebecca Janzen's observation that, "in literary works, less powerful characters appear sick or disabled, especially as they participate in public education, as they try to access health care or are rejected from unions" (6). Unlike the authors of Janzen's study, however, Fernández does not use imageries of sickness and disease to undermine the legitimacy of the postrevolutionary government. Rather, his representations of diseased indigenous characters and medicalized women serve to showcase state power as federally funded doctors and teachers export modern medicine to the rural countryside. Far from being "excluded from the cosmic race" (Janzen 6), then, "El Indio's" sickly characters are able to assimilate to the patriarchal, mestizo order as they submit to the state and allow it to heal them. Indeed, their infirmities become a precondition of their ultimate "redemption"; the medication that they receive modernizes their bodies and transforms them from Amerindians or "immoral" women into mestizo/as whose articulation of race and gender is more appropriate according to postrevolutionary paradigms.

Fernández's films build on a distinctly Mexican understanding of medicine and race that began to emerge during the Porfiriato in which hygiene became a key component to eugenic projects that aimed to modernize the nation through mestizaje. The postrevolutionary government followed in the footsteps of its Porfirian counterparts and dedicated numerous resources to hygiene in both rural and urban areas.[6] The fact that state thinkers from both periods expressed a eugenic faith in hygiene reflects how Lamarckian principles—particularly the idea that physical improvements to the body would alter the national genotype—guided domestic policy. According to Nancy Leys Stepan, the preference for Lamarckism in Latin America signaled a perceived need for nonwhite populations to overcome their supposed backwardness by improving their bodies (18; see also Suárez y López Guazo, *Eugenesia* 98–101). Mendelian genetics, which precluded hygiene's ability to amend the genome, would not suffice in the country because any eugenic project based on that paradigm would code indigenous and mestizo bodies as irredeemably dysgenic. Lamarckism's influence in the country extended beyond the Secretariat of Public Health [Secretaría de Salubridad Pública] to other secretariats like the SEP. Just as medicine would hybridize the body with technology, education would create culturally hybrid indigenous subjects who would become fluent in Hispanic language and culture. Thus the cultural missions—which consisted of rural education and hygiene (Mijangos Díaz and López Torres 51–52)—were eugenic projects that, according to Lamarckian paradigms, would convert Amerindians into not only cultural, but also biological and genetic, mestizos.[7]

With the notable exception of *The Torch*, the medical segments from "El Indio's" movies function as SEP-funded treatises on the state's "sanitary dictatorship" (Aréchiga Córdoba, "Dictadura" 119), which the Nuevo León congressman José María Rodríguez proudly referred to as "the only dictatorship that civilized societies tolerate" ["la única [dictadura] que toleran los pueblos civilizados"] (310). Fernández used his "celluloid school" to promote these coercive state hygiene projects whose principal aim was the dissemination of medicine and education to rural (indigenous) populations (Tuñón, "Una escuela" 454, 466–68). In his indigenista films, access to adequate health care converts indigenous bodies into technologically hybrid entities who, similar to Donna Haraway's cyborg, trouble the reigning body politics.[8] The destabilization of outdated structures of power—like caciquismo and indigenous serfdom—allows Amerindians to claim mestizo privileges if they modernize their bodies through medicine and education and abandon their "backward" heritage (Nahmad Rodríguez 113–14). In *The Torch*, "El Indio's" English-language remake of his masterpiece *Enamorada* (1946), a zapatista general and an American doctor fail to contain an influenza outbreak. The resulting death and carnage challenges the simplistic notion that the presence of medicine automatically equals adequate health care and modernity. Here Fernández suggests that Mexico must follow a homegrown path toward the future. One of Janzen's most important observations is that it is not enough for "weak" individuals (particularly women and indigenous people) to undergo medical procedures; rather, they must submit to the institutions and authority of the state (6). Seeing as *The Torch* takes place during the Revolution, it is impossible for the state to intervene in the flu epidemic. As such, the principal characters have to depend on the expertise of the foreign doctor, Edward Roberts. If Fernández were to permit his film's U.S. medic to contain the epidemic, he would invalidate a nationalistic premise that underlies the majority of his cinema in which *statist* medical endeavors hold the keys to modernization. Within the discursive framework of his films, national (mestizo) doctors initiate and interpellate (potentially) threatening bodies into their "proper" place in the patriarchal order of official mestizaje. Beyond immunizing people against harmful disease, medics also redeem such bodies from their own, apparently unacceptable, racial and gender performativities.

Far from existing as a mere metaphor for nation-building and indigenismo, "El Indio" viewed medicine as a key contributor to projects of social immunization. Roberto Esposito can shed some light on medicine's immunological role—both medical and social—within postrevolutionary Mexico. Building on the work of Haraway, who discusses the immune system to theorize "what may count as self and other in the crucial realms of the normal and the pathological" (204), he asserts an "immunization paradigm" that resonates within both biopolitical and posthuman thought (45–77; Campbell vii–xlii). According to Esposito, biopolitical states must constantly balance the tensions that emerge between the individual (*immunitas*) and the community (*communitas*): two selves, as it were, whose existence "is inscribed reciprocally in the logic of the other" (Campbell ix). Within Esposito's view, the community—which paradoxically includes the individuals who compose it—represents threats against which individuals must immunize themselves. This theory translates strikingly well into the Mexican context, where José Manuel Puig Casauranc—José

Vasconcelos's successor as secretary of public education—wrote that hygiene projects aimed to "defend teachers and students from the dangers of life in the *community*" ["defender a maestros y alumnos de los peligros de la vida en *comunidad*"] (quoted in Urías Horcasitas 61–62, emphasis mine; see also Puig Casauranc 160–67). Rather than frame hygiene primarily as a means for improving life in indigenous communities, the bureaucrat suggested that the principal goal of state-sponsored medical efforts was to protect modernized (and especially modernizing) individuals from the supposed excesses of a dangerous, indigenous community.

State doctors provided medicine to all individuals who desired it (and even to many who did not). Nevertheless, government leaders conceived of immunization as a tool for protecting "enlightened" individuals from a perceived indigenous swarm. This unflattering representation of indigenous subjectivity has led numerous scholars to view Mexican and Latin American indigenismo as a biopolitical project that exhibited many of the characteristics that Giorgio Agamben enunciates in his book *Homo Sacer* (Janzen 89–93; Acosta 41–48). Agamben argues that biopolitical states divide the world between bios (the good life) and zoê: the homo sacer subjects whose killable, "bare lives" exist beyond the protection of the law (9–14).[9] According to postrevolutionary dogmas, rural Amerindians represented a curious form of zoê that, while (generally) not killable, certainly lacked the legal protection that urban mestizos enjoyed. This was by no means a mistake; rather, it reflected the biopolitical values of the state. As Abraham Acosta argues, "the bare life that resides on the borders . . . becomes the very thing against which biopolitics emerges as a pre-emptive social defense" (44). Acosta's observation signals the paradoxical nature of indigenista thought; while ostensibly pro-indigenous, the state tried to defend its population from indigenous subjectivity and "primitivity." In light of his observation, it appears that we can best understand the biopolitical nature of indigenismo by synthesizing the thought of both Esposito and Agamben. On the one hand, the focus on redeeming the (indigenous) individual meant that Amerindians were a childlike entity whom the state had to modernize and incorporate. While paternalistic, such an approach to indigeneity fell short of Agamben's killable homo sacer. On the other hand, even as they celebrated the redemption of the individual, indigenista discourses and politics continued to devalue indigenous communities at large. State dogmas interpellated individuals who chose not to assimilate to the mestizo order into bare life and zoê.

Official ideologies denied the possibility that indigenous subjectivities could form part of the mestizo bios. Indeed, Matthew J. K. Hill shows that the redemptive potential of Fernández's Amerindian characters was their status as "mestizos in embryo" (41). "El Indio" thus asserted that, in order to achieve bios (and the Agambian good life), Amerindian individuals had to abandon their ethnic communities and become mestizos. Because "redeemed" individuals necessarily joined the mestizo community (and left the indigenous one behind), indigenous communities remained perpetually bare by definition. This fact can help reconcile my understanding of postrevolutionary biopolitics with that of Gareth Williams, who argues that postrevolutionary thinkers wished "to immunize the *collective* against the random and heterogeneous elements inherent in the social body" (6, emphasis mine). Within the context of this chapter, Williams's argument exemplifies the interconnectedness of Esposito's twin notions of *immunitas* and *communitas*. State actors focused on immunizing and assimilating indigenous individuals, but they did so with the goal of expanding mestizo subjectivity collectively throughout the nation. They wished to redeem the masses at large, but they could do this only if they reached (and redeemed) every indigenous individual within their reach. Medicine proved especially useful to projects of indigenous assimilation; it simultaneously modernized indigenous individuals, separated them from the "bare" communities from which they came, and transformed them into members of the mestizo community through technological hybridity.

Viewed in this light, it becomes obvious that state actors intended for this medicating act to amend the biopolitical landscape. Writing from the U.S. context, Chris Hables Gray argues that state-sanctioned immunization campaigns are coercive projects of forced cyborgization that attempt to improve the health of the population at large by stripping individuals of their rights to accept or refuse treatment (*Cyborg Citizen* 95–97).[10] Viewed alongside Esposito's, Gray's work seems to suggest that immunization campaigns exist to force individuals out of an undesirable, unmedicated community and into a sort of Agambian "good life." These claims take on greater weight in postrevolutionary Mexico, where the state aimed to transform Amerindians into mestizos through technological hybridity. Official hygiene campaigns served the dual purpose of initiating Mexican bodies to the state and immunizing individuals against the pitfalls of their pre-mestizo (and hence premodern) communities. Upon receiving medication, immunized individuals and their progeny would be entitled to mestizo privileges and responsibilities. The state certainly had laudable intentions to better the lives of its people—a goal that it achieved in spectacular fashion in rural communities (Flisser 356)—but it achieved this end by further subordinating marginalized peoples to a top-down articulation of national character.

Statist articulations of mestizaje necessitated strict prescriptions about what constituted proper racial, gender, and sexual performativity. The fact that disease was most common in indigenous communities and urban brothels led many to equate bad health with immorality (Bliss, "Health" 205–14; "Science" 5–40). The state charged itself with the task of "purifying" problematic societal actors and educating their children so that it could instill proper values of performativity and modernity in both parents and offspring (Schell 559–60). As it equated health with character, the state laid the foundation through which "bare lives" could be redeemed through repentant hybridization. It is perhaps for this very reason that "El Indio" constantly juxtaposes medicine's redemptive properties with Catholic imageries. This discursive strategy is especially interesting because, according to Benjamin T. Smith, the state conflated equitable health care with anticlericalism (41). In a sense, one performative failure that the state wished to eradicate from the (indigenous) masses was its excessive piety. The historian Gretchen Pierce, for example, notes that rural teachers often "led expeditions to local churches to smash and burn statues of saints" (508). Nevertheless, Fernández's focus on representing "authentic" Mexicanness often led him to reify at times contradictory ideals, particularly regarding the relationship between the Mexican people and the Church. Adriana Pacheco notes that Fernández's cinema championed such antithetical ideals as "progress, modernization, populism, anticlericalism, Catholicism, and Guadalupism" ["progreso, modernización, populismo, anticlericalismo, catolicismo y guadalupismo"] (33). The director constantly tapped into his country's latent religiosity to buoy official discourses. His most positive representations of Catholic faith were the folkloric, sincere practices of the nation's female and indigenous populations; however, he also extended a privileged position to men of the cloth since his films received their moral compass from the conflation of God with the state.

Regardless of the director's own purported anticlericalism (Hershfield, *Mexican Cinema* 70–71), he ascribed a key immunological role—both medical and societal—to the Church within midcentury Mexico. Each film discussed in this chapter depicts the clergy differently, but the overriding narrative of the Church in Fernández's oeuvre is its ability to intervene and temper the performative excesses—racial, gender, or socioeconomic—of Mexican subjects of all social strata. The Church effectively immunizes the individuals of the community against themselves as it shows them their "proper" place in society. This ideological function underscores a key tenet of Catholic and other Christian belief systems that holds that people undergo deep metaphysical and spiritual changes as they repent, an idea that alludes to the very physical change to indigenous genes that will occur according to Lamarckian paradigms. We see hints of the Church's immunological role in *Enamorada/The Torch*, where the village priest aids in establishing social cohesion across class lines. The religious imagery is much more pointed in *María Candelaria* and *Río Escondido*, where the female protagonists represent "goodness, purity, and sacrifice" (Hershfield, *Mexican Cinema* 70), traits that equate them with the Virgin of Guadalupe.

Cyborg Virgins: Redeeming Mexico through Traditional Modernity

It is perhaps ironic that María Félix and Dolores del Río, actresses whose "dazzling beauty" established them as sex symbols in Mexican popular culture (Monsiváis, "Mythologies" 123), would emulate the Virgin in these films. Yet both actresses interpret characters who signal a redemptive path in part by invoking their ties to Mexico's most popular saint. As we have already seen, Rosaura ushers a new era of modernity into the remote village of Río Escondido by medically and educationally immunizing its rural population. Given her strong ties to the postrevolutionary state, Rosaura is a full-fledged member of mestizo society. María Candelaria, however, has no direct ties to the government, so her redemptive qualities are more mythic in nature. The film codes her as Amerindian because she was born to an indigenous prostitute in the village of Xochimilco. Nevertheless, because Dolores del Río was fair-skinned, her character's articulation of indigeneity is highly problematic. According to Tierney, the criolla actress's whitened representation of indigeneity distinguishes her from the movie's other Amerindians; as such, the film celebrates "modern" Amerindians whose spiritual and phenotypic whiteness aligns them with official mestizaje (*Emilio Fernández* 90–95). María Candelaria's fair features lead an unnamed painter to signal her apparently indigenous body as a symbol of implicit hybridity and national potential. Beyond their emulations of the Virgin, both female protagonists have medically enhanced bodies; María Candelaria takes quinine to treat malaria while Rosaura is vaccinated for smallpox before the film begins. These female protagonists' ties to both technology and the sacred take on greater significance given the theoretical framework that I have developed throughout this book. The implicit technological hybridity of these types and shadows of the Virgin of Guadalupe suggests that we read them as a cyborg Virgin, an entity whose paradoxical nature serves as the perfect construct for a country that aimed to achieve modernity through technological advances and traditional morality.

Brief plot summaries will facilitate the discussion of how these female protagonists appear in both films, and they will allow me to further show why it is useful to categorize them as cyborg Virgins. In *Río Escondido*, the Mexican president personally designates Rosaura as a *maestra rural*. He is only filmed from behind, and his voice equates him with God. We never see his "holy" face, yet he presides over the nation's "benevolent" projects of indigenous incorporation. Rosaura goes to the town of Río Escondido, where she stands up to caciquismo and immunizes the indigenous peasants from their prerevolutionary performative failures, thus initiating them into modern society. She does this first through modern medicine when she helps Felipe, a rural doctor, administer vaccinations to combat a smallpox outbreak, and later by teaching official doctrines that oppose caciquismo and promote capitalist expansion and mixed-race identity. Because she undermines his power, the local cacique, don Regino, attacks her in her home. She kills him, but dies of a resulting heart attack.

The inhabitants of Xochimilco despise María Candelaria because her mother was a prostitute. They refuse to allow her to sell flowers within the city limits, which makes it difficult for her to pay off a debt that she owes the cacique, don Damián. This in turn makes it impossible for her to marry her fiancé, Lorenzo Rafael (Pedro Armendáriz), because they cannot afford a dress nor a ceremony. She and her fiancé go to a nearby town where a criollo painter—who emulates Diego Rivera (Tuñón "Femininity" 91)—sees her and wishes to paint her, but she refuses. Later, she gets malaria from a mosquito bite and requires quinine pills that don Damián refuses to provide. Lorenzo Rafael breaks into the cacique's store by night and steals the medicine and a wedding dress. He saves his fiancée but is sent to jail. María Candelaria agrees to pose for the artist if he will post bail; however, after he paints her face he asks her to undress. She refuses, and the artist finishes his portrait using another model's body. The village's indigenous inhabitants see the incriminating image and stone María Candelaria to death.

Rosaura and María Candelaria provide a type of secular salvatory potential for their countrywomen and men that paradoxically draws strength both from traditional notions of performativity and from the hybrid body's resistance to outdated body politics. These characters' articulations of technological hybridity thus serve as a fascinating counterpoint to what Sara Anne Potter classifies as a "technified muse": a cyborgian woman whose technologized body becomes a site for challenging cultural memory and official constructs of gender (x). Both the cyborg Virgin and the technified muse depend on the technologized body's ability to disrupt the reigning body politics, but they carry out contradictory roles in postrevolutionary society. While Potter identifies technified muses in avant-garde art and literature that questioned postrevolutionary tenets of cultural nationalism, the cyborg Virgins that I discuss below appear in state-sponsored films that celebrated state power and traditional norms of gender and race. Both Rosaura and María Candelaria articulate their bodies in ways that conform to statist understandings of proper gender performativity, for example. These female protagonists thus set an example for their audiences, who will presumably incorporate similar values into their own lives. Rather than contest official discourses of race, gender, and sexuality, then, the female protagonists of these films validate them and even aid in their construction. My juxtaposition of the cyborg Virgin with the technified muse shows that, far from carrying a predetermined ideological value, the technologized body functioned as a disruptive force from which artists of all stripes could both construct and contest official doctrines of race, gender, and sexuality during the postrevolutionary period.

The cyborg Virgin figure is especially intriguing in these films because it deconstructs the classic binary of the deified femininity of ecofeminism and an ambiguous cyborg that resists many constructs of femininity, including that of goddess (or saint) (Haraway 162). For Haraway, the cyborg's ability to resist interpellations of the body is a greater tool for feminist liberation than is an appeal to an essentialistic femininity that imbues women with supernatural power (181). Of course, Haraway does not have the last word about the interconnected nature of cyborg and goddess subjectivities. J. Andrew Brown, for example, notes that Latin American cyborg figures—particularly women—frequently strive to recuperate, rather than transcend, their gender (*Cyborgs* 43–76); as such, the binary between goddess and cyborg loses much of its appeal. Nina Lykke maintains a general distinction between both entities when she asserts that "both the cyborg and goddess metaphors recast the non-human other in the role of subject, actor and agent in her/his own right" (82), a fact that alludes to both figures' ability to interface with and challenge the patriarchy. Fernández's cyborg Virgins may not undermine patriarchal society, but they are excellent examples of marginalized subjects who become key agents of the state after achieving bios through the combination of their traditionally gendered, sacred, and cyborg identities.

As "El Indio" films secular, cyborg Virgins, he further extends a discourse of hybridity already inherent to Guadalupan imageries and articulates a figure that resonates differently for mestizos, criollos, and Amerindians. Although Lykke probably did not have Golden Age Mexican cinema in mind when she asked that we "explore the potentials of cybergoddesses" (85), Fernández's films provide fertile ground from which to gauge her ideas. As a construct of the modernity-driven state, these cyborg Virgins' liberatory potential is necessarily limited to assigning racial and gender Others their proper roles within the paradigm of official mestizaje. That said, the mere act of employing Guadalupan discourses in any way "challeng[es] the dominant versions of national identity with an Indian-inflected, insurmountably dual, vision of mestizaje" (Feder 231). This is, of course, due to the many similarities between the Virgin of Guadalupe and several pre-Columbian goddesses like Tonantzin, Coatlicue, and Mayáhuel (Oleszkiewicz 241–46; Feder 244–46). Indeed, the Virgin of Guadalupe's ties to indigenous deities explain why Mexican Catholicism tends to emphasize the Virgin more than even Christ. The multiple significations of the Virgin of Guadalupe's hybrid etymology emphasize the need to validate both European and indigenous heritage within a system of institutionalized mestizaje. Imperializing forces have long tried to subjugate the Virgin of Guadalupe to Eurocentric patriarchy; as indigenous deities were syncretically tied to Catholic saints, they necessarily subordinated their will to that of Christ and the Church. Of course, the Virgin of Guadalupe also bore a message of inclusion since her reported appearance to Juan Diego during colonial times asserted a special place for Amerindians within the Church and even the Spanish Empire. Thus, while the Virgin of Guadalupe is a European appropriation of indigeneity, she also reminds mestizos and criollos to include Amerindians in their constructs of nation.

As Mexico has reimagined itself over the years—during the colonial, the republican, and postrevolutionary periods—it has constantly returned to this goddess/saint. Her paradoxical knack for including everyone yet coaxing them to conform to the reigning racial and patriarchal ideologies makes her an excellent figure for nation-building (Noble, *Mexican National Cinema* 82; Feder 242–44). "El Indio" exploits this potential with his own technologically hybrid, female protagonists to construct and question an autochthonous national identity. Mirroring Mexican Catholicism's ultimate subordination of the Virgin of Guadalupe/Tonantzin to patriarchal religious structures, the postrevolutionary director ties technologically hybrid female bodies to the modernity-driven, equally patriarchal discourse of official mestizaje. Fernández certainly was not privy to cyborg or ecocritical debates as he filmed in the 1940s, but his work sheds light on the extent to which those in power can invoke cyborg, feminine deities to proclaim liberation even as they perpetuate their own hegemony. Rosaura and María Candelaria bear the inclusive token of modernity to the masses, but Amerindian communities cannot partake of said modernity without first accepting the imperialistic, mestizo narrative of nationhood. What is more, because these cyborg Virgins' worth comes from upholding traditional norms of sexuality, the articulation of their bodies problematizes tendencies toward both the sacred and the cyborg in ways that stretch current understandings of both posthumanism and ecocriticism.

Perhaps one of the most interesting things that we can take from these performances of technologically hybrid—yet traditionally "chaste" and "pure"— women is the constructed nature of even the most "liberatory" of discourses. Both characters seem like perfect midcentury articulations of what Jerry Hoeg calls "cybermestizas," an inclusive category "in which both performativity and material body are in constant flux, and therefore immune to rigid categorization" (99). Nevertheless, these cyborg Virgins remain susceptible to rigid interpellations of the body that require both to "remain . . . virgin[s] for the benefit of the nation" (Hershfield, *Mexican Cinema* 70). Fernández's cyborg Virgins clearly represent nationalistic liberation despite conforming to racial and gender norms. What is more, their bodies—as well as those of the indigenous peasants of their towns—most certainly are "in constant," but not infinite, "flux." Rosaura succeeds in tapping the redemptive potential of these shifting notions of performativity by encouraging the indigenous population of Río Escondido to assimilate to the dominant class. María Candelaria, however, is never able to inspire the Amerindians of her town to adopt a more modern worldview. This remarkable distinction between the characters not only determines the effectiveness of each; it is key to understanding the resistant role that "El Indio" imagines for his cyborg Virgins in general.

Both films show mestizo caciques who oppress the indigenous peasants of their towns in part because the postrevolutionary state continued to struggle against local strongmen well into the mid-twentieth century (Brewster 105–6).

These strongmen represent a distinct articulation of racial hybridity from that of official mestizaje. Rather than incorporate indigenous Mexicans into the body politic, they perpetuate racial differences that have historically exalted mestizo/criollo subjects while relegating Amerindians to serfdom and peasantry. Don Regino, for example, owns all the property in Río Escondido, and as a result the peasants cannot evade him even in their (his) homes. He controls the town's two wells and warns that he will kill anyone who "steals" water from the one he has designated for himself. Like don Regino, don Damián controls Xochimilco's flow of money. He owns the only store, is the lone creditor, and most employment goes through him. Both men benefit from a position of privilege along racial and gender lines, so they jealously strive to maintain the biopolitical status quo. This is especially the case regarding how they handle state hygiene programs and their respective cyborg Virgins. Because medicated bodies—both indigenous and mestizo, male and female—necessarily alter the reigning body politics, the strongmen must suppress the democratizing effect of modern medicine in their towns. Don Regino cannot curb an immunization effort after a smallpox epidemic engulfs Río Escondido, nor can he silence the redemptive discourses that Rosaura disseminates in the school. Don Damián, however, controls access to medical privilege by only providing health care to those who recognize and respect his authority. What is more, he contains María Candelaria's salvatory potential when he has the people of Xochimilco stone her to death.

María Candelaria's failure to inspire change in the people of Xochimilco is especially surprising when we consider "El Indio's" obsession with producing a redemptive, educational cinema (Tuñón, "Una escuela" 441–45). Mónica del Carmen García Blizzard argues that the movie still makes sense within a postrevolutionary paradigm; because it takes place prior to the Revolution, "the film's tragedies are presented as a result of a faulty governing structure that does not effectively rule or integrate different social sectors" (159). "El Indio's" indictment of prerevolutionary society is especially strong with regard to rural hygiene, which careless government officials incompetently oversee. In one telling scene, two doctors arrive while don Damián yells at his indigenous laborers and violently forces them to work. After witnessing the cacique's abusive nature, the doctors give him jars of quinine with instructions to medicate those who contract malaria. Both the medics and don Damián harbor racist and sexist thoughts; when don Damián mentions that it is strange that only female mosquitoes bite, one of the doctors points out that "all the world's ills come from females" ["todo lo malo viene de las hembras"]. The prerevolutionary medic's assertion grates against the grain of an official discourse that hoped to incorporate women as full-fledged members of the postrevolutionary state. The doctors and the cacique also view Amerindians as incompetent. Don Damián exemplifies these beliefs as he paternalistically force-feeds the pills to his workers (Hershfield, *Mexican Cinema* 55).

Don Damián may medicate the town, but his actions do not constitute social—or even medical—immunization. The people whom he treats, for example, are already healthy, a fact evidenced by their hard work only moments before. Quinine will do little for them, because, as an antimalarial, it is only effective for combating infections already present in a diseased body. Most doctors emphatically recommend against using the drug to prevent illness due to the possibility of serious side effects (U.S. National Library of Medicine). Don Damián, then, wastes precious medical resources, places his workers in danger, and frustrates the proliferation of a redemptive form of technological hybridity as he ineffectively medicates the town. The cacique's actions are even more oppressive at a societal level because he establishes that all access to health care goes through him. Rather than facilitate indigenous assimilation, the presence of medicine further coerces the people to support the local cacique. Indeed, don Damián punishes those who challenge his authority by withholding medical privilege from them. This is especially visible in the cases of María Candelaria and Lorenzo Rafael; María Candelaria has constantly rebuffed the cacique's sexual advances and sworn herself to her poor, indigenous fiancé. Don Damián has opportunities to medicate each of these indigenous protagonists on separate occasions, yet he refuses to do so out of spite. What differentiates María Candelaria from other medicated characters in the film, then, is that she receives treatment against the cacique's will. This medical act constitutes a social immunization as it undermines don Damián's authority, modernizes her body, and aligns her with the more benevolent actors of the state.

María Candelaria's ties to technology and hybridity result from a raft ride she takes with Lorenzo Rafael. Figueroa's high-angle shot of the actress invokes the image of the Virgin of Guadalupe as it captures her surrounded by lilies. While in this saintly position, she melodramatically swats a mosquito that has bitten her. This scene fits into the paradigm of educational film that Fernández constantly produced; by showing his protagonist contract malaria from a mosquito bite, he implores his audience to take care in swampy areas. However, any practical lessons we can extract from this scene take a back seat to mythic discourses that juxtapose her saintliness with an infection that will ultimately lead to her medication and technological hybridity. When Lorenzo Rafael attempts to buy quinine at the cacique's store, don Damián points a rifle at him from the merchant side of the sales counter and orders him to leave. Figueroa masterfully represents the separation of bodies by filming this (en)counter from an oblique angle, a technique that "creates two vanishing points rather than the normal one, to the left and to the right of the frame, and initiates tension between them" (Ramírez-Berg, "Figueroa's Skies" 35). The artistic tension on the screen alludes to the social discord that results from the racialized structure of medical privilege as the cacique and peasant stand in different planes. The shot thus reaffirms the existence of biopolitical structures that block Lorenzo Rafael from acquiring the quinine through legal means. After stealing the medicine, the indigenous man arrives at his fiancée's home; finding her unconscious, he medicates her.

Like all of the indigenous characters discussed in this chapter, María Candelaria cannot accept or reject medication and technological hybridity; instead, other people impose it on her, thus producing a type of forced cyborgization. Lorenzo Rafael brings a criollo doctor—who is almost certainly an agent of the state—to medicate his fiancée, and María Candelaria recovers. This sequence underscores the fact that indigeneity, which according to Fernández entails an aversion to modern medicine, is still a vice against which the state must immunize its citizens in a top-down manner. This is not to say that state efforts to medicate ill indigenous bodies are immoral; María Candelaria would die without treatment. However, as the state reserves the right to technologically hybridize its Amerindian population, it also becomes a colonizing force that coerces indigenous actors into abandoning their cultural heritage. The threat that modernization represents to indigenous cultures and ways of knowing leads many to resist modern medication. Because they oppose progress and advancement, however, the director rarely permits Amerindian arguments to come across as intelligent.[11] Perhaps the most outspoken critic of modern, Western medicine in this film is the local *huesera*, who also tries to cure María Candelaria. She voices her displeasure upon seeing that Lorenzo Rafael has invited a doctor, telling him to choose between the medic and herself. The medic quells the tension by allowing the indigenous healer to finish before he treats María Candelaria. In her reading of this scene, García Blizzard argues that "El Indio" posits indigenous healing as "obsolete" but "benign" because the *huesera* ultimately allows her patients to receive more competent care (255–57). "El

Indio" does not directly antagonize indigenous healing and medicine, but he makes it clear that the medic—and not the healer—saves his heroine. Given the film's didactic nature, Fernández also invites his audience to support the state's modernizing hygiene mission.

Upon receiving medication, María Candelaria is initiated both genetically and culturally into the mestizo mainstream. Immunized against her own sickly and "premodern" condition, she now speaks with an "other voice" (Deanda Camacho 71) and undermines oppressive structures of power. María Candelaria's body becomes a blueprint that other indigenous people in Xochimilco can follow in their own quests for corporeal modernization and assimilation to the mestizo order. What is more, María Candelaria has—along with Lorenzo Rafael—challenged don Damián's monopoly over the town's health care; her living body's very presence in Xochimilco attests to the cacique's incomplete hegemony. Her resistant potential comes to the fore when don Damián arrives at her wedding and has Lorenzo Rafael arrested. She cannot convince the local authorities to forgive her fiancé, but she enlists the help of the priest and the painter. This leads Tierney to argue that "the film aligns María Candelaria and Lorenzo Rafael with these 'good' and 'reasonable' white characters" while at the same time distancing her from "bad" characters like don Damián and the indigenous community at large (*Emilio* 90). Viewed from the perspective of Esposito's immunization paradigm, it becomes clear that the director ties the titular character's redemptive nature to her ability to separate herself from the dangerous indigenous community that surrounds her. Indeed, the combination of María Candelaria's medication, her phenotype, and her association with mestizo/criollo characters, signals her as more modern—and hence more mestiza/o—than even the mixed-race cacique. As such, she represents the ideal blueprint for national progress and redemption. Nevertheless, her prerevolutionary Mexico is not yet ready for her articulation of racial and technological hybridity.

This fact comes to the fore through her relationship with the painter, who metafilmically embodies the cultural values that the SEP hoped to promulgate through art and film (see chapter 2). This artist has long attempted to fuse indigenous culture with European art to initiate the native population into the wonders of Western culture, but he has never found an adequate subject to depict. Upon finding María Candelaria, he believes he has met an Indian princess who can inspire the masses toward mestizaje and modernity. His obsession with María Candelaria's body, which he wishes to paint nude, reminds us of her body's overall significance throughout the film. Though Haraway's cyborg delegitimizes constructions of racial and gender performativity, the redemptive nature of María Candelaria's body is firmly rooted in both technological hybridity and traditional gender norms. Interestingly, and perhaps paradoxically, she remains discursively chaste precisely because of her refusal to associate with the high culture of European nude art.[12] This is one of the most paradoxical aspects of the film; on the one hand, Fernández's indigenista films aimed to incorporate the indigenous community into the modern state by instilling European cultural norms in the masses, yet here we see that María Candelaria would lose her redemptive value if she were to cede to Western culture. Regarding the painting, Laura Podalsky argues, "what had scandalized the villagers probably would not have the same effect on the spectator." This suggests that one key element of the film is that of re-instilling an indigenous innocence, and even spirituality, in the audience. Because mestizaje is ultimately a process of hybridization, official discourses had to recognize that certain elements of indigenous identity would necessarily persist in mestizo Mexico forever.

The painter may believe that he holds all the keys to redeeming the indigenous masses, but it is his subject's refusal to fully assimilate to his European artistic and cultural tendencies that signals her as the ideal example of racial, technological, and cultural hybridity. Thus my reading of María Candelaria as a cyborg Virgin leads me to emphasize her rejection of Western culture in favor of (what Fernández saw as) indigenous values. Upon seeing that María Candelaria will not pose for him nude, the painter decides to superimpose another model's body on his depiction of María Candelaria's face, an act that creates a type of Frankenstein's monster. Tierney argues that the fact that the artist must connect the body of another model to María Candelaria's head suggests that the Indian princess "has 'no body'" (*Emilio* 94), particularly in a sexual sense. Renae L. Mitchell takes this point further by observing that Fernández deliberately leaves his audience wondering "what the portrait of a young woman of 'pure Mexican race' would look like" (4). We can only know that such a painting depicts a hybrid body; indeed, as a type of the Virgin, María Candelaria's body can only become sexed when fused with that of another woman with "lower" values. The hybrid fusion of two female bodies becomes a way to explore the (cyborg) Virgin's forbidden sexuality without defiling her innocence. Of course, this hybrid art results in an incriminating painting that testifies (falsely) against María Candelaria's chastity. When the peasants and don Damián view the image, the cacique whips them into a frenzy, charging them to punish and kill her. The cacique's actions go beyond *machista* jealousy; in seeing this painting, he recognizes the chance to kill María Candelaria and reassert his preeminence in Xochimilco.

In the following sequence, Fernández and Figueroa crosscut between a terrified María Candelaria, the torch-wielding indigenous mob that angrily pursues her, and Lorenzo Rafael, who, upon hearing his love's calls for help, breaks out of his jail cell. These parallel actions converge outside of the prison, where Lorenzo Rafael finds María Candelaria mortally wounded. Her final words, "I have done nothing wrong" ["no he hecho nada malo"], serve as a testament against her attackers. This sequence underscores the irony of Fernández's indigenista film: "El Indio" argues for the incorporation of Mexico's indigenous peoples, but the state must meticulously oversee such efforts. Left to their own devices, the Amerindians of *María Candelaria* are petty, violent, and woefully unaware of their own best interests (Noble, *Mexican National Cinema* 88–91). If the painter is correct in asserting María Candelaria's redemptive potential, then the people of Xochimilco have rejected and slain their secular savior. By killing the person who could have shown them how to enter a modern, mestizo world, María Candelaria's murderers have condemned themselves to generations of second-class citizenship. The film ends as Lorenzo Rafael rows his fiancée's dead body—decorated once again like the Virgin of Guadalupe—away from Xochimilco on a raft.

This tragic ending signals the extraordinary scope of the postrevolutionary state's mission; rather than content itself with turning a few "exemplary" indigenous subjects to technological hybridity and mestizo modernity, it aimed to immunize each individual of the indigenous community against its own perceived performative failures. This endeavor stretches Esposito's understanding of *immunitas* and *communitas* to their limits as the immunization of every individual member of the community (theoretically) produces a new bios. The state necessarily fails to discursively immunize all the indigenous characters in *María Candelaria* in part because the film takes place prior to the Revolution. However, this does not necessarily mean that the film is "an isolationist fantasy rather than a parable on modernization" (Tierney, *Emilio* 96). By positing María Candelaria as a technologically hybrid incarnation of the Virgin, Fernández suggests a nascent potential to redeem all the nation's Amerindians. Indeed, his protagonist's death merely postpones the inevitable march toward national, mestizo modernity. He centers postrevolutionary indigenous redemption on

Rosaura Salazar, another female protagonist in *Río Escondido*. With the help of enlightened state actors and government officials, Rosaura succeeds where her predecessor could not. It is largely due to her work that official programs extend immunization—both through medicine and the school—to the indigenous peasants of Río Escondido, thus incorporating them into official, mestizo modernity. Viewed in this light, Rosaura's ties to both modernity and the sacred invite us to view her as a cyborg Virgin; indeed, this theoretical approach allows for more sophisticated analyses about the relationships between technology, religion, and the body in the film.

Rosaura faces many of the same obstacles to modernization that Fernández identifies in the prerevolutionary society of *María Candelaria*. A few scholars offer against-the-grain readings of *Río Escondido*, asserting that it critiques the Alemán administration's failures to combat continued "widespread poverty, illiteracy and disease" along with caciquismo and systemic racism in rural communities three decades after the Revolution's end (Tierney, *Emilio* 150; see also Higgins 140; García Riera, *Emilio* 108). Fernández certainly preferred Cárdenas over succeeding presidents (Tuñón, "Emilio Fernández" 183–84), but the aforementioned readings contrast with most scholarship, which follows the lead of Carl J. Mora, who refers to the movie as "an outstanding effort of official interest filmmaking" (78; García Benítez, "Construcción"; Hershfield, *Mexican Cinema* 61; Fein 123; Chávez, "Eagle" 121). Throughout the film, "El Indio" celebrates the state actors—particularly rural doctors and teachers—who redeem the nation by entering hostile territory and helping the people of rural Mexico despite a serious lack of funds (Kapelusz-Poppi, "Physician" 35–38). Beyond challenging Alemán's cuts to education (Niblo 222–24; Segre 93), then, the director charges that the administration has tasked teachers and medics with duties more appropriate for police and even the military (Segre 157). Through his film, "El Indio" suggests that the only way to carry out the idealistic goals of the Revolution is to have a competent government sitting at the helm; if Alemán wants Mexico to continue modernizing, then his administration must not betray the nation's revolutionary values.

The film represents the power struggle between the nascent, postrevolutionary government and regional *caudillos* in a Manichean light. At the beginning of the film Rosaura goes through the Palacio Nacional, where the murals of Diego Rivera—particularly *México a través de los siglos* (1935)—and the images of past presidents (re)teach her of her national heritage and "articulat[e] three theses: that there is a historical-cultural bias to the Revolution, that public education is important in helping that project adhere together, and finally, that the national cultural establishment . . . play[s] a substantial role in ensuring the success of that project" (Acevedo-Muñoz 24). This scene both initiates Rosaura into officialist projects of indigenous assimilation and immunizes her against the contaminating effects of the actress, María Félix, who plays her. María Félix constantly eschewed "proper" articulations of gender performativity, claiming at one point to have "the heart of a man" ["corazón de hombre"] (Félix 33; Pizarro 186). Rather than admitting a transgender identity, the actress was probably signaling her drive to inhabit spaces previously restricted to men—a fact that made her a highly polemical figure whose scandalous private life bled through in her performances on the silver screen (Ocasio 274; Castro Ricalde and Irwin 233–34; Pizarro; Drake 3).[13] Susan Dever sees Fernández's decision to cast María Félix in this role as especially useful because it "underscore[s] the transformation of the independent woman to dutiful charge of the state" (60). As a redeemed (read: immunized) individual herself, Rosaura is uniquely positioned to lead a cultural mission that will incorporate rural Amerindians through education and modern medicine.

When Rosaura arrives to Río Escondido, she tells don Regino that the president has commissioned her to open a school; however, the cacique replies, "I am the only president here" ["aquí no hay más presidentes que yo"]. Despite obvious allusions to the tension between federal and local governments, the film challenges a simple binary of center/periphery. The mutual antagonism between Rosaura and don Regino revolves around the teacher's statist assertion that rural Amerindians deserve full citizenship and don Regino's attitudes that relegate indigeneity to zoê. Beyond representing the will of the center, then, Rosaura aligns herself with the rural peasantry that composes the majority of Río Escondido, an alliance that becomes especially clear when she finds a mother of three who is dying of smallpox. The teacher takes the children out of the home, telling them that they will get sick if they stay inside, and sends for the medic, Felipe. Rosaura adopts the children and helps the doctor attend to the dying woman. This scene highlights both Rosaura's maternal instincts and her virginity, thus drawing an implicit parallel between this protagonist and the Virgin of Guadalupe. By equating Rosaura with the Virgin, Fernández imbues the teacher with a secular moral authority that borders on the divine. Less obviously, this scene also alludes to her technological hybridity, and by extension, her cyborg condition. The fact that she and Felipe can freely enter the infected home alludes to their past vaccinations. What is more, the protagonists also show that, despite coming from the national center, their Mexico City–based cultural mission serves the best interest of rural Mexicans on the periphery who live at the mercy of brutish caciques.

Given that the Constitution of 1917 decreed access to education and health care as human rights (Aréchiga Córdoba, "Educación" 57–58), it should come as no surprise that medical doctors and teachers would enjoy such prominence in "El Indio's" oeuvre. For Fernández, both medics and teachers play significant immunological roles in postrevolutionary racial projects. The former modernize the primitive body through medicine while the latter purify the national soul by instilling proper behavior and performativity. "El Indio" further exalts these state-appointed actors as he juxtaposes them with don Regino, who irrationally forbids Felipe and Rosaura from burning the deceased woman's home, thus impeding their efforts to contain the smallpox epidemic. The cacique shows that his refusal goes beyond mere indifference to indigenous "zoê" when he forbids any attempts to vaccinate the indigenous population. Clearly, he views the threat of an alliance between the local peasants and the state—catalyzed and symbolized through medical immunization—as a greater threat than he does infectious disease. Only after taking ill does don Regino desist. He asks Felipe to cure him, and the doctor does so after the cacique agrees to open Rosaura's school and to allow him to immunize the town's population—"You are just one individual, and I have to save the entire town [people/*community*] from contagion" ["Usted es un sólo individuo y yo tengo salvarle del contagio a todo el pueblo."] (emphasis mine). The doctor's words embody Esposito's biopolitical thought; that said, Felipe's desire is not merely to immunize a few individuals against a dangerous community. Rather, he must reach all of the individuals who, in their totality, form an indigenous community in need of protection against medical and societal contagion. It is doubtful that Felipe truly heals don Regino; because smallpox is a virus, no cure exists beyond an individual's immune system (Mayo Clinic). This cacique's ultimate survival results from naturally beating the infection without the help of medical technology. The indigenous bodies that Felipe will soon vaccinate, then, can claim cultural, technological, and—in a Lamarckian sense—genetic mestizaje in a way that don Regino cannot.

As in *María Candelaria*, medication occurs without the people of the town being consulted. This fact underscores Fernández's elitist attitude that "portrayed Mexico's indigenous peoples as pure and simple, like children who had to be led to ... consciousness by the intellectual elite" (Hershfield, "Screening the Nation" 268–69). Here, the state, like a parent, must guide its indigenous children toward hybridity and modernity, even if this goes against the community's collective will. The resulting lack of agency leads Tuñón to view Fernández's indigenous characters as beings "without opinions of their own" ("Femininity" 86). Nevertheless, we should note that Fernández's Amerindians frequently harbor opinions that run contrary to statist dogmas. When don Regino decrees their vaccinations, for example, the peasants, understandably suspicious of the cacique's motives, run away. The ensuing scene crosscuts among indigenous peasants who flee; don Regino's lackeys, who lasso and even shoot those who try to get away; and Rosaura, who, along with the village priest, watches hopelessly. Don Regino's lackeys can apparently maim and kill indigenes with impunity because, as homo sacer subjects, local peasants exist outside of the (local) law's protection (Agamben 12–13). The immunization of indigenous bodies, however, modifies the reigning body politics and undermines the old system of power. As such, this act ushers in a new body politics where technologically hybrid bodies represent the new bios of the institutionalized revolution.

Significantly, it is Rosaura—a character with clear ties to traditional values, modernity, and even the divine—who finds a peaceful resolution to the roundup. She convinces the local priest to ring the church bell, and the violence abruptly ends. To the ruffians' surprise, the peasants immediately congregate outside the church building. Figueroa captures this event with a low-angle, deep-focus longshot of the church framed between a tree and clouds, while small indigenous bodies move toward the ringing bell. He later fades to an image of the priest, who assures the people that the doctor only wishes to help. This sequence both taps into the visual symbols of postrevolutionary cultural nationalism and aligns medicine with the divine. Viewed within the context of the current discussion, Rosaura's juxtaposition with the Church further underscores her messianic nature as a teacher and as a cyborg Virgin. By aligning both the Church and medicine one with another, Fernández emphasizes the redemptive role that he ascribed to the postrevolutionary state's medical efforts. Of course, despite Fernández's reification of these endeavors, the attempts to incorporate indigenous Mexicans into the mestizo state were hardly innocent. The director's film emphasizes that the act of hybridizing Amerindian bodies ultimately serves to immunize them against their native culture and performativity. As a result, this scene also represents an attempt to domesticize Mexico's indigenous population through the symbol of the

Church, a practice that dates back to the Conquest. Medical immunization represents a new form of cultural imperialism as the state uses it to coax Amerindians to assimilate to the dominant culture.

Rosaura and Felipe immediately start vaccinating the peasants. Coupled with the education that will follow, these injections play a key immunological role in combatting performative "failures" that have supposedly kept indigenous peoples on the periphery. In a scene that draws to mind N. Katherine Hayles's observation that "human beings are conceived, gestated, and born.... Machines are designed, manufactured, and assembled" ("Life Cycle" 322), the peasants line up and, one by one, receive their vaccinations with an impersonality and efficiency that reminds the viewer more of a Fordian assembly line than a medical procedure. This scene challenges Esposito's notion of immunizing the individual against the community because the indigenous masses are never treated as anything but a collective entity. Thus, we should view this segment more precisely as the conversion of an entire previously zoê community into bios. After this dramatic scene, the Amerindians can no longer be killed with impunity. The newly technologically hybrid masses can finally interface with the modern state, but they must do so through Rosaura, who intercedes between them and the government in a way that mirrors a Catholic saint's intercession with God. Even after achieving technological hybridity, these indigenous actors remain children whom the state must nurture through its messianic actors, particularly medics and teachers.

Fernández does not show individuals of certain communities being immunized; indeed, the scant filmic evidence suggests that don Regino's henchmen do not receive medical attention. This becomes especially clear as Brígido, the cacique's right-hand man, stays in his boss's room and watches from the window as Felipe and Rosaura immunize the masses. At one point, don Regino orders his henchman to draw nearer to him; Brígido lifts a handkerchief to his mouth and nose and inches toward his boss. The bandit's fear in this sequence suggests that we never see Brígido's vaccination because he never receives one. This is entirely possible; Felipe's ultimatum is silent on the fate of don Regino's posse. It makes sense within the discursive framework of the film that the cacique's henchmen would not deserve technological hybridity. The fact that neither the criollo/mestizo antagonists nor the indigenous population are technological hybrids upon the teacher's arrival signals a key, understudied discursive element of how postrevolutionary thinkers and artists like Fernández understood official mestizaje. Statist officials and thinkers certainly prescribed assimilation to the modern state through technological hybridity as necessary to Amerindian redemption, but they also believed that criollos—and even mestizos—who had not accepted the state's articulation of mestizo modernity must also embrace the tenets of official mestizaje. The film's mixed-race ideal is not attached specifically to European blood ties, but to the fusion of all cultures and races to build an "authentically Mexican," future-oriented nation.

The need for even mixed-race people to achieve technological hybridity comes out especially clearly through the previous *maestra rural*, Mercedes, who has never received a vaccination. This is especially significant because it seems unlikely that the 1940s Mexican state that was obsessed with its hygiene program would have commissioned an unvaccinated *maestra rural* to a place like Río Escondido. Mercedes's technological bareness signals her, like the rest of the characters, as a member of the premodern zoê whom the state must redeem through Rosaura. Fernández amplifies the former teacher's need for a redemptive immunization by showing how she has ceded to don Regino's machismo by both acquiescing to his romantic advances and allowing him to convert the schoolhouse into a stable. Viewed within the context of our current discussion, it would seem unsurprising that Mercedes does not qualify as a cyborg Virgin. Her failure to uphold official doctrines of race and gender makes her incapable of teaching the inhabitants of Río Escondido any alternatives to caciquismo. In direct contrast to Rosaura, Mercedes represents an unvaccinated (and thus technologically bare) type of la Malinche.[14] Despite Mercedes's failures to uphold official ideals of performativity, she is the only explicitly mixed-race character that we see vaccinated. This is because Mercedes ultimately is not an active oppressor. Due to her gender, she, like the local inhabitants of Río Escondido, is one of the victims of patriarchal caciquismo that the state must liberate and redeem. The fact that Felipe and Rosaura withhold medical privileges from the male, mestizo ruffians does not preclude these figures from immunological discourses. Instead, it emphasizes that, while the state can immunize itself against the shortcomings of its indigenous and female communities through technological hybridity, it must cure caciquismo through forceful removal.

Rosaura heads the statist effort to "civilize" rural Mexico through a two-pronged effort that entails assimilating the Amerindian population and ending caciquismo. After Felipe initiates the peasants into modern culture through technological hybridity, the children start attending school. We cannot overstate the discursive significance of Rosaura's dominance in this space. The historian Elena Jackson Albarrán notes that postrevolutionary schools functioned as a sort of secular church where the regime could expound official doctrines and encourage "the exchange of ideas among local authorities, parents, and schoolteachers" (Albarrán 50). Rosaura's dominance in this space emphasizes her secular saintliness, and the example she sets for her students prepares them to move forward in the quickly modernizing nation. If we wish to extend the religious metaphor further, immunization serves as a type of baptism in that it initiates indigenous characters—still babies in postrevolutionary ideologies—into secular, mestizo society, but these newly assimilated individuals still have much to learn. Rosaura foments what Benedict Anderson terms as a nationalist "communion"—itself a term with heavy religious connotations—through education (6), which will require further knowledge and immunization. Before her first class, the camera rests on a poster of a drunken, passed-out Amerindian dressed in a sarape. The caption reads: "This has finally ended. Mexico fights for economic greatness" ["Esto ya se acabó. México en lucha por la grandeza económica."]. Although the state has modernized the bodies of Río Escondido's indigenous children through medical immunization, it still must socially immunize the town by eradicating supposed performative failures like drunkenness. Of course, the state achieves this end through a robust education program, headed by Rosaura, that will amend and modernize the national genotype. In abolishing alcoholism, then, Rosaura performs a medical act that, within Lamarckian paradigms, reprograms the genome at least as much as Felipe's smallpox vaccines do.

During her first lesson, she shows the children an image of the revered president Benito Juárez, who served from 1858 to 1872, telling them that he is the proof that they can become "useful" members of society (García Benítez, "Identidad"). Her focus on utilitarianism lays bare the modernity-driven discourses that run rampant throughout the film; upon overcoming their "Indianness," these children will become successful workers in the capitalistic, mestizo state. Her invocation of Juárez is especially noteworthy given that the former president had become a symbol within postrevolutionary Mexico of the greatness that indigenous citizens could achieve. Of course, as Lund notes (*Mestizo* ix–x), Juárez's allure was not his indigenous identity per se; rather, officialist thinkers emphasized how the popular president had assimilated to the modern state and become a quintessential mestizo.[15] While Rosaura celebrates Juárez, she paints people like don Regino—who opposes indigenous assimilation—as evil actors whom the state must confront (Rangel 64–65). During one class, Rosaura explains that the country consists of "good Mexicans," all of whom are technological hybrids at this moment, and "bad Mexicans," such as the cacique and his lackeys, whose unvaccinated bodies parallel their backward racial ideologies. She explains that the "good Mexicans" should not simply kill the "bad," but she also makes it clear that resorting to violence becomes necessary when the "bad" refuse to change.

Don Regino fails to recognize that Rosaura represents the greatest threat to his power, and instead focuses on Felipe. In one instance, he chances upon the medic as he instructs many elderly women to boil water before drinking it. After telling them of the bacteria and amoebas that live in the water, the medic says, "It is preferable to boil the water and put an end to the microbes, because if we don't they will kill us" ["Es preferible hervir el agua y acabar con ellos [the microbes] porque al contrario nos matan a nosotros."]. At the surface, Felipe's words reflect the attempts of many contemporary medics to teach rural Mexicans how to avoid disease.[16] Beyond teaching these women—and by extension his filmic audience—about health and hygiene, however, Felipe also equates don Regino with the microbes. As Felipe speaks, scientific rhetoric and paradigms become thinly veiled attacks on don Regino and any other "parasite" that would harm the Mexican nation. The cacique immediately takes Felipe away from these women and orders him to leave town. Given the recent shift in the structures of power, don Regino must be clandestine as he banishes Felipe; the camera itself is excluded from their conversation. The state-run immunization effort has challenged don Regino's racial privilege, and his decision to banish the doctor reflects not his power but his impending impotence. His decision to banish Felipe while allowing Rosaura to stay serves as the cacique's biggest miscalculation in the entire movie. The cyborg Virgin continues to appear before her students even after the medic leaves, and her redemptive lessons inspire the people of Río Escondido to oppose the racist structures of caciquismo.

Don Regino attempts to subdue the unruly teacher by offering her a luxurious home if she will accept him as her lover and soften her rhetoric. This strategy has worked before with Mercedes; unfortunately for the cacique, Rosaura indignantly refuses the proposition. Along with denouncing the evils of caciquismo, the film also exalts the traditional qualities of motherhood and chastity that official ideologies continued to prescribe. Rosaura may not denaturalize the reigning discourses of appropriate gender performativity in this scene; nevertheless, it remains instructive to view her as a cyborg Virgin precisely because the combination of her ties to technological hybridity and the Virgin of Guadalupe makes her so redemptive within the context of the film. By eschewing the cacique's advances—and the comfortable lifestyle that he offers—she opts for self-renunciation and abnegation. Like the Virgin of Guadalupe, she remains a champion for the masses. Don Regino later tries to apologize by visiting Rosaura while she is teaching class, but she and her students shame him out of the school. This signals the first time that technologically hybrid, immunized Mexicans withhold privileges from don Regino. Rosaura effectively erases the ruffian from the master narrative of mexicanidad, relegating his practice of exploiting Amerindians to the status of a failed "pre-revolutionary social structure" (Hershfield, *Mexican Cinema* 63). The fact that Rosaura's camaraderie lies with her indigenous pupils—who, like her, are technological hybrids—signals a biopolitical shift in the village. Technologically hybrid bodies now represent the authentically Mexican, eugenic ideal in Río Escondido.

Fernández shows the results of this new body politics when the village well dries out and don Regino shoots Rosaura's adopted son, Goyo, as he draws water from the cacique's personal well. In a departure from the scene where his henchmen murder fleeing Amerindians without repercussions, the cacique now faces the town's united wrath. Goyo's funeral visually attests to the newly installed structures of power as Figueroa films his casket using a slightly off-center oblique angle, thus juxtaposing the injustice of Goyo's death with nationalistic imageries and filmic techniques. Fernández and Figueroa compound this fact as they cut to a scene in a bar, where they film don Regino and his men straight on—rather than at an angle—as they sit at a table. Unlike Goyo, these characters are not shown using distinctively Mexican aesthetics; the juxtaposition of these two shots artistically asserts that don Regino and his henchmen can neither aesthetically nor ideologically form part of an enlightened Mexico. The bandits' continued presence—and not that of the indigenous peasants—is the true hindrance to Río Escondido's modernity; thus the peasants must forcibly remove their oppressors if they want their town to progress.

The indigenous peasants carry out this immunological act near the film's end. Don Regino breaks into Rosaura's home intent on raping her and scorning her out of town, but Rosaura preserves her virginity by shooting him to death. As Rosaura defends herself with a pistol—a type of phallic device—she emphasizes that don Regino cannot sexually dominate her. This last affront to don Regino's mestizo, male authority is intimately tied to his loss of corporeal privilege following the democratizing effects of medical and educational immunization. After don Regino's death, the peasants swarm upon the remaining ruffians and lynch them while a triumphant march plays in the background. The people of Río Escondido have overcome their performative failures through immunization, and they have learned how to act in accordance with the discourses of official mestizaje. Afterward, Río Escondido is a modern space where every body, regardless of phenotype, has assimilated to the national genotype of official mestizaje. Rosaura suffers a heart attack following this triumph and, after receiving a letter of gratitude from the president, she dies. Susan Dever reads Rosaura's death as a narrative necessity because strong-willed *maestras rurales* "were ultimately antithetical to the long-term goals of this [postrevolutionary] project; consequently their primary service to nation-building had to be carefully controlled" (59). Similar to Vasconcelos's Indian, Fernández's female rural teacher's greatest gift to Mexico is the sacrifice of her own life in order to give rise to a new mestizo nation. The last great immunization, then, is that of Rosaura herself; having lain the foundation for the redemption of the village, she has fulfilled her role. Her (cyborg, Virgin) body, now buried in Río Escondido, testifies of her monumental achievement of transforming the town's indigenous zoê into full-fledged participants in the mestizo bios.

Immunizing the Shrew: Negotiating Class and Gender in (Post)Revolutionary Mexico

Technological hybridity does not automatically equate redemption in all of Fernández's movies. This is especially the case regarding *The Torch*, where an influenza outbreak weakens a zapatista general's occupying army, thus clearing the way for federal forces to retake the town of Cholula. The desperate attempt by both the general, José Juan Reyes, and a North American doctor, Edward Roberts, to contain the epidemic ultimately fails. The remarkable inability of the protagonists to restore order opens a series of questions for the scholar of Fernández's cinema. If, as many critics argue, one of "El Indio's" key motivations was to create a distinctly Mexican cinema that affirmed the country both aesthetically and technologically, then why would he represent Mexican futility in a movie targeted at a North American audience? This may be in part because the director can blame the American doctor. The failure of Roberts's medicine to immunize the town from disease reflects the fact that overdependence on foreign actors—even medical doctors—impedes the creation of national technological and cultural hybridity. As this film so masterfully shows, medicine can be redemptive only insofar as it correlates with state power. Medical campaigns can serve no nationalist good when people depend on foreign entities to provide their health care needs for them. The medical emergency in *The Torch* sheds light on the biopolitical discourse of another section in this film, and also *Enamorada*, where José Juan (Armendáriz in both films) and Miss Peñafiel (María Félix in *Enamorada*; Paulette Goddard in *The Torch*), an aristocratic woman from the town's richest family, cure each other of their transgressions of proper gender and socioeconomic performativities through love.[17]

Despite similar storylines, both *Enamorada* and *The Torch* have followed very different trajectories in both the academic and the popular sectors. The former remains one of the director's most successful and canonical films, while the latter is largely forgotten.[18] The scant criticism that acknowledges the existence of *The Torch* follows Alfredo Michel Modenessi's observation that Fernández directed "an apparently frame-by-frame American remake [of *Enamorada*] . . . in 1950" (101; Mahieux; García Riera, *Mexico visto* 58). Part of *The Torch*'s poor reception results from its stilted English dialogue and generally weak performances. For example, many viewers expressed dissatisfaction with the performance of Paulette Goddard, a Hollywood actress who, despite previous successes, was now in the twilight of her career (Mahieux). Indeed, her interpretation of a young, aristocratic Mexican woman faced harsh criticism in the Mexican press, especially when compared to María Félix's legendary performance only four years earlier (García Riera, *Emilio* 163). Rather than dwell on aesthetic considerations, however, the present study focuses on how the strangely placed medical emergency in the middle of *The Torch* elucidates the parallel immunological discourses of gender and class in both films. The protagonists' failure to overcome the flu outbreak in *The Torch* speaks to an even more urgent need to reconcile competing revolutionary factions (or communities) within Mexico, an immunological process that will come about through heterosexual romance.

I will briefly summarize both films to highlight their many similarities and key differences. In each movie, José Juan occupies Cholula and rounds up the richest men of the town. One of these is Carlos Peñafiel, an elderly man whom the zapatista general incarcerates. The general later meets Miss Peñafiel, Carlos's fiery daughter, who is engaged to the wealthy American Mr. Roberts.[19] When José Juan learns of her parentage, he orders her father's release. He tries to win Miss Peñafiel's heart, but she resists his advances in several slapstick scenes that both critique the general's overly zealous machismo and her own "manly" behaviors. At one point José Juan pays a mariachi band to serenade Miss Peñafiel with the classic song "La malagueña," but she still does not accept him. Here the stories diverge; in *Enamorada,* José Juan approaches Miss Peñafiel and declares his undying love for her in a church. In *The Torch*, however, the general sees a coughing man—whose sarape codes him as indigenous—fall dead to the ground. This man is the first of many victims of Spanish flu. José Juan, Miss Peñafiel, and her fiancé try unsuccessfully to contain the epidemic. After this divergent segment, the film returns to the storyline from *Enamorada*. The zapatista general learns that federal troops will attack the city, and rather than unnecessarily risk his men's lives, he retreats. Miss Peñafiel, who is about to take marital vows with the American, learns of the general's decision and leaves her fiancé for the revolutionary.

These movies open themselves up to distinct analytical readings precisely because Fernández directs them at such different audiences. Almost all of the criticism situates *Enamorada* within didactic, officialist expressions of mexicanidad, nation-building, and proper gender roles. Such studies view the romance between José Juan and Miss Peñafiel as a filmic example of a Latin American foundational fiction, and they emphasize the national reconciliation that occurs through the protagonists' heterosexual romance (de la Mora 155; Mraz 114; Mahieux).[20] Such nationalist readings become necessarily complicated when applied to *The Torch* because Fernández probably did not aim to instill mexicanidad in his U.S. audience. At the very most, he may have attempted to foment transnational dialogue, while at the least he may have exploited Mexican stereotypes in hopes of success at the box office. Nevertheless, this remake's explicit treatment of physical immunization can help resolve contradictory readings of *Enamorada*. For example, Jean Franco asserts that the film—which is based on Shakespeare's *The Taming of the Shrew*—celebrates José Juan's domination of Miss Peñafiel as a restoration of the patriarchal values of the Revolution (*Plotting Women* 149). Tierney diverges from this reading by positing the film as a screwball comedy that undermines official doctrines of gender by focusing on love's "feminizing" effect on José Juan (*Emilio* 105–8). Rather than argue about whether the film sees machismo or tomboy behavior as the main antagonist to national progress, it is more useful to question how the film attempts to correct both characters' shortcomings regarding gender performativity. Indeed, the lead characters' heterosexual romance also facilitates a deeper immunization against socioeconomic, racial, and political division. Esposito's immunization paradigm proves especially useful in navigating the gender contradictions that occur throughout.

The need for national reconciliation is especially obvious through the performance of José Juan, who dresses as a zapatista, a *federal*, and a *villista* during different junctures of the film.[21] John Mraz explains,

> The crucial officialist myth of the Mexican Revolution is that it is a struggle of the "good guys"—Zapata, Villa, Carranza, Madero, and Obregón—against the "bad guys," Porfirio Díaz and Victoriano Huerta. Fernández replicates the official line and, in accordance with his essentialist and ahistorical vision, goes it one better by conflating Zapatismo, Villismo, and the Federal Army through the device of Juan José's [sic] uniforms. (115–16)

Fernández's costuming emphasizes the fact that, while the movie takes place during the Revolution, it resonates with the 1940s cultural referent in which it was filmed. Three decades after the supposed end of hostilities, the government still struggled to reconcile the competing interests of its various revolutionary factions; even those who had ostensibly "won" the armed conflict (such as the *villistas* and the zapatistas) often found themselves at odds with other "victors" (particularly Venustiano Carranza, Álvaro Obregón, and their successors). Given this lack of unity, it should come as no surprise that even the film's "good guys" exhibit imperfect tendencies. José Juan's excessive brutality alludes to both his machismo and his uncompromising *zapatismo*. Statist art and cultural production lauded Zapata at a mythic level in the years following the Revolution, but the leader's demand for "land and liberty" ["tierra y libertad"] came across as anarchic to most PRI officials during the 1940s. One of the overarching themes of the film, then, is the softening of José Juan and his assimilation to a postrevolutionary state that only partially reflects his ideals. Given "El Indio's" obsession with national reconciliation, it may surprise many viewers that José Juan never dresses as a *carrancista* or as an *obregonista*. Far from an oversight, however, this fact reflects Fernández's need to symbolize the reconciliation of the zapatistas with the state through more than mere costuming. Indeed, the director brings these groups together through heterosexual romance. While clearly not zapatista, Miss Peñafiel ultimately expresses her support for the Revolution. As such, Fernández aligns her with the carrancistas, and the obregonistas, both of whom belonged to the more conservative revolutionary faction. As "El Indio" puts these two protagonists together, he imagines a deeper communion between Mexicans regardless of political ideology. José Juan's hatred for the rich subsides as he falls in love with Miss Peñafiel; at the same time, his love interest's classist prejudices fade as she acquiesces to his advances. Thus, the film documents the immunization of its protagonists against the twin devils of bourgeois self-righteousness and the proletarian/peasant envy that many associated with *zapatismo*.

The allegorical reconciliation of the love story also informs our reading of the health crisis in *The Torch*, where, beyond highlighting the American doctor's failures, Fernández uses immunological discourses to overcome the threats of internal division. Given the disjointed relationship of this segment to the rest of the film, it feels as if the director tried to force an epidemic into the story. Because this was one of only a few films he directed in the United States, and considering his obsession with (particularly rural) health care, this certainly may be the case. Regardless of Fernández's reason for including a flu outbreak in his film, however, the very existence of disease opens this segment up to immunological readings. This is especially the case in light of Carlos Tabernero Holgado and Enrique Perdiguero-Gil's assertion that Spanish flu in this film represents "a complete threat for the ... survival of whole human *communities*" (emphasis mine). Viewed in this light, the reactions of the film's protagonists are especially interesting; the main characters lend their unique skills to the cause of containment, and in this way help maintain order. The general decrees martial law—indeed, he threatens to charge any individual who leaves the town with treason—and attempts to quarantine the sick. Miss Peñafiel donates her family's fine linens for a makeshift hospital, and Roberts puts together a hurried vaccination campaign.

Fernández alludes to the United States' own imperfect health care system by setting this film during the 1918 flu epidemic that many argue killed more people than did the violence of the Mexican Revolution or World War I (Billings).[22] This strategy makes his film especially ahistorical; the revolutionary conflict—at least that between the *federales* and the opposition—formally ended with the ratification of the new constitution in 1917. Fernández's decision to set a movie about the Revolution in the year of the Spanish flu sheds light on his obsession not with historical fact but with myth and Mexican modernity. If the movie's epidemic were a preventable ailment like malaria or smallpox, "El Indio" would play to an imaginary of Mexican inferiority to U.S. medicine. However, the director's focus on a sickness that has continued to afflict the "developed world" well into the twenty-first century—particularly the historically catastrophic Spanish flu epidemic—allows him to comment on rural health care without calling Mexican modernity into question. By the 1950s, state initiatives to improve national health through preventive medicine had been so successful that Mexican officials turned their attention to First World medical problems (Fajardo Ortiz and Salcedo Álvarez S11). One key distinction between the medical efforts in *The Torch* and those of *Río Escondido* is that the SEP and the Secretariat of Public Health play no role in the former. The fact that the American doctor fails where the state will later triumph—at least in *Río Escondido*—promotes a mythos of homegrown Mexican modernity that need not depend on foreign validation.

Given their respective roles in the crisis, we should consider Roberts, Miss Peñafiel, and José Juan as allegorical representations of their national, racial, and classed communities. Such a reading fits with most of the criticism on *Enamorada*, which already views the love story in such a light. Of course, the context of a national emergency necessarily amends the symbolic nature of each character. This is especially true with José Juan, who transcends the role of poor zapatista and becomes the town's political authority. Miss Peñafiel represents Mexico's moneyed upper class, whose foreignness bleeds through the American actress's performance. Roberts represents U.S. technological and medical aid. Although they work together to contain the outbreak, their ultimate failure challenges the overly simplistic notion that cross-class and transnational cooperation alone hold the keys to Mexican progress. Even so, the epidemic forces the bourgeoisie and the peasantry—associated with the carrancistas and zapatistas respectively—to work together and recognize their "proper" roles within the institutionalized revolution.[23] Rather than use her money to escape the crisis, Miss Peñafiel stays in Cholula. As she tears her fine sheets to succor the sick, she moves beyond the stereotypical, self-interested bourgeois woman and becomes a key contributor to the national good. The disease decimates José Juan's forces, and he realizes that, while he has good ideals, he is not the best political leader, a fact that implicitly validates the more conservative carrancistas who will eventually come to power. The disease humbles both characters—and by extension their class and political ideologies—which in turn opens a space for national reconciliation.

José Juan controls the town with an iron fist as he and Roberts team up using techniques not unlike those of don Regino in *Río Escondido*. For example, he both decrees that everyone receive medical treatment and that they not leave the town. José Juan is no cacique, and he is trying to act in the best interest of the people, but when compared to the postrevolutionary state's vaccination efforts in *Río Escondido*, the zapatista's work is certainly incompetent. After his decree, the desperate inhabitants of the town line up like machines on an assembly line to receive their medication. Even after receiving treatment, however, many people still take ill. In this way, the film demystifies U.S. foreign aid, a fact that is especially significant given that Fernández directed the production at a U.S. audience. "El Indio" is careful not to question the good intentions of his North American protagonist; as Viviana Mahieux notes, Roberts is not an enemy. The medic's failure does not come from his lack of character, but because the circumstances overwhelm his finite abilities.

Fernández centers the terrible effects of the disease in Mexico on Adelita, José Juan's adopted daughter. Tierney observes the gentle relationship between the general and this little girl in *Enamorada*, arguing that it hints at "cracks in his macho image" as the film begins (*Emilio* 110). Her observation resonates even more in the remake, where "El Indio" greatly expands the girl's role. After the influenza outbreak, José Juan orders Adelita to stay home at all times, but despite his greatest efforts, the girl takes ill and dies as the local priest prays over her deathbed. Adelita's demise is especially poignant when viewed alongside postrevolutionary ideologies and foundational fictions, both of which emphasize the possibility of regenerating the nation through one's posterity. Adelita's death allegorically signals lost potential that even an alliance with the United States could not resolve. When viewed alongside successful immunizations in films like *Río Escondido*, Adelita's death attests to the state's need to create its own competent medical programs. One would think that the modernizing changes to the bodies of the people of Cholula would immunize them against disease and initiate them into official mestizaje. However, the doctor's medicating acts create technologically hybrid subjects that are explicitly coded as foreign. The state certainly fetishizes hybridity, but it wishes for racial and cultural mixtures that occur among Mexicans of different races and social strata. Roberts's immunological failures are obvious during the flu epidemic, but they are subtler—yet more central to both films—in his inability to cure Miss Peñafiel of her "manliness." "El Indio" shows this character's weakness shortly after Carlos's arrest. Miss Peñafiel holds a shotgun (a revolver in *Enamorada*) in an excessively phallic manner, and shouts that she will kill José Juan herself if Roberts will not intervene. Roberts takes the gun and places it under the couch, telling her to calm down, but Miss Peñafiel simply grabs the firearm again.

Not until she runs up against the strong machismo of the general will she act in a more socially acceptable manner. Mraz correctly asserts that the zapatista "beat[s] her into submission" (114), but we should recognize that Miss Peñafiel uses violence against the general as well. In one scene, for example, she throws a lighted firecracker under his horse that, upon exploding, sends him flying into the air. As such, José Juan's fists and Miss Peñafiel's "coarseness"—both elements of improper gender performativity according to postrevolutionary doctrines—become the medicines that cure each member of the couple of their individual performative shortcomings. Similar to how a vaccination uses a potentially dangerous strand of a virus to build the body's resistance (Esposito 50), both characters employ their social "diseases" against their love interest to produce the films' only successful immunization(s). The romance of José Juan and Miss Peñafiel produces a synergetic union that creates an entity—modern Mexican subjects—whose strength is greater than the sum of its parts. The suitors do not immunize each other on their own; instead they must go through Father Sierra, the local priest (Fernando Fernández in *Enamorada*; Gilbert Roland in *The Torch*). Franco notes that in *Enamorada* (and by extension *The Torch*), "religion, in the person of the androgynous and classless priest, becomes the only logical mediator between the landowning class and the new revolutionary leadership, and between the sexes" (*Plotting Women* 149). In the scene where José Juan arrests Miss Peñafiel's father, the priest implores the general not to act rashly. This is his first of many attempts to temper the general's overzealous aggression and machismo, and he has similar conversations with Miss Peñafiel about her manliness. Despite initially opposing a romantic relationship between the two, the priest constantly acts as an intermediary between them as he helps them recognize their own faults.

None of the current criticism has explicitly mentioned how Father Sierra's role in facilitating the protagonists' compatibility underlies his immunological function in the town. Separate meetings between the priest and each of the suitors in a room behind the chapel help him in this endeavor. Here the priest sees José Juan's soft side as the general moves a picture of the wise men bowing before the Christ child to a spot where it will catch the sunlight. Several critics note that part of José Juan's affinity with the painting is that, upon learning that the painter's name was Juárez, he mistakenly thinks of the anticlerical president (Franco, *Plotting Women* 150; Tierney, *Emilio Fernández* 116). For Franco, this shows how representation can "mediate conflicts," because the priest later mentions José Juan's reverence for the painting when, in a fit of rage, Miss Peñafiel shouts that she wishes she were a man so that she could hit the general. After hearing the priest's words, the girl realizes that "lower classes might harbor 'noble' feelings" (*Plotting Women* 150). Tierney, on the other hand, argues that José Juan—who views himself as a revolutionary, redemptive figure—realizes that he has only achieved this status through violence, and the painting shows him that he needs to lead with the humility of the Christ child (*Emilio Fernández* 116–17). Neither analysis explicitly engages with Father Sierra's immunological role: he helps Miss Peñafiel to overcome her sentiments of socioeconomic superiority (and unladylike performativity) and he aids José Juan in overcoming his machismo, yet the priest's function lies in the background of both analyses.

The general—admittedly with "divine" assistance—immunizes Miss Peñafiel (and vice versa) where his American counterpart has failed. Thus, the director asserts shared nationality, rather than social class, as the key variable in determining a couple's compatibility. Viewed in this light, "foundational fictions" such as *Enamorada* and *The Torch* represent an interesting articulation of Esposito's immunization paradigm because it is through heterosexual romance that the state defends its individuals from the dangers of the communitas. Notably, neither José Juan nor Miss Peñafiel represents zoê in either film; both embody two separate bios communities that cannot peacefully coexist without negotiating their relationship one with another. The strategy that these films choose, then, is that of fusing the two together through heterosexual romance to create a single hybrid, immunized community through their progeny. The couple's shared national identity, coupled with the Church's approval, explains why José Juan can immunize his romantic interest where the more highly educated foreign suitor has failed. The key to Fernández's nation-building project is not the establishment of transnational economic ties between elites, but the reconciliation of Mexico's rich and poor.

José Juan calls on Miss Peñafiel's family after releasing Carlos from prison, and he and Miss Peñafiel flirtatiously banter with one another through the door. Several parallel edits allow the audience to see the expressions and reactions of both characters during this comedic back-and-forth. The ensuing scene affirms both characters' problematic articulations of gender. Tierney states that this sequence creates the violence and instability of the screwball comedy that was a staple of 1940s Hollywood films, especially as it exemplifies "the exchange of comic banter where both Beatriz [Miss Peñafiel] and José Juan call each other names or trick each other with language" (115). At one point, Miss Peñafiel gets José Juan to put his ear to the door and then she hits it with a wooden log. In retaliation, the general pretends to walk away, Miss Peñafiel puts her ear to the door, and the general kicks it, saying "women are like mice; curiosity always traps them!" Jairo Antonio Hoyos Galvis notes that, because José Juan's (apparently) feminine curiosity hurt him only moments earlier, this scene attests to the general's gender fluidity. When Miss Peñafiel hits the general through the door after he acts in an "effeminate," "gossipy" manner, she becomes the male, with the log in her hand becoming an overtly phallic representation of her adoption of masculine performativity. At the same time, her act underscores the contradictory nature of machismo, where men frequently exhibit the same traits that they criticize in women. More pertinently, the couple's mutual antagonism paradoxically signals them as compatible: even their differences make them into better Mexicans.

No healthy relationship can depend solely on a mutual predisposition toward violence. When José Juan punches both Miss Peñafiel and Father Sierra outside of the church, he later decides he must apologize not with simple words, but with a live rendition of "La malagueña." This scene was clearly meant for María Félix, whose signature eyebrows embodied the strong personality that she exuded on the screen (Paranaguá, "María Félix"; F. Miller). As such, despite Goddard's solid performance, María Félix's absence becomes palpable during this scene of *The Torch*. Figueroa does not content himself merely with capturing the actress; instead, in both films, he goes from seeing her eyes to seeing *with* her eyes. He cuts among close-ups of her face; numerous extreme high-angle shots of Armendáriz, who stands below her window; and several much softer high-angles of the photographs of Roberts in her bedroom. These shots clearly communicate José Juan's social inferiority as the camera angle and Miss Peñafiel's eyes diminish his presence on the screen. Because she can see "without being seen" (Tierney 111), Miss Peñafiel is the active agent in this encounter. The general's passivity is especially noteworthy; he must rely on other men to sing for him in falsetto, which emphasizes his status as a "soften[ed]" macho (Franco, *Plotting Women* 151). One small difference between the films in this segment is that Goddard throws an empty piggy bank down at José Juan to remind him of his poverty. In *Enamorada*, María Félix's character says no words, but it is obvious that the general has won her heart.

Despite the song's effect, the upper-class Miss Peñafiel does not agree to leave her American suitor until Father Sierra announces—moments before the wedding ceremony—that General José Juan Reyes will not stand against the oncoming federal troops. This scene carries a very different discursive punch in each film; Fernández teases his U.S. audience by subverting a common trope from westerns and letting the Mexican—rather than the American—get the girl (Tierney, *Emilio* 117). He trumpets the Mexican suitor's success in *Enamorada* as well, but because he aims this one at a Mexican audience, it is perhaps more cathartic than resistant. Mraz argues that a central tenant of *Enamorada*—and perhaps both films—is that "*gringos* may be good at money, but Mexicans are better at love" (114). Before leaving Roberts at the altar, Miss Peñafiel inadvertently breaks a pearl necklace that her fiancé has given her as a wedding gift. In *Enamorada* she takes a sarape from her indigenous servant before exiting the home. Notably, in *The Torch* she also breaks the necklace, but she does not put on a sarape. This scene is especially key in *Enamorada* as it marks Miss Peñafiel's initiation into mestizo Mexico. Until this moment, she has been both racially and culturally criolla; however, here she eschews European jewelry and chooses instead to wear traditionally indigenous garb. This act signals her initiation into mestizo society; what is more, any children she bears with José Juan will inherit these same qualities. She has forsaken her racial and socioeconomic privilege in favor of greater social justice. Interestingly, she has learned how to empathize with her fellow citizens only as she has adopted gender performativity that is more in line with statist values. This suggests that she only undergoes change after meeting the zapatista general because he represents ties to her country that Roberts will never have. By joining José Juan in his retreat, Miss Peñafiel abandons a good, but incompatible, foreign man who has been constantly unable to "cure" her of her performative shortcomings.

When focusing on Miss Peñafiel's immunization, we must take care not to ignore the changes in José Juan as well. At the film's beginning, the male protagonist is both *machista* and nonnegotiable. This is not to say that Fernández would count him among the "bad Mexicans," but José Juan's hardline views no longer work in the modern, postrevolutionary—and especially post-*cardenista*—context from which the movie was filmed. The general becomes more reasonable after Miss Peñafiel cures him of his machismo. He will never abandon his beliefs, but he also will not spill unnecessary blood defending them. As part of the national reconciliation that we see here, he realizes that he should recognize the conditions on the ground before acting rashly. The general's decision to flee rather than die means that his ideals will continue through to his posterity despite suffering a military defeat. The couple's continued centrality within the Mexican nation-state comes through filmically in the closing shot, which employs the typical big skies, curvilinear perspective, low angle, and iconic Popocatépetl. José Juan sits in the center of the shot on his horse, and Miss Peñafiel walks by his side, her hand subserviently on his steed's rump. Franco views this as the reestablishment of proper gender roles (*Plotting Women* 152), while Tierney argues that it represents a "mutual escape from a world in which they do not belong" (*Emilio Fernández* 117–18). Despite their differences, both critics allude to the fact that the film optimistically foretells that this couple will reproduce a new, greater society and regenerate the race.

The lovers' reproductive potential rings especially clear as we consider Adelita's erasure from each film. In *Enamorada*, the girl does not ride alongside her adopted father—which seems strange given that the general claims that he always takes her with him when they travel. Of course, *The Torch* explains the girl's disappearance by including her death during the epidemic. Adelita's absence is key because the presence of an adopted child would undermine the portrayal of the union between the zapatista general and the aristocratic (and symbolically carrancista) young woman as a foundational fiction. This does not erase the tragic nature of Adelita's death in *The Torch*. The fact that a flu virus kills her attests to the need for better access to health care and sanitation in rural areas. However, while her death is a great loss, her passing is paradoxically necessary for the immunization of gender and the reconciliation between classes that occurs in the love story. What is more, this scene shows that the nation's eugenic redemption must go beyond hygiene and also resolve the conflicts between people of different social strata through heterosexual romance. Fernández signals his protagonists' union as the nation's future as they move through the authentically Mexican landscape. Perhaps Spanish flu has hurt the zapatistas in *The Torch*, but the relationship between Miss Peñafiel and José Juan produces a social immunization that opens a space for national reconciliation.

Conclusion

With the possible exception of the muralists, no artists shaped national identity more profoundly than did the duo of Emilio Fernández and Gabriel Figueroa, whose melodramas educated generations as to what mexicanidad meant in the postrevolutionary era. This chapter has extended the scholarship on "El Indio" by showing how the director inscribed modernizing discourses on the bodies of his characters. In the context of the cultural missions, which used hygiene and education to change the indigenous genome, it should come as no surprise that the director's didactic cinema postulated the fusion of the body with technology as a means for creating an appropriate mestizo identity. His films express numerous paradoxes—like cyborg Virgins whose potential to undermine prerevolutionary interpellations of the body comes from their adherence to traditional performativity—that reflect the implicit tensions of any "official," homogenizing identity. The analysis of *Enamorada / The Torch* further complicates Fernández's view on rural hygiene, because in this movie medication does not immunize Mexican bodies against medical threats, nor does it initiate them into the mestizo state. Here, proper hybridization will occur only through the reproduction of a new Mexican subject through heterosexual romance across class and racial lines. The immunological discourse of these films alludes to a morally ambivalent tension in which the state aimed to carry out internal colonialism (*Río Escondido*; *María Candelaria*) while at the same time denouncing foreign imperialism (*Enamorada*; *The Torch*). As the Golden Age came to a close and masked *luchadores* replaced *charros* and revolutionaries as the main protagonists of the silver screen, Mexican cinema would emphasize this colonial ambivalence to an even greater degree.

4

Colonizing Resistance

Liminal Imperiality in the Cinema of El Santo
and in Carlos Olvera's *Mejicanos en el espacio*

The events of October 2, 1968, marked an apparent climax of numerous confrontations between student-led demonstrations and a postrevolutionary government that fetishized the appearance of modernity. In the weeks preceding the Olympic games—which Mexico would proudly host—several demonstrations erupted across the nation that demanded both the release of political prisoners and the institution of a truly democratic regime (Preston and Dillon 65–66; Paz, *Labyrinth of Solitude* 229–30). Realizing that the student movement undermined government attempts to present itself favorably, the PRI and President Gustavo Díaz Ordaz decided to "stop at nothing to project an image of stability and modernity" (Joseph and Henderson 553). On that fateful night, the government deployed military forces with the ostensible task of restoring "law and order," which effectively meant silencing the embarrassing demonstrations through violence if necessary. The army surrounded an unarmed demonstration at the Plaza de las Tres Culturas in Tlatelolco and started shooting. Hundreds of students were killed and injured, while so-called friendly fire hit many soldiers. The blatant nature of this abuse of state power led numerous activists like Elena Poniatowska to claim that the massacre undermined the authority of the PRI more than had all of the previous demonstrations combined.[1]

Scholars of Mexican studies have recently started to challenge the narrative that Tlatelolco changed the trajectory of the postrevolutionary state. Noting the lethargic nature of the transition that (supposedly) followed, Samuel Steinberg asserts that "the PRI's endurance benefitted from the massacre" (9). Steinberg comes to this conclusion primarily by looking forward from the massacre and noting that, despite supposedly losing legitimacy, the party won the next five presidential elections; it later came back to power after a brief, twelve-year reprieve with the election of Enrique Peña Nieto in 2012. Tlatelolco was neither the first nor the last case of state violence that the PRI perpetrated against its own people. As early as 1959, party leaders had crushed the Ferrocarriles Nacionales railroad strike and arrested union leaders (Preston and Dillon 65; Sergei 2295–97).[2] In the decade following the events at Tlatelolco, President Luis Echeverría ordered paramilitary strikes against peaceful student demonstrators that left twenty-nine dead; his government later "disappeared" hundreds of rebels (Preston and Dillon 88–89).[3]

State violence constituted a key component of the mission that the PRI viewed for itself. Gareth Williams argues that "by the late 1950s . . . [the PRI] portrayed itself as a universal state and, as such, as the police horizon for the essential suppression of the political" (124). Because the party asserted itself as the only legitimate defender of the Revolution, it coded any and all opponents as enemies of the state (Williams 124). Viewed in this light, the PRI's actions and governing structure constituted a form of internal imperialism; the party forced its modernity fetish on the masses, but it paid for this posture in the areas of human rights and the democratic rule of law. The victims of state violence often belonged to the racial and ethnic majority, but their political activism signaled them as Others who did not uphold the ideals of mestizo modernity. This in turn caused them to cede their racial privilege and become peripheral bodies whom, in a self-fulfilling prophecy, the government had to contain through projects of internal empire. Given that many Western powers had employed similarly violent acts against their own protesters earlier that same year (Volpi 154–61), Díaz Ordaz correctly assumed that the West would sympathize with his cause. It thus appears that the president ordered the massacre at Tlatelolco in order to gain favor with the United States and other Western nations. What is more, this hardline approach probably discouraged his neighbor to the north from meddling in his country's internal affairs. As these cases of state violence show, Mexican officials could (and did) champion projects of internal imperialism even as they simultaneously opposed external attempts to interfere with the country's domestic affairs.

The notion of being both oppressor and oppressed comes through in many midcentury Mexican discourses, but it is especially salient in Mexploitation cinema and countercultural literature, particularly that of la Onda.[4] In the pages that follow, I view Carlos Olvera's 1968 countercultural novel *Mejicanos en el espacio* alongside the Mexploitation cinema of El Santo, El Enmascarado de Plata. Postrevolutionary Mexico's liminal colonial position as both an imperialized and imperializing nation lies at the heart of both examples of midcentury cultural production. Both El Santo's cinema and *Mejicanos* use supernatural, fantastic genres to make their critiques; some of the most common genres of lucha libre cinema are science fiction (SF), horror, and fantasy. Viewed in their totality, masked-wrestler films allude to the country's contradictory pro- and anti-imperialism. On the one hand, luchadores like El Santo save Mexico and its people from foreign imperialists (particularly aliens and European mad scientists like the Frankensteins); on the other hand, they contain the ghosts of the nation's indigenous past (la Llorona, indigenous mummies, and so forth). Mexploitation thus asserts mestizo Mexico's right to oppose external imperialism even as it validates statist projects of internal empire. *Mejicanos en el espacio*, a SF space opera, tells of a twenty-second-century "Centromexican" state whose incompetent attempts to mimic U.S. imperialism ironically validate the very systems of domination that continue to relegate it to the periphery. These works' antithetical treatment of mestizo imperialism exemplify the tensions that emerged between a new generation of writers and weakening projects of state-funded cultural nationalism. They also dialogue with Octavio Paz, who argued that, because Mexicans have inherited the traditions of both the conquerors and the conquered, they must constantly and consciously decide whether to assert themselves as "chingones" (those who fuck/those who oppress) or allow themselves to be "chingados" (those who are fucked/those who are oppressed) (*Labyrinth of Solitude* 78). Nevertheless, these works move beyond Paz's vulgar dichotomy by showing a modern state whose inhabitants simultaneously both oppress and are oppressed. This chapter paints a more complete picture of the political discourses and mythologies that informed the state violence of the 1960s and 1970s, and it shows how the political discourses of these years were grounded in the country's contradictory, racially charged history.

Mestizo imperialism did not suddenly emerge at the conclusion of the Revolution; ever since achieving independence, Latin American countries have tried to assert their subjectivity and resist foreign incursions into their territory by "imitating" European cultures and political systems (Schwarz 1–2). According to Roberto Schwarz, one key component of this imitation came about shortly after Latin American countries like Mexico gained independence and "the socio-economic structure created by colonial exploitation remained intact, though now for the benefit of local dominant [mestizo/criollo] classes" (12).

Even as they created internal empires, elites in Latin American countries like Mexico could never fully shake off their own colonial status due to their servile relationship with—and perceived modernity deficit to—European countries and, later, the United States (Krauze 45–47; Santiago 1–8). As Claudio Lomnitz explains, Mexican "internal colonialism" reflected the country's "weakness in the international arena" (*Deep* 128). The state carried out projects of internal empire to prove its modernity to itself and to the international community. However, these practices were largely doomed to fail because the postrevolutionary state lacked the international prestige necessary to leverage its imperial gains for an uncontested place in the so-called First World.

The mestizo/criollo drive for internal empire largely resulted from state officials "mimicking" the actions of those countries that challenged their sovereignty. According to Homi K. Bhabha, mimicry—or imitation in Schwarz's terms—occurs as colonizing agents produce a "reformed, recognizable Other, as *a subject of a difference that is almost the same, but not quite*" (126, emphasis in original). As European conquerors instilled their culture in Mexico, they differentiated themselves from mestizos even as mixed-race people tried to assert their own subjectivity and assimilate to the governing class. Rather than provide a means for resistance and self-expression, mimicry amplified Mexican and Latin American Otherness. Systemic conditions made it impossible for the subordinate—(mestizo) Mexico in this case—to achieve equality simply by mimicking the colonizer. One reason that mimicry cannot emancipate an oppressed individual is that such behavior is rarely authentic. James C. Scott illustrates this fact through his concept of the "public transcript," a space where "public performance of the subordinate . . . [is] shaped to appeal to the expectations of the powerful" (2). Mimetic behaviors within colonized societies conform to the oppressor's worldview, but they also produce the fissures necessary to assert intelligible Otherness (Bhabha 128). Adapted to the Latin American and Mexican context, Bhabha's assertion that "to be Anglicized is . . . not to be English" (128) would become "to be Westernized is not to be Western." Despite mimicking imperial powers, Latin American countries remain on the global periphery. This in part occurs because, as mestizo elites assert their racial superiority over the indigenous population, they affirm a racial hierarchy that affords them less privilege vis-à-vis their whiter peers.

Latin American mimicry differs from that described by Bhabha (130–32), whose primary focus is the mimetic drive's effect on the day-to-day life, cultural tastes, and prejudices of the subaltern. Within the Mexican and Latin

American contexts, imitation produces an aspiring imperial power. Mimicry extends beyond the public transcript and into the "hidden transcript," which is performed "beyond direct observation by powerholders" (J. C. Scott 4). One example of this within Mexico occurred as state-sponsored discourses of cultural nationalism asserted internal empire—exemplified by the modernization of the indigenous body—as a key component of mexicanidad. Mestizo colonizers' own colonized experiences clearly informed their understandings of race and modernity. This complicated history led state officials to assert that national progress could be born only out of projects of racial domination. At least within Mexico, then, the hidden transcript often ceased to be a site of liberation and instead became a space from which the subaltern could articulate their own dreams of imperial grandeur. One could argue that internal colonialism still represented a form of resistance because mestizo actors believed that they could only discourage other powers from meddling in their domestic affairs through robust imperial projects. Far from an inclusive, anticolonial construct, then, mestizaje functioned as a strategy of domination articulated through a European model. We cannot justify the resulting policies of state violence on these grounds, but we should note that the "hidden transcript" became a site from which mestizo actors could authentically mimic their imperial masters.

Mexploitation and *Mejicanos* show how mimicry, when coupled with nationalism, condemns foreign actors who try to imperialize (mestizo) Mexico even as it celebrates mestizo attempts at internal—and even external—empire. The notion of mimicry may strike some as problematic in this discussion because both the literary style of la Onda and the idea of masked-wrestler superheroes are very much Mexican innovations. Clearly, neither of these examples of midcentury cultural production constitutes stylistic or genre-based mimicry. Lucha libre movies depended on cosmopolitan aesthetics and international markets for their diffusion, for example. But these films also followed distinctively Mexican protagonists on heroic escapades. The colonial mimicry of Mexploitation cinema thus takes place from within Scott's "hidden transcript," often hidden in plain sight from U.S. and European viewers. Indeed, Mexploitation's colonial mimicry is most apparent at the discursive level as it represents internal colonialism as a natural—and even positive—component of (mestizo) modernity. Olvera also articulates *Mejicanos* from the "hidden transcript." Beyond articulating his story outside of the reach of (monolingual) U.S. readers, he also uses a genre and medium that will meet less resistance—or recognition—from state officials. Rather than validate systems of internal colonialism like its Mexploitation counterparts, Olvera's work openly criticizes the imperial projects of the PRI. The novel ridicules statist attempts at internal empire by satirically displacing the country's colonial drive onto a Martian population. In this way, the novel denaturalizes notions of colonial mimicry and suggests that the only ethical way forward for the nation is to identify a different means of self-representation.

My focus on how midcentury literary and cultural production interfaces with Mexico's liminal coloniality redeems both Mexploitation cinema and *Mejicanos* from an academy that has generally ignored and even scorned them. Part of these works' exclusion from the academic canon is genre-based; as J. Andrew Brown and M. Elizabeth Ginway observe, Latin American SF's historically poor reception resulted from the critical expectations of an academy that preferred magical realism (1). Nevertheless, Ignacio M. Sánchez Prado argues that Mexican SF literature—though not necessarily film—struggled in large part due to the low quality of the work of "unknown" authors like Olvera ("Ending" 113); indeed, he characterizes *Mejicanos* as "aesthetically and narratively" limited (129n8).[5] Similar assertions abound regarding Mexploitation cinema. Carl J. Mora, for example, grudgingly recognizes some good from Santo's work, mostly due to its commercial success, but he also charges the wrestler's films with sacrificing aesthetics for profit (148–49; see also Ayala Blanco 296). As these critiques show, most of the negative reactions to *Mejicanos* and Mexploitation center on their (apparently) low cultural value. Innovative insights emerge as we look beyond these works' apparent aesthetic shortcomings and instead focus on the discursive significance inherent to each.

Both Mexploitation and *Mejicanos* depict their country's imperial drive through allegorical representations of colonizing or colonized monsters. According to Elaine L. Graham, monsters have a subversive effect on the popular imaginary because they denaturalize cultural beliefs that deny the humanity of the "Other" (39). The fact that monsters may have humanlike characteristics does not make them any less terrifying; rather, their similarity to the self emphasizes commonalities between the oppressor and the oppressed. Monsters often call colonial hierarchies into question, but they also frequently validate structures of domination by providing heroes with an obviously "evil" (read: dehumanized) opponent to kill. Marco González Ambriz et al. document numerous types of Mexploitation monsters in their 2015 book *Mostrología del cine mexicano*; their tongue-in-cheek analysis highlights the comical aspect of these low-budget creatures, but they ignore how Mexploitation monsters allegorically depict the country's problematic relationship with an imperial world. Some of these creatures represent imperializing agents from afar, while others hail from an indigenous past that mestizo society supposedly must domesticize. In Mexploitation films, for example, European and pre-Columbian villains both harbor threatening tendencies that supposedly lie dormant within mestizo society (and identity) at large. El Santo symbolically tempers the excesses of both the European and indigenous sides of the national race equation by containing these threats through violence. This is especially significant because Mexploitation—and indeed *Mejicanos*—takes place in contexts where racial hybridity affords people and nations sufficient privilege to oppress Amerindians (or primitive aliens) while at the same time subordinating mixed-race subjects to "whiter," European actors and nations.

Masking the Officialist Projects of Mexploitation Cinema

Mexploitation cinema differed from that of the Golden Age in large part because of its lower quality. When viewed alongside the films of the previous epoch—where the national film industry had received foreign and national moneys for its productions (Castro Ricalde and Irwin 53–54)—Mexploitation seemed especially lowbrow. As funds dried up, directors largely had to fend for themselves, and the B-movie reigned. Notwithstanding this new economic model, Victoria Ruétalo and Dolores Tierney note that, unlike exploitation cinema in the U.S. context, which often challenged state ideals, Mexploitation was "often made within certain national industries" (4, 1–7). Despite its aesthetic shortcomings, then, Mexploitation cinema continued the tradition of the Golden Age by buoying nationalistic and statist doctrines from within.[6] Not all government figures viewed lucha libre and Mexploitation favorably; Andrew Coe documents the intriguing fact that Luis Echeverría's brother tried to block the production of these films (30). This seems to have been more personal than political, however, because the bureaucrat's acting career had been limited to minor roles in masked-wrestler movies. Despite this detail, Mexploitation remained at its core a nationalistic genre, and nobody had more success in this new cinematic environment than Rodolfo Guzmán Huerta. Huerta was an ordinary everyman from Tulancingo, Hidalgo, but his silver mask transformed him into El Santo (del Pozo Marx 199). Already a hero in the ring and in *fotomontajes* or photographic comic books (Wilt 211–12), he made a smooth transition to cinema. According to Rafael Aviña, "Santo had the luck of arriving precisely at the end of the so-called Golden Age, when the national cinema navigated its worst financial and thematic crisis" ["Santo tuvo la suerte de llegar en un momento preciso, cuando el cine nacional se debatía en su peor crisis financiera y temática al término de la llamada 'época de oro'"] ("Santo" 30). The luchador filled a void in the national cinema, but most critics ignore his oeuvre even though his popularity rivaled that of the greatest stars of the Golden Age.

Lucha libre films were born out of professional wrestling, a popular spectacle that sits at the threshold where sport, theater, and ritual meet (Levi xvi). Because they were performed in local rings, these performances brought (urban) communities together, and they often played a conservative, cathartic role for the working class.[7] As Heather Levi notes, lucha libre matches "paralleled a political system in which electioneering took place behind closed doors, elections ratified decisions that were already made, and people who appeared to be opponents were really working together" (192). The relationship between this sport and the state probably ran even deeper than she claims. Because the audience engaged in a back-and-forth with the luchadores, many people had the sensation that they could contribute to the outcome of the fights even though the results were decided long before anyone entered the ring (Villarreal, "Simulacro"). At the very least, wrestling matches tacitly buoyed the regime by allowing audiences to vent their frustrations in a politically safe environment. Given its cathartic potential, it is not surprising that lucha libre's conservatism extended beyond the ring and into the political arena. During his presidential campaign, for example, Gustavo Díaz Ordaz invited El Santo to accompany him at his rallies. The wrestler's ability to draw large, excited crowds led Díaz Ordaz to say, "I greatly appreciate his cooperation, but at this rate the people will elect him instead of me!" ["Le agradezco mucho su cooperación, pero al paso que vamos, ¡él terminará siendo presidente!"] (quoted in Illescas Nájera 52). Because no other political parties could field competitive presidential candidates, we should not necessarily conflate El Santo's political performances with personal ideology. The luchador often transcended political differences and served as a uniting force across a divided nation. Nevertheless, as he appeared on the silver screen, El Santo promulgated the same cathartic, statist discourses that he produced in the ring.

The conditions that would lead to El Santo's cinematic career came in 1955, when the government banned lucha libre fights from television. Given the sport's generally conservative role in society, it is surprising that the PRI chose to impede its diffusion throughout the nation. Heather Levi provides some insight as to why this may have occurred as she argues that the sport posits "lo naco"—or the urbanized Amerindian who fails to fully incorporate into mestizo society—as the new incarnation of *lo mexicano* (196–99). Many have speculated that the ban was instated out of fear that televised contests would infect the middle and upper classes. After its removal from television, wrestling was limited to people living in working-class neighborhoods like Mexico City's Tepito. Ironically, this censorship resulted in the production of some 300 lucha libre films, 52 of which starred El Santo. To a large extent, these movies were an underhanded means for exporting lucha libre to people who could not attend live events (Lieberman 5; Levi 177–214).[8] Lucha libre films, then, participated in an act of narrow resistance. Each movie showed at least one fight in the ring, always televised, as if imploring the government to lift its ban. In a strategic move to placate the censors, these films adopted Hollywood-style horror and SF monsters—as well as various specters of the indigenous past—as stand-ins for the *rudos* (Syder and Tierney 43–44), or villains of the ring, whom the government specifically targeted in its television ban (Levi 181–84). The films could thus celebrate the heroic *técnicos* (good guys) while at the same time avoiding actual *rudos*. Because the villains of these films hailed from foreign lands or the pre-Columbian past, Mexploitation buoyed the dominant narrative of a mestizo state that believed it faced existential threats both internally and externally.

Santo's cinema generally promotes an imaginary of Mexican (mestizo) moral superiority that, according to Anne Rubenstein, stems from its hero's status "as an exemplary counter-macho" (577). Rather than embodying macho brute force, a quick temper, and a taste for alcohol the luchador exerts self-control and exudes wisdom (Fernández Reyes 152–54). Such traits signal him as the perfect hero to promulgate statist discourses and defend the nation from internal and external threats. No film emphasizes discourses of mimetic imperialism more clearly than does *Santo contra la invasión de los marcianos* (1966), a movie that pits the masked wrestler against a host of extraterrestrial invaders. As Miguel Ángel Fernández Delgado argues, "ever since [aliens] appeared in literature in the eighteenth century . . . they have been used to critique and relativize social conventions" (143). Indeed, aliens become natural bearers of colonial discourse(s), by nature of their status as quintessential foreigners. As a result, these figures' presence in a text or on the screen often invokes racial, political, and colonial structures of power (Rieder 1–33). Directed by Alfredo B.

Crevenna, *Santo contra la invasion de los marcianos* begins with spliced footage of several U.S. rocket launches—which reference both the space race and the rampant nuclear testing of the Cold War—while ominous music plays in the background. The director cuts to more borrowed footage, this time of a spacewalk, while a dubbed voiceover states, "As human science advances, a great mystery comes to the fore: Is our planet the only world inhabited by rational beings like us? If not, will we travel to and conquer these worlds, or, on the contrary, will their inhabitants come and subject us to their dominion?" ["A medida que la ciencia del hombre avanza, surge una tremenda incógnita: ¿Será nuestro planeta el único habitado por seres racionales como nosotros? De ser así, ¿llegaremos a conquistar estos mundos, o por el contrario, sus habitantes vendrán a someternos a su dominio?"]. As this voiceover ends, Crevenna cuts to an alien spaceship—which looks like two frying pans stacked on top of each other—that moves clumsily across the screen, thus foreshadowing an imminent Martian invasion.

In what Doyle Greene calls "the most overtly political of the Santo films" (70), the Martians' decision to invade Mexico City reflects an imaginary in which the capital city's modernity makes it a logical site for a Martian invasion (Negrete and Orozco 189). The film explicitly ties the Martians to Europe and Western imperialism when the aliens adopt Greek names and proclaim themselves as the original inhabitants of Atlantis (Greene 68–83). The aliens are almost indistinguishable from other humans; what sets them apart is their dress—males wear luchador garb while women wear short, flashy skirts—and their greater technology, which is signaled by a third, cybernetic eye. The aliens' imperialist actions mirror those currently practiced on Earth, where human beings use technological advantages to conquer and dominate members of their own species in faraway lands. Crevenna cements the invaders' ties to Europe when they take control of Mexico's television signals. Their leader, Argos (Wolf Rufinskis), admonishes the earthlings to abandon their nuclear experiments—which endanger even Mars—or face destruction.[9] Throughout this scene, Crevenna crosscuts between Argos's solemn declaration of war and the Mexican viewers, most of whom laugh at his message and praise the television company's creativity. Just as Spanish *conquistadores* would read "El Requerimiento"—a Spanish-language document that demanded that local Amerindians adopt Christianity and recognize the supremacy of the Spanish Crown or face destruction—prior to attacking indigenous cities, the Martians give an ultimatum that their victims are not meant to understand. Under these circumstances it is not surprising that Argos fails to convince the people of Earth to change their ways. Crevenna further accentuates the ties between the Martian attackers and colonial Spain by having Argos address the nation using the *vosotros* form, which, while common on the Iberian Peninsula, rarely occurs in Latin America. Significantly, three people do take the Martian seriously: a Catholic priest, a famous scientist, and El Santo.

If the broadcast has connected the Martians with the Spaniards, the demand that the earthlings follow enlightened Martian ideals or face extermination equates them with the 1960s United States—a country that appealed to democratic and humanitarian ideals that many Mexicans felt it contradicted in Vietnam. Like Mexico's northern neighbor, the Martians are willing to kill innocent children in defense of their supposed values. One early scene shows Hercules, a Martian scout, teleport to a playground in Mexico City, where he starts vaporizing innocent men, women, and children with invisible rays from his third eye. Luckily, El Santo is offering a clinic to young children at this same site. He confronts the alien attacker and, after an impressive show of lucha libre, chases him away. After Hercules teleports back to his base, the aliens decide that they must capture El Santo alive because he is the perfect physical specimen. The pro wrestler, the scientist, and the Catholic priest—all of whom have believed in the Martians from the beginning—represent the crown jewels of a Martian eugenic project in which the invaders will identify the "best" humans and return them to Mars, where they will continue to propagate the species after the destruction of Earth. Greene asserts that the professor and the priest show science and religion as two complementary pillars of Mexican society (72); however, we should not forget that El Santo is a third pillar. The wrestler's very body symbolizes modern, mestizo masculinity; indeed, his physique is one of his greatest assets and liabilities across his cinema, especially when imperial actors try to use science to subjugate the people of Mexico.

Throughout his work, El Santo stood against numerous enemies, and the storylines across his films were at times contradictory. The criticism is divided on how to approach El Santo's cinema in its entirety: David Wilt asserts that "the only consistent facet of the movies was Santo himself" (218), while Mora argues that "[Santo's] films reinforced each other over the years, amounting to a single Mexican-style fairytale of good versus evil played out on the wrestling mat" (148). When read alongside one another, these almost antithetical arguments explain how El Santo established his mythos across the totality of his work despite the inconsistencies in continuity that inevitably emerged between films (Fernández Reyes 15, 156–74; Illescas Nájera 53–62). They also assist us in identifying what aspects to include in a cross-film discussion of race and modernity in his cinema and which ones to ignore. Any time that a director assigns discursive significance to the wrestler's body, we should consider how that furthers Santo's identity as a larger-than-life superhero. Santo's antagonists generally attempt to subjugate his body in search of personal gain. Along with the Martians, the Frankenstein family admires his specimen to the point of infatuation. In *Santo contra la hija de Frankenstein* (1971) and *Santo y Blue Demon contra el doctor Frankenstein* (1973), we see antagonists whose family name, as well as their penchant for unethical science experiments, signals them as imperializing Others despite their highly Mexicanized Spanish.

In the first of the aforementioned films, Frida Frankenstein (Gina Romand), the century-old daughter of the famous villain of Hollywood horror, learns that the effects of her age disappear when she injects herself with Santo's blood.[10] This is due to a mutation that has caused abnormally high levels of the "TR factor," which causes the body to recover from injuries and aging. Her supply of the needed fluid—which she acquired from a nosebleed at one of his matches—has begun to dwindle, so she orchestrates a plan to kidnap the luchador's girlfriend and draw him into her lair. Although she posits a biological reason for Santo's eternal youth, the story responds to a perceived ageless quality that many people have ascribed to El Santo due to his profession as a masked wrestler (Monsiváis, *Rituales*). Frida, for example, reveals that she started to suspect Santo's condition after noticing that after thirty years of professional wrestling, the luchador still showed no signs of physical wear. When this movie was produced, Santo was almost sixty years old; nevertheless, his mask concealed his true age. Even after Rodolfo Guzmán Huerta's death, El Santo continued on through his son, who still wears the mask in his fights. Throughout Santo's career, the slippage between the mask and the body produced interesting narratives—such as a mutation that leads to his eternal youth—that linked him to posthuman identity.

The luchador's biological advantages tie him to discourses of official, Vasconcelian mestizaje. When José Vasconcelos decreed the inevitable aesthetic triumph of mestizaje, he did so with the assumption that such eugenics would produce a type of humanity heretofore unknown to the world. The genetic changes that the human race would undergo would lead to Mexican—and world—redemption. In a way then, Vasconcelos's cosmic race is a mutant people that harbors genetic combinations that were previously unknown. What separates Vasconcelos's utopia from the rest of humanity is the way in which it fetishizes and consciously aims to improve human genetics. As the philosopher states, in Mexico, "the mixture of races [*sangre*: blood] has taken place and continues to be consummated.[11] It is in this fusion of ethnic stocks that we should look for the fundamental characteristic of Ibero-American idiosyncrasy" (19). Most studies on official mestizaje focus on the state's indigenista movements, but we should bear in mind that this philosophy held that Europeans would also benefit from breeding with the descendants of Mexico's pre-Columbian past as their progeny joined the fifth race.

The film emphasizes the redemptive value of mestizaje on the European body through an especially literal incarnation of Vasconcelos's notion of the mixing of blood, where the European, Frida Frankenstein, forcibly extracts the fluid from her prisoner and later injects herself with it. As a result, her body takes on (fleetingly) the same mutations as those of the iconic wrestler, and she becomes young once more. This film also transgresses certain aspects of Vasconcelian thought, where the European subject was necessarily male and the indigenous object female. Frankenstein's daughter attempts to exploit the Mexican mutant in a scene that harks back to the historical European oppression of the inhabitants of America. Here Santo is captured, bound, and locked away in a room. The woman enters, faces him, and strips him of his mask in an act of figurative castration. The camera pans to the side so that we can only see the hair on the back of his head—the actor is a double. This scene plays out the racial undertones of the Conquest, but it once again inverts the gender roles. In the language of Paz's vulgar dichotomy, the female is now the active *chingona*, and the man is the passive *chingado*. Frida extends this imagery as she forcefully kisses her captive. Her exploitation of El Santo's body does not end here; she later commissions the wrestler's hypnotized girlfriend to pluck out her lover's eyes, which is another clear allusion to sexual violence and castration. Frida's plans to keep the luchador alive reflect her imperial need to harvest his body. Unfortunately for Frankenstein's daughter, true love proves stronger than hypnosis; in an offscreen confrontation, the girlfriend remembers her love for the luchador, unties him, and returns his mask.

The assertion that this film—and others—communicates officialist, mestizophilic discourse requires us to understand this superhero as explicitly mestizo. Given the slippage among terms like European/criollo, mestizo, and indigenous within the Mexican context, simple observations of phenotype will not suffice. Instead, we must show how the wrestler is associated with modernity, and thus with mestizaje, while at the same time recognizing his ties to pre-Columbian indigeneity. Nothing illustrates Santo's equation with indigenous Mexico more convincingly than his mask. Interestingly, the first professional wrestlers to wear masks came from the United States, and only afterward did Mexican luchadores adopt them. According to Heather Levi (106–9), masks remained popular in Mexico precisely because they resonated with urbanized, Amerindian spectators. Indeed, the mask becomes the focal point for one of the great divergences between the professional wrestling of Mexico and that of other countries. According to Roland Barthes, one of the great draws of professional wrestling is its excessive and unapologetic violence, a fact that holds especially true when a contestant is hurt and "exhibits for all to see his face, exaggeratedly contorted by an intolerable affliction" (19). Mexican lucha libre presents significant questions for Barthes because popular masked fighters cannot make—or at least showcase—such expressions. Critics like Nelson Carro attempt to reconcile Barthes's theorization of the sport with its Mexican articulation by noting that masked wrestlers still "grotesquely signal" any injuries they may have incurred (16). Nevertheless, masked wrestlers conceal their suffering from the audience when they showcase their injured extremities. The distinction between injury and (overt) suffering takes on renewed significance in light of Paz's assertion that the Mexican "ideal of manliness is never to 'crack,' never to back down" (*Labyrinth of Solitude* 29–30). Rather than display their pain for all to see, injured masked wrestlers become heroic figures who stoically endure their pain and continue to fight. A masked wrestler never truly "cracks" unless his foe unmasks him, thus making his shamed face known to all. Beyond invoking the pre-Columbian past, then, Santo's mask also alludes to Mexican constructs of heroic masculinity by allowing the luchador to suffer without sacrificing his (counter) macho image.

Perhaps no film exaggerates the myth of Santo's mask more than *El hacha diabólica* (1964). In this film a professor looks at the wrestler's mask—which Santo's family has handed down from generation to generation—under a magnifying glass and finds the inscription "ABRACADABRA." He informs Santo that this inscription comes from a man who practiced "the science of the Good" ["la ciencia del bien"]. We should note that the Spanish "ciencia" has slightly different connotations from the English "science," particularly in early modern societies such as that of Santo's progenitors. In this context, the word probably means knowledge, or even magic. In any case, it is significant that the film attributes supernatural properties to Santo's mask. During this same conversation, the wrestler admits that his mask gives him strength when he feels unable to continue his fights. The hero's words suggest that, beyond a simple costuming device, his mask is a living, prosthetic extension of his body that assists him in defending the Good.[12] The fusion of the wrestler and his mask produces a technologically hybrid protagonist that fits neatly in a tradition of superheroes whose power is rooted in a cyborg condition.[13]

Santo's cyborg status is not limited to a symbiotic relationship with his wrestling costume; rather it extends to his place within modernity. Brown asserts that "posthumans can have artificial implants [such as prosthetic masks] but they can also have an identity based on the relationship between them and their machines" (11). Here Brown is referring specifically to the internet, but the luchador uses radio and video technology in a way that foresees the interconnectedness of the World Wide Web. Evan A. Lieberman sees Santo's technological competence as the discursive proof of the wrestler's place within modern, and hence mestizo, society. Indeed, the critic asserts that these movies show that "the world is technological, and it might be used for good or evil, but it will be used and there is no retreat back to a pre-technological age" (11). In *Santo contra los zombies* (1962), the wrestler uses his lab to detect and thwart zombie movements such as an attack on an orphanage. The wrestler's ability to detect faraway events in his impressive laboratory associates him with cyborg identities through his relationship with technology, while his ties to indigeneity are especially clear through his mask. Given his ties to both sides of the nation's imagined racial equation, El Santo becomes a full participant in a mestizo state that fetishizes modernity. Unlike Haraway's ambiguous cyborg that deconstructs notions of gender and race (161–65), El Santo ultimately accentuates these constructs by articulating and performing a hyper-mestizo masculinity. Even so, he remains liberatory within the discursive framework of official mestizaje because his exemplary performance of both race and gender allows him to contain other monstrous threats to the nation.

His strength also makes him an especially attractive target for Frida's family member, Dr. Irving Frankenstein (Jorge Russek), who himself poses an external threat to Mexico. The films are silent on the relationship between Dr. Frankenstein's grandson and Frida; however, the age discrepancies between them present one of the more obvious situations where continuity fails to carry across films. This apparent lack of consistency is especially surprising given that Miguel M. Delgado directed both movies. The plot inconsistencies notwithstanding, in *Santo y Blue Demon contra el doctor Frankenstein*, the hundred-year-old grandson of the famous Dr. Frankenstein has recovered his grandfather's technology for controlling dead bodies. Hoping to capture Santo and enslave his body, he sets up an elaborate trap that results in the wrestler being subdued on an operating table. Unfortunately for Frankenstein's heir, Blue Demon enters right before the medics can euthanize Santo and insert electronic gadgets into his body. Both luchadores escape, and shortly thereafter, in a match between El Santo and one of Frankenstein's disguised cadavers, Mexico's dynamic duo confronts and kills both the scientist and his creation.

Frankenstein's practice of killing people and controlling their bodies through technology constitutes the especially uncanny colonialization of Mexican bodies through a posthuman entity that is difficult to categorize as either cyborg or zombie because it shares similarities with both. Part of this results from the time in which these movies were produced; the cyborg began to enter explicitly into the human imagination only in the 1960s, when it became apparent that only a body coupled with technology could survive the rigors of space travel (Clynes and Kline 29–31). It would take another two decades for popular culture, Haraway, and other intellectuals to further test the figure's liberatory potential. Likewise, the figure of the zombie has undergone numerous transformations, but imperialism has always sat at the entity's core (McAllister 476–77; Dendle 46–48). What began as the perfect servant from the imagination of black Haitian slaves has more recently morphed into "an embarrassingly literal incarnation of the drive to cannibalize and consume that seems to reflect, perhaps a little too neatly, our own late capitalist moment" (Laraway 133). As David Laraway notes, this recent version of the zombie entered public discourse after films like *Night of the Living Dead* (1968) and especially the 1978 film *Dawn of the Dead*, which came out near the end of Santo's cinematic career. The zombies of the Santo films are difficult to categorize from a twenty-first-century perspective in that they are undead, cybernetic cadavers.

In *Santo contra los zombies* we see a paradigmatic version of this Mexploitation entity that deconstructs any clear distinctions between zombie and cyborg. Here an evil, masked scientist has kidnapped Professor Sandoval, a man who has done a great deal of work on zombies. We later learn that the villain has converted the professor into one of his legions of undead minions. Interestingly, the professor continues to employ the knowledge he gained before dying to help the masked scientist convert dead bodies into new slaves. If one of the defining traits of modern zombies is a lack of cognitive abilities (Laraway 135; Lauro and Embry 92–96), then it becomes clear that these undead—whose expertise facilitates complex surgeries—are somehow different. The professor's condition underscores Sarah Juliet Lauro and Karen Embry's assertion that "unlike Donna Haraway's 'Cyborg Manifesto,' we do not propose that the position of the zombie is a liberating one—indeed, in its history, and in its metaphors, the zombie is most often a slave" (87). In many ways, the professor embodies what Lauro and Embry call the "zombi": a soulless precursor to the modern zombie who must always do the bidding of a voodoo master (90). As such, he suffers a form of what Peter Dendle refers to as "psychic imperialism" (48) because the villain controls his mind. The colonial aspect of zombie subjectivity rings especially clear in *Santo contra la magia negra*, where a white witch, played by Sasha Montenegro, conjures black zombies against the wrestler to sabotage his mission with Interpol. The zombies of *Santo contra la magia negra* are subjected to an Orientalized representation of voodoo that emphasizes racial privilege. In *Santo contra los zombies*, Professor Sandoval has found a way to reproduce identical behavior in corpses through cybernetics.

Santo contra los zombies highlights the cybernetic aspect of these undead at its climax when Gloria Sandoval (Lorena Velázquez), the professor's daughter, is taken to the masked scientist's lair. In several impressive shots, the villain agrees to let her see her father. Standing behind the woman, he activates certain switches on his belt, and the camera cuts to the front of the room; Gloria's undead father appears, waves, and turns away. Gloria realizes afterward that she has seen a zombie, but in a disturbing sense, this cadaver is still her father. As we have already seen, Professor Sandoval exhibits upper-brain function even if he lacks agency. This point makes the aforementioned scene especially horrific because the father helplessly witnesses his daughter's impending execution. Professor Sandoval can comprehend her plight, yet he can do nothing to prevent it because his brain no longer controls his body. The fusion of his corpse with technology has turned him into a perfect slave who literally cannot oppose his master's will. Professor Sandoval's undead, posthuman condition toes the line between zombie and cyborg from a technological standpoint, yet it enjoys no liberatory potential. Far from providing an escape by producing Haraway's "pleasurably tight coupling[s]" between the organic and the inorganic (152), the fusion of the body with technology becomes key to enslaving bodies. This trope appears time and again in Santo's films, and in most cases, it is a European scientist who enslaves "decent" Mexicans.[14] In *Santo contra los zombies,* the villain turns out not to be a foreign criminal, but Professor Sandoval's brother. When Gloria asks Santo why her uncle would murder his own brother, the hero replies that the man committed these atrocities "due to unrighteous ambition and a lust for riches and power. When men challenge the laws of God, they fall victim to their own wickedness" ["por ambición, por riquezas y por poder. Cuando los hombres desafían las leyes de Dios, caen víctimas de sus propias maldades"]. The luchador's pessimism about science and technology bleeds through this quote because it is through advances in these areas that humanity most explicitly challenges God (Fernández Delgado 141).

The evil Sandoval becomes a clear example of a colonizer of modern, mestizo Mexicans who must be defeated precisely because he steals agency from those whom he oppresses. In most cases, Mexploitation juxtaposed internal threats to postrevolutionary Mexico with specters of the country's colonial and pre-Columbian history. Indeed, Mexploitation evoked the Golden Age through problematic narratives that decreed mestizo Mexico's right—and even duty—to domesticize the Amerindian. With titles like *Santo contra la venganza de la Llorona* (1974) and *La venganza de la momia* (1970), it comes as no surprise that Lieberman and others have asserted Santo's role in rescuing Mexico from its own past (14). Alfonso Morales notes the multiplicity of Santo's villains when he writes that "whether they derive from myth or legend, whether they are the spawn of Hell or technology, all embodiments of Evil are the same when slammed to the floor" (183). This quote captures the essence of Santo's films and problematically posits Mexico's indigenous past as an evil that must be overcome. Carlos Monsiváis claims that Santo's titles condense his films' storylines into a few words (*Rituales*), but we run the risk of misinterpretation if we fail to look beyond the cover. Indeed, in neither of these movies does El Santo confront the specters of the past directly. Both advertise a monster in the title, but their true villains are corrupt, modern-day Mexican men who are willing to kill for treasures from the nation's painful history. Santo inadvertently defuses the threat of la Llorona by securing a treasure that a crime boss has stolen. When he donates it to a children's hospital, the luchador frees Mexico's most famous ghost from her pact with the devil, thus liberating the country from this specter of the past. Because he never sees her, the luchador remains unconvinced that la Llorona ever existed.

La Llorona represents a form of monstrosity distinct from the posthuman beings we have dealt with up to this point, but she poses equally serious questions about mexicanidad. Indeed, as the product of oral, rather than written, histories, la Llorona lends herself to associations with protohumanity. If we build on Dale J. Pratt's definition of the protohuman as a prehistoric, incommensurable, and even exotic Other (17), then it becomes clear that protohumanity accentuates the Otherness of a group even as it recognizes a degree of humanity. According to Pratt, the term "protohuman," beyond referring to cavemen, signals prehistoric civilizations—often composed of *Homo sapiens*—whose ways of knowing will remain forever in secret because we lack the necessary records to tap into their culture and society. The lack of (readable) records from prior to the Conquest certainly aided the postrevolutionary state in associating pre-Columbian society with the protohuman. María Herrera-Sobek notes that la Llorona comes from at least two interweaving sources. In one incarnation of the myth, she is a mestiza whose Spanish lover betrayed her for a European woman. In another, she is an indigenous prophetess who foretold the destruction of Tenochtitlán prior to the arrival of Cortés (106–8). There are many other accounts that inform the legend of la Llorona as well: Rosario Castellanos, for example, equates her with la Malinche ("Otra vez Sor Juana" 468). The figure's ties to indigeneity ring especially clear as we realize that a colonial paradigm would have coded any one of the aforementioned women as indigenous. What is more, the combination of these women's race and gender would have relegated them to the periphery (Steven Stern 16). The film in question unfortunately sidesteps la Llorona's indigenous nature by depicting her as a phenotypically white, blonde woman whose husband left her for a richer woman. By side-stepping the racial discourse inherent to la Llorona, the film nullifies internally subaltern societies and cosmologies and appropriates their stories into a mestizo paradigm.

The drive to domesticate indigenous stories and histories appears across many of Santo's films, but it is perhaps most visible in Carlos Aured's *La venganza de la momia*, a movie where El Santo proudly disproves an indigenous boy's "superstitious" beliefs. In this movie, the wrestler accompanies a group of mestizo intellectuals who enters the ancient tomb of an indigenous mummy. Upon discovering this relic of the past, they celebrate their great "scientific" advancement, and the group's indigenous guide, taking exception to their hubris, quips, "The advancement of whom? The whites?" ["¿El avance de quién? ¿De los blancos?"]. The westernized team ignores much of the lore surrounding this mummified corpse, but the surrounding community knows that the mummy will reawaken if anyone disturbs it. Perhaps a little too conveniently, the guide himself will be the monster's first target because his ancestor condemned the mummy to death centuries ago. This sets the tone for a fairly formulaic Mexploitation horror film; however, the movie shocks its audience's generic expectations when the villain ends up being Sergio Morales (Eric del Castillo), a member of the expedition who dresses up as a mummy and starts killing the crew so that he can have the mummy's treasure for himself. The threat, then, comes not from the past per se, but from how modern subjects appropriate it for their own exploitative ends. The mummy's (in)existence effectively strips the indigenous characters of their own history; as their knowledge proves inadequate and demonstrably false, official mestizo histories are validated. The result is what Edward Said would call the Orientalization of the Olpache civilization—both past and present (31–49). Present-day Olpaches are, at best, individuals whose folkloric knowledge may help parse together what constitutes "real" history, and at worst they simply get in the way of scientific research. This becomes especially clear when the lead archaeologist finds a manuscript near the mummy's tomb and orders his guide to interpret it. This scene is problematic on many levels; firstly, it ignores the fact that Spanish conquerors eradicated indigenous writing—which was limited to the Mayans—shortly after the contact period. It would be impossible for an Amerindian man, regardless of education, to interpret this text based on a supposed shared racial/ethnic identity. The guide refuses to interpret at first because he does not wish to offend the dead, but he reluctantly agrees when the archaeologist says that he knows others who will interpret it if the guide refuses. This back-and-forth presents modern-day Amerindians as obstacles to mestizo attempts to unlock the mysteries of pre-Columbian societies and greatness.

The story that the guide recounts greatly resembles Hollywood's *Mummy* films, where a man is condemned to death and is mummified alive because of a forbidden love. While the film is hardly original, it becomes much more interesting as we consider how it is represented filmically. The guide simultaneously reads the indigenous script and interprets it into Spanish. He speaks with a monotonous, rhythmic cadence while the camera cuts to actors from the past. The guide continues to speak, now functioning as a voiceover, while the actors carry out highly folkloric representations of the nation's indigenous past. The scene employs wind music and simple percussion that, when coupled with the guide's narration, produces an essentialized past that conflates Mexican indigeneity into a single, monolithic entity. The Olpache are a fictitious nation whose name connects them to the Apaches, an indigenous nation from Mexico's northern border region. Yet the film's present-day setting in the jungle equates them geographically with both the Mayans and Olmecas. The actors play out the guide's words in Teotihuacán, thus tying the Olpache to the Aztecs through architecture. Noting that the state (as opposed to the country) of Mexico and the coastal areas of the Yucatan Peninsula enjoy vastly different flora and fauna, Aured employs high-angle longshots that place the pyramids in the center of the screen and minimize the background. This cinematography seems especially amateur when juxtaposed with the Golden Age techniques of such masters as Gabriel Figueroa, whose longshots employed low-angles, curvilinear perspectives, big skies, and deep focus to oppose Hollywood's influence and project an autochthonous mexicanidad (Ramírez-Berg, "Cinematic Invention" 15–17). The cinematography in *La venganza de la momia* uses more standardized Hollywood techniques than do its Golden Age forebears; if there is a distinction between U.S. film tradition and this one, it is mainly due to the latter's lower quality.

It would be unfair to compare almost any cinematographer in the world to Figueroa—one of the most gifted cameramen of all time (Lieberman and Hegarty 33)—based on aesthetics alone; instead we should consider the discursive implications of these competing cinematographic techniques. Golden Age indigenismo communicated a discourse of official mestizaje that aimed to modernize contemporary Amerindians while reifying the pre-Columbian past. Such films suggested that Mexico's Amerindians could reclaim their lost greatness if they assimilated to the state. Figueroa's shots conveyed the greatness of both modern (mestizo) Mexico and its pre-Columbian ancestors. Such is not the case in *La venganza de la momia*. Like the Golden Age, this latter film asserts a clear distinction between pre-Columbian and contemporary indigeneity; however, it posits both as backward. The film posits contemporary Amerindians as childish and superstitious, while "prehistoric" Olpaches are both murderous and—as evidenced by the figure of the mummy—monstrous. Unlike the official mestizaje of the 1930s and 1940s, then, this film proposes a rupture between the indigenous cultures of the past and present through urbanization. The goal is not to emulate the greatness of past civilizations, but to overcome indigenous tendencies, both historical and contemporary, through modernization. It would thus be unnecessary, and perhaps even counterproductive, to depict the Olpache civilization using the low-angle longshots that would have romanticized pre-Columbian civilizations. The mummy may not pose a physical threat in this film, but its very memory holds the potential to unravel the nation.[15] Despite the mounting evidence in favor of a resurrected mummy wreaking havoc, at no point does Santo truly believe that the murders are supernatural.

After confronting the "mummy" and killing him with his own spear, El Santo—like the good luchador that he is—unmasks his foe. He looks at a young indigenous boy and says, "The dead do not come back to life. It is the evils of the living that harm their fellow men" ["Los muertos no resucitan. Es la maldad de los vivos la que siempre hace daño a sus semejantes."]. This comment feels especially unnatural coming from a superhero with firsthand experience facing Martians, zombies, and vampire women. Indeed, Santo's very next film, *Las momias de Guanajuato*, placed him alongside Blue Demon and Mil Máscaras as they struggled against reanimated mummies, a fact that largely invalidates his discourse here. The luchador's words come across as something similar to a parent who shows a terrified child that there is no monster under the bed, but they also demonstrate his colonialist mentality. Here the wrestler becomes a parental figure who must lead Amerindian children—both literal and figurative—to consciousness. After escaping from the "mummy," Santo takes the boy to one of his wrestling matches in Mexico City, and, after winning, invites him onto the ring. If Levi is correct in asserting that lucha libre became "naco" as it represented the indigenous transgression of urban space, then we should recognize that "naco" identity emerged as Amerindian subjects left their rural communities. The boy, in occupying this space, has effectively left his roots behind and assimilated—albeit imperfectly—to the modern, urban state. El Santo's victory is complete; he has overcome the specters of the past, slain an overly ambitious villain, and initiated a young indigenous boy into mestizo modernity. When juxtaposed with his other films, *La venganza de la momia* makes a clear contribution to our understanding of the colonial projects that Mexploitation cinema imagined. Threats to Mexico could come from indigeneity—both past and present—or they could result from imperial forces that challenged Mexico from beyond its borders. At least within Mexploitation, mestizo superheroes like El Santo would strive to protect their nation from both sources.

Criticizing Mexico's Imperial Drive in *Mejicanos en el espacio*

Unlike Mexploitation, which tended to promulgate official discourses, *Mejicanos en el espacio* challenges and undermines statist ideals.[16] The difference between how Olvera's novel and El Santo's cinema engage with the midcentury state reflects, in part, the type of media that both employ. Unlike film, which had to get past government censors, literature could largely critique the state unchecked. Indeed, Sánchez Prado argues that the written word represented "a space of greater contention and conflict where debates over the nature of nationalist articulations of mexicanidad—and the form that these should take in the national culture—permitted the development of more diverse postures than in other cultural manifestations" ["un espacio de mayor contención y conflicto, donde los debates sobre la naturaleza misma de 'lo nacional' y la forma que esta naturaleza debería tomar en la cultura permitieron el desarrollo de posiciones más diversas que otras manifestaciones culturales"] (*Naciones* 16). The relative freedom of expression in literary discourse allowed for the creation of la Onda. Spearheaded by incredibly young writers like José Agustín, Gustavo Sainz, Margarita Dalton, and Parménides García Saldaña, it should come as no surprise that la Onda broke with previous Mexican literary movements. Indeed, its general irreverence toward postrevolutionary doctrines and social mores set it apart.[17] Olvera's playful, satirical style leads Gabriel Trujillo Muñoz to place *Mejicanos* in the tradition of la Onda as well, thus aligning the author with the countercultural youth movements that linguistically, morally, and critically challenged the 1960s PRI (*Biografías* 170). A comparative discussion of la Onda and Mexploitation would provide interesting insights into midcentury Mexican culture based on the simple fact that they were contemporary movements with different aims. The comparison becomes even more pertinent in the case of *Mejicanos*, a novel that carries out the irreverent projects of la Onda while also building on the same SF tropes as its Mexploitation counterparts do.[18] As Olvera transposes SF discourses and ideas to la Onda, he produces severe critiques against midcentury Mexico's colonial aspirations.

Mejicanos is one of a handful of twentieth-century Mexican SF novels that engages utopian notions of official mestizaje. One thing that separates Olvera from his predecessors is his Onda-inspired, unabashed criticism of statist articulations of official mestizaje and the resulting projects of internal colonialism. A quick discussion of how key SF texts from the early part of the twentieth century engaged with postrevolutionary doctrines of official mestizaje will provide a useful backdrop from which to view Olvera's novel. Early twentieth-century SF generally treated postrevolutionary eugenics and internal colonialism with a moral ambiguity and ambivalence that was especially salient in the cases of Eduardo Urzaiz and Rafael Bernal, two letrados who wrote fiction while holding positions of importance in the postrevolutionary regime. Urzaiz, a Cuban-born Yucatecan medic, practiced medicine when the reigning paradigms of eugenics had politicized his profession. His futuristic novel *Eugenia* (1919) blurs the distinction between utopia and dystopia. As the title suggests, it tells of a future Mexican state that aggressively carries out projects of eugenics. As the novel closes, readers question whether they have read a work in favor of postrevolutionary eugenics or a critique of it. A similar effect emerges with Bernal, whose novel, *Su nombre era muerte* (1947), tells of a culturally mestizo anthropologist who exiles himself to an indigenous community, where, with the help of the locals, he learns to communicate with mosquitoes. The novel criticizes indigenista paternalism even as it essentializes indigenous communities and ways of knowing by equating them with insects. One more novel worth mentioning is Diego Cañedo's *El réferi cuenta nueve* (1943). Unlike Bernal and Urzaiz, Cañedo did not hold a government position. In many ways, however, he upholds postrevolutionary tenets of official mestizaje to a greater degree than do Urzaiz or Bernal. Cañedo's novel urges Mexico to side with the United States against Germany during World War II, and one of its principal arguments is that Aryanism poses an existential threat to Mexican mestizaje. As each of these examples shows, Mexican SF—while relatively rare in the first half of the twentieth century—often engaged with postrevolutionary doctrines of mestizaje, indigenismo, and modernity.[19]

Olvera addresses many of the same themes as his predecessors do through satirical representations of an inept yet brutal twenty-second-century "Centromexican" state. His depictions of government incompetence serve as critiques of the corruption that plagued 1960s Mexico. This comes through especially clearly as Olvera explores (and condemns) the Centromexican drive for empire. Centroméjico's liminal coloniality comes through with his decision to spell the word *Mejicanos* with a *j* rather than an *x*. During much of the nineteenth and twentieth centuries, there was a debate about how to properly spell the country's name in Spanish. The Spanish Academy mandated the proper spelling to be *Méjico* with the publication of the eighth edition of *Ortografía* in 1815; however, the Mexican Congress passed a law that codified *México* as the proper spelling in 1823 (Coester 109).[20] In a 1925 article, Alfred Coester stated that "Mexican nationalistic pride refuses to conform to a decree of the Spanish Academy" (109). Viewed in this light, debates surrounding the "proper" Spanish spelling of *México* have long entailed questions of colonization and resistance. Mexican leaders justified their decision to spell the country's name with an *x* rather than a *j* by problematically asserting that the spelling with an *x* did a better job of maintaining and respecting the name's Náhuatl influence.

Of course, given that Náhuatl never used a Latin alphabet until after the arrival of Cortés, this argument has always found itself on shaky ground. The decision to spell the country's name with an *x* ultimately has always had less to do with respecting the country's indigenous heritage and more to do with resisting Spain's influence. By adopting the *j*, then, Olvera's Centroméjico acknowledges its servile relationship to Spain and, by extension, other Western countries like the United States.

Even as Centroméjico conforms to the demands of its oppressors, it attempts to become a colonial power in its own right by carrying out projects of domination against weaker populations. Olvera's critical subject matter, coupled with the novel's playful vocabulary, leads José Manuel García-García to posit *Mejicanos* as an example of "gelasto-political literature," which he defines as a style in which the writer "passes judgment, above all, on the unconsciousness of the governed and the cynicism of those who govern" ["enjuicia sobre todo la inconciencia de los gobernados y el cinismo de los gobernantes"] (ii). García-García further notes that the novel's principal targets are soldiers, politicians, and officialist intellectuals (18–20). One early example of Olvera's critique of official discourses comes through his protagonist's favorite radio program, *El ermitaño en el espacio*, which tells of a Mexican space-drifter who has inherited superhuman strength from his "ancestors of bronze" ["antepasados de bronce"] (39). García-García views this seemingly innocent radio show as a rebuke of statist actors who continually refashioned Vasconcelos's words to conform to present-day doctrines (69). The novel thus challenges the most sacred tenets of the postrevolutionary state by satirizing one of the foundational philosophies upon which official articulations of mestizaje were predicated. Olvera focalizes his novel through his protagonist Raúl Nope, a first-person narrator who has left a position as a university instructor after growing tired of the Party's chafing control of the education system.[21] However, the military career that he ends up pursuing provides no relief from government propaganda. Olvera's Centroméjico functions as an obvious allegory for 1960s Mexico; as this country (and, by extension, 1960s Mexico) engages in imperial activities, it ironically validates the social hierarchies that allow the United States to continually treat it as an inferior.

Olvera is one of many midcentury Mexican writers whose work fits nicely within the theorizations of the French mystic Simone Weil, who rather bluntly states that "the notion of oppression is, in short, a stupidity.... And the notion of an oppressive class is even more stupid. We can only speak of an oppressive structure of society" (156). For Weil, oppression results from systemic, rather than personal, failures; indeed, socially constructed hierarchies of power often turn otherwise good people into oppressors. One especially interesting argument that she makes is that subordinate people gain a false feeling of control as they exert power over those who sit institutionally below them (156–58). The mystic's writings were especially influential in how another 1960s Mexican author, Rosario Castellanos, used literature to critique official discourses and to show how social hierarchies of race and gender abounded throughout Mexico (O'Connell 238–39; Dalton, "Educating" 157–58).[22] Olvera's connection to Weil is probably more roundabout than that of Castellanos, but the French mystic's theories still elucidate the power relations that he exposes throughout his novel. Centroméjico takes a great deal of satisfaction from its colonial holdings on Mars, but these imperial projects occur within a structure of power that has already designated the country as racially and culturally mediocre. As such, Centroméjico cements its subordinate position in the solar system by validating and working from within a hierarchy of power that favors the United States.

The novel emphasizes how Centromexican imperial endeavors do little to improve the country's position in international politics as Nope's squadron is ordered to investigate unclaimed territory on Ganymede, one of Jupiter's many moons. The *espaciero* narrates the events thusly:

> Well, the spaceship displayed the vast knowledge of those who built it as it descended gently in a small valley. People back on Earth followed the landing step-by-step in hopes that we would find something worth our while. But we didn't find anything. Absolutely nothing. Of course, we didn't expect to, so no one felt disillusioned or defrauded.
>
> [Bueno, pues la astronave descendió suavemente en un vallecito, haciendo alarde de los conocimientos de sus constructores. Desde la Tierra seguían paso a paso las etapas del aterrizaje en espera de que encontráramos algo que valiera la pena. Pero no encontramos nada. Absolutamente nada. De cualquier modo no lo esperábamos, así que no hubo desilusión por parte de nadie ni hubo quien se sintiera defraudado.] (9)

We soon learn that this is because Centromexican astronauts only investigate worthless territories that the more powerful "güeros"—a term that Nope uses loosely to denote U.S., European, and even Chinese citizens—have already explored and decided not to annex. The imperial powers' control of Centromexican expeditions is so all-encompassing that the explorers are not even allowed to retrieve lunar rocks. This last restriction proves problematic for Nope, who schemes to forge the apparition of the Virgin of Guadalupe on a Ganymedean stone to install a basilica and cash a major profit. Centroméjico's commitment to space exploration underscores the fact that the country feels greater power as it exploits other lands even though this behavior requires it to acquiesce to the desires of other, more powerful nations.

The state clearly uses these expeditions to defend unjustifiable claims of Centromexican technological sophistication and military might. Perhaps because García-García recognizes that Centroméjico will never achieve its modernity through these imperial projects, he asserts that these military maneuvers never move beyond mere propaganda (86). His argument ignores the fact that these actions constitute a concrete foreign policy strategy: Centroméjico's Party leaders sincerely believe that they will be able to leverage their country's imperial gains for greater prestige with the United States and other imperial powers back on Earth. The Party's steadfast imitation of U.S. and European imperialism anchors this futuristic society clearly in 1968. The zeal with which Centroméjico executes its space program mirrors the excitement leading up to the Olympic Games (*Labyrinth of Solitude*, Paz 248–53). Rather than viewing themselves as the first "Third World" country to receive this honor, national leaders saw the games as their initiation into modern society (Zolov 119–20). Díaz Ordaz ordered the harsh intervention at Tlatelolco, then, to defend his country's internationally validated modernity. The similarities between *Mejicanos* and 1960s society have led many scholars to assert that the novel uses the trope of futurity to make countercultural commentaries on contemporary (1960s) society (García 38; Vargas 31). López Castro argues that the novel was forgotten after the massacre (122); if he is correct, then the academy has failed to recognize how it interfaces with and challenges the attitudes within the PRI that allowed the massacre to occur.

As with 1960s Mexico, Centromexican attempts to assert themselves in international politics entail high human costs and relatively few rewards from the international community. The nation imagines itself embroiled in a colonial conflict, but its adversaries never view Centroméjico as an equal. The novel comically emphasizes international contempt for the nascent empire when it reveals that the United States has placed a top-secret base on Ganymede right next to Centromexican territory. Rather than take extreme security measures, the North Americans depend on their southern neighbor's incompetence to hide their actions. In response to this humiliation, the Party assigns Nope to lead "Operation Gunsmoke" ["Operación Gunsmoke"], which is a spy expedition that he will carry out on the nearby U.S. base. Perhaps as proof of national leaders' inexperience regarding international relations—where opposing powers hide any intelligence they have acquired—the Party's scheme goes no further than simply publishing the results of Nope's discovery. Centroméjico does not seek empire for strategic purposes; instead, it seeks subjectivity through a mechanical reproduction of the oppressor's model.

Far from working on behalf of national security, Nope must beat the Americans at their own game and showcase Centromexican modernity. If the operation's success remains clandestine, the country will not receive public praise for outsmarting the United States. One key component to Operation Gunsmoke is the presence of Lobelto, a Martian mercenary who has spent time in the South American guerrillas and in Martian political demonstrations in Los Angeles that clearly allude to the 1960s civil rights movement in the United States. By implicitly aligning Lobelto with twentieth-century U.S. activists like Martin Luther King Jr., Malcolm X, and César Chávez, Olvera asserts the need for recognizing and protecting Martian and subaltern rights. This strategy also grounds his novel in the student movements of 1968 that patterned their own civil disobedience after the demonstrations that had rocked the United States just a few years earlier (Zolov 122; Volpi 143–50). Olvera alludes to the unequal power dynamic between Centromexicans and Martians through the relationship that emerges between Nope and Lobelto. As they plan their expedition, they determine that Nope will lead the infiltration of the base while Lobelto will serve as the liaison between Centroméjico and any Martians found in U.S. territory. Despite the Martian's key role in the Centromexican strategy, Nope constantly insults him. The espaciero's behavior is telling when juxtaposed with Centroméjico's own submissive role in the solar system's social hierarchy. Although Centromexicans express outrage when other countries automatically relegate them to the periphery, they are more than happy to exert their own supremacy vis-à-vis the Martians.

In a series of events that emphasizes how Centroméjico's attempts at empire never subvert—and, indeed, generally affirm—U.S. hegemony, Nope and Lobelto embark on their mission. As soon as they cross into the U.S. territory, an alarm sounds, and when Nope attempts to escape, a soldier shouts "Stop, Mexican! Stop or I'll shoot!" (75). It is surprising that U.S. forces immediately know the nationality of their invaders. Dressed in their space suits, both Nope and Lobelto are quintessential cyborgs whose bodies are hidden and ostensibly unidentifiable. They probably have not entered with any obvious markings that would associate them with Centroméjico. Instead, this seems to be one of many cases that shows Centroméjico's technological—and hence modernity—deficit to the highly efficient Americans. Unlike Donna Haraway, who views the cyborg as a destabilizing figure that can easily undermine entrenched power structures, Olvera suggests that unequal access to technology neutralizes the liberatory potential of technological hybridity because one group is inevitably favored over another. At the end of the ill-fated operation, U.S. officials return Nope and Lobelto to the Centromexican base without so much as acknowledging Nope's commanding officer—a breach of decorum that leaves the captain fuming about American contempt for himself and his country. The captain's outrage is comical because the U.S. decision to view Nope's trespassing as an act of incompetence—rather than espionage—shields him and his country from the consequences of committing an act of war. Of course, while they avoid an international scandal, Nope and the captain still must answer to angry Party leaders. In a fit of desperation, Nope invents a story where he captured Lobelto from the U.S. base. This account exonerates him and the captain, but it also means that Party officials will subject the Martian to torture and certain death. Realizing he has acted immorally, the novel's protagonist repents of his lie and attempts to sneak off the base with Lobelto. Unfortunately, Party officials capture him and send him to an insane asylum.

In his essay "Madness and Society," Michel Foucault argues that insanity is a construct of the state that marks and removes undesirable actors from social discourse. As such, we should investigate what enables the state to interpellate the espaciero as insane. García-García deftly explains the trigger for Nope's condition when he likens him to a twenty-second-century Don Quixote who has listened to too many radio shows (65), but he never addresses the deeper discursive ramifications of Nope's apparent mental status. According to Foucault, the insane asylum emerged during early industrialism as a confining space for those who could not contribute to capitalist society ("Madness" 372). Nope's failure to execute "Operation Gunsmoke" marks him as incompetent, but given that none of the novel's characters are particularly good at their jobs, this explanation for his incarceration is unsatisfying. Instead, we must note that the protagonist poses an existential threat to Party politics. Nope's narrative voice refuses to conform to any aesthetic or political standard, and as a result he becomes Foucault's "individual who reveals the truth with spirit" ("Madness" 374). Party leaders show that Centromexicans should ignore him by denoting him as insane, yet his very mental status suggests that Nope bears "the truth that ordinary men [can]not state" ("Madness" 373). Indeed, Nope's voice undermines the intolerance of the Party (and that of the speaker himself) through biting satire and harsh ironies. The espaciero's words expose mimetic imperialism as a self-defeating process that must fail by its very definition. The state cannot permit Nope to speak uninhibited, so it attempts to "cure" him. Returning to Foucault, this action effectively becomes an act of forced assimilation in which Nope must remain in a treatment center until he can properly function in society ("Madness" 376–77). In other words, the state will keep him removed from public discourse until he has internalized the official ideology.

The most subversive truth that Nope communicates is that of Martian equality to the earthlings. Throughout the novel, he emphasizes numerous traits that these extraterrestrials share with Mexico's own indigenous populations—both pre-Columbian and twentieth-century. In each case, the hegemonic race (Spaniards, criollos, mestizos, Centromexicans) views the subservient race(s) as subhuman despite empirical evidence to the contrary. The Centromexicans, for example, project their essentialist understandings of race onto a complex and varied Martian (proto)humanity. In one of many telling sequences, Nope condemns U.S. experiments that have used the Martians for lab rats even as he pejoratively refers to these aliens as "natives" ["nativos"] (59). Ironically, his language dehumanizes the Martians on the one hand, yet on the other hand it recognizes certain traces of humanity that other organisms from Mars—such as the flora and fauna—lack. Nope's discursive strategy establishes an interplanetary and interethnic union and calls into question the denial of certain rights to the "native." Both Centroméjico and the United States brutalize their Martian subordinates. The differences in how these two countries handle their colonized subjects reinforce popular imaginaries of conquest and virtual extermination of Amerindians in the United States and the racial and cultural mestizaje that ostensibly occurred in Mexico.[23] The United States does not exterminate native Martians per se, but it does use them to carry out inhumane scientific experiments. Speaking of how U.S. experts understood the Martians upon arriving on the planet, Nope narrates,

Everyone thought they were animals, primates, or some sort of monkey not known on Earth. Because they looked so much like us, it was always kind of awkward to see them jumping around and growling and kicking every time that we tried to get close to them. They were buck naked, females and males, and they looked like they were never cold, despite the extreme Martian climate.

[[Se] pensó que se trataba de animales, de simios, de changos de alguna especie no conocida en la Tierra. Como son tan parecidos a nosotros siempre era medio feo eso de verlos dando brincos por todas partes y gruñendo y pataleando cada vez que trataban de acercárseles. Andaban completamente encuerados, hembras y machos, y parecía que nunca tenían frío, a pesar de lo extremoso del clima marciano.] (59)

Returning to Graham, the monstrous aspect of the Martians is not their animal-like characteristics but their similarities to Earth-based humanity. These aliens may lack language and culture when the first earthlings arrive, but they already share numerous traits in common.

Nope contrasts the five years of meticulous, failed U.S. experimentation with an accidental discovery by his compatriot, Güicho Reyna, who discovered, or rather catalyzed, Martian intelligence. In a story that cements the parallels between the Martians and Mexico's indigenous populations, we learn that Güicho was on watch in a remote Centromexican territory when a group of Martians attacked him and escaped with his tequila. When the Martians returned, they could speak. Within two hours, U.S. officials arrived and took both the aliens and Güicho into custody, where, after exhaustive tests, they concluded that "ethanol distilled from a cactus and oxygenated in the Martian organism produces considerable psychic changes in the Martian metabolism" ["un etanol destilado de cactos y oxigenado en los organismos marcianos produce en su metabolismo considerables cambios síquicos"] (61). The fact that the Martians gain language only after coming in contact with a traditional (Centro)Mexican beverage, coupled with the ensuing U.S. invasion of both Centromexican and Martian rights, suggests that the Martians and Centromexicans are connected in their similar plight as colonized subjects. On the one hand, because a Centromexican discovered Martian intelligence, it seems that the earthlings should affirm the country's modernity. Arguably no other nation has left a more significant mark on humanity's understanding of the solar system. On the other hand, it is precisely at this moment of glory that U.S. officials arrive. Not only do they annex all of the results of Güicho's discoveries, but they take him prisoner as well, thus committing a clear violation of sovereignty that would never occur between equals. Any illusions of grandeur immediately fade away as Centroméjico loses its claim to humanity's greatest astrobiological discovery and achievement.

The novel seems to imply that the inhabitants of Mars and Centroméjico should come together against their U.S. oppressors, but the Party instead chooses to colonize the newly intelligent Martians within its territory as if liberation could result from this mimetic imperialism. Centroméjico draws from the example of its own historical colonizer in New Spain as it goes about its imperial project, but there are several key differences in how the newer empire administers its colonies. For instance, Centroméjico never institutionalizes Spanish in the Martian population. Part of this is due to twenty-second-century technologies that have produced American-made interpreting machines that facilitate communication between speakers of different languages. These devices become a sort of prosthesis or cybernetic organ upon which both interlocutors depend. Joanna Zylinska understands the prosthesis as "an articulation of the slippage between the self and its others" (216). This is certainly the case regarding the interpreters; it is through this apparatus that the Self can interface with an alien Other. As they communicate through this object, both the Centromexican conqueror and the conquered Martian become cyborg entities where the fusion of the body with technology allows for a level of unification that would otherwise be impossible.

The prosthetic mouthpiece invokes certain liberatory aspects of Haraway's thought as it literally brings different groups in contact and facilitates their communion while at the same time permitting both interlocutors to maintain their own language and, to a certain extent, culture (150). Indeed, these devices become a great example of what N. Katherine Hayles sees as the privileging of the flow of information over the body within posthuman societies (*Posthuman* 2). Information is no longer trapped due to limitations of the body; instead, it is transformed as it leaves one speaker and is changed into something that the listener can process. One unintended consequence is that, given their dependence on this communicative prosthesis, the two races do not develop a means of training their own bodies to communicate with one another. This in turn leads to even greater social fragmentation than that of colonial Mexico. In New Spain, for example, although most indigenous subjects never learned Spanish, there were many who did. At the same time, numerous Spanish bureaucrats learned Náhuatl and other regional languages to more efficiently administer in indigenous colonies (de Reuse 226). In both cases, people trained their bodies to move and communicate across cultures. On Mars, however, technological advances result in neither colonizer nor colonized learning the Other's language. Ironically, then, the interpreting machines allow Centromexican colonizers to ignore Martian bodies unless they specifically engage them.

In many ways, the Centromexican Empire is even more totalitarian than that of its Spanish forefathers; as it controls technology, the Party also controls interracial relations. Systemic exclusion from the language makes it impossible for the Martians to follow the counsel of Roberto Fernández Retamar (30), who implores the subaltern to appropriate the colonizers' language in subversive ways. These aliens, then, become true subalterns in the tradition of Gayatri Chakravorty Spivak, for they are literally incapable of speaking (294–308). The novel emphasizes Lobelto's subalternity as the interpreter fails to convey certain types of discourse in his communications with Nope. The espaciero often reverts to insults and slang, but the machine simply buzzes, reminding the Centromexican that they are not speaking the same language. The espaciero's inability to express himself through pejorative language sears his discriminatory thoughts in his mind. At one point he complains, saying, "You can't imagine how hard it is to try to be decent when talking to a Martian" ["No se imaginan lo terrible que es tratar de ser decente frente a un marciano."] (63). Of course, the fact that the Martians have no voice when engaging with earthlings does not mean that they never speak. José Rabasa has argued that "Spivak's question [can the subaltern speak?] is only pertinent when the subaltern is expected to interface with the state" (4). The question becomes moot when colonized people, or Martians in this case, choose to "remain *outside* the state and history" (4, emphasis in original). Obviously, Martian communities continue to interact among themselves; the problem is that their discourse is illegible to state officials like Nope. Like the indigenous populations of midcentury Mexico, the technologically bare Martians remain on the fringe of society. The state generally ignores them, but it does engage them if it has a vested interest.

One of the main factors that causes Centromexican astronauts to engage with Martians (particularly Martian women) is a desire for sexual gratification. Nope generally avoids sexual contact with female aliens; as Alexander P. Shafer argues, the espaciero "is queer (though not gay); he rejects a heteronormative life of marriage and family and subverts traditional masculine roles of husband and father" (48). Nope's commentaries about the sexual politics of the Centromexican empire thus come from the perspective of a man who, beyond being "insane," is also a sexual outsider. Similar to what happened under Spanish colonial rule in New Spain, sexual relations occur between colonizing Centromexican males—with the exclusion of Nope—and colonized Martian females. Such relationships are then moderated from the center of the colonizing nation. This reflects a historical reality where, according to Elizabeth Anne Kuznesof, indigenous (and perhaps mestiza) women's status as sexual objects provided them with certain avenues for accessing European privilege that were unavailable to men (161). A similar dynamic emerges in the fictitious case of Centroméjico's colonization of Mars, where explorers frequently pursue sexual relationships with Martian women. Beyond catalyzing sexual competition between Centromexican and Martian males, these actions also provide a path by which Martian women can use their gender to offset their racial stigmatization. Perhaps for this very reason, Martian women have established some of the most scandalous brothels in the solar system.

Olvera uses Nope's queer voice to undermine attempts to dehumanize Martian women (and by extension men). The espaciero's parents suspect that he secretly plans to have a Martian mistress, so his mother warns him against interstellar sex and reproduction through a racist letter: "They were telling me about all the embarrassing diseases that those filthy space chicks get. That is not natural at all. Nasty! They look like animals" ["Ya me estuvieron platicando todas las vergonzosas enfermedades que pescan con esas horribles viejas que salen de los otros mundos. Si eso es nada natural, fuchi, hasta parecen animales."] (27). As Nope reads these words, he denaturalizes his mother's assertions of Martian inferiority. Indeed, the simple fact that earthlings and Martians can have reproductive sex validates claims of Martian humanity. If they are biologically compatible, then they must somehow belong to the same species. It is an evolutionary anomaly that species from two different planets would have developed the necessary anatomy to carry out heterosexual reproduction. Of course, the fact that both races exhibit high intelligence would make it problematic to deny Martians an equal status to Earth-based humanity even if they did not have sexually compatible bodies. Haraway explains it best as she considers humanity's unexceptional evolutionary condition: "By the late twentieth century in . . . scientific culture, the boundary between human and animal is thoroughly breached. . . . Language, tool use, social behavior, mental events, nothing really convincingly settles the separation of human and animal" (151–52). Western society continues to assert a distinction between human and other forms of life; Rodney A. Brooks acknowledges this fact when he observes that Western society confers greater levels of "beingness" to animals depending on their evolutionary similarities to humans and on the complexity of their nervous systems (154). Throughout his novel, Olvera shows that the Martians have the mental capacity necessary to carry out even the most complex of human tasks, such as piloting spacecraft and using language. If this were the only similarity between the inhabitants of the fourth planet and those of the third, it would be enough to require equal rights.

When we consider both the Martians' intelligence and their sexual compatibility with earthlings, we can disprove any claims of Martian inhumanity as racist constructs. Of course, there are cases in nature where males and females from separate species can procreate; however, these are confined to organisms whose evolutionary lines only recently diverged, and who therefore still have similar DNA (Cochran and Harpending 48–54). These exceptions prove the rule; interspecies breeding remains possible due to genetic similarities that are so strong that it is difficult to bestow more "beingness"—and hence greater rights—on one of the two progenitors or on the progeny. The fictional case of earthling-Martian reproduction does not result from a recent shared ancestor because these races evolved independently. Evolutionarily speaking, each respective race is more recently related to its planet's most prehistoric bacteria, plants, and fungi. Given the historical improbability that they would have a shared genetic ancestor—beyond the possibility of a Martian bacteria arriving to Earth via asteroid—the most probable explanation for their ability to interbreed stems from a type of convergent evolution that is not only phenotypic, but also genetic.[24] Their corresponding evolutionary histories have both produced genetic humans, and any progeny that comes from interbreeding represents an ironic, literal variation of José Vasconcelos's "cosmic race." Any denial of rights to Martians, earthlings, or any possible interplanetary progeny is based not on objective, verifiable differences in "beingness," but on social constructs that favor earthlings.

The Centromexican treatment of the Martians is a thinly veiled critique of policies—both in 1960s Mexico and throughout the world—that denied humanity to the subaltern. What is more, the novel shows how mimetic imperialism ultimately validates U.S. incursions into the imitating country's territory. It is against this backdrop that the novel so effectively criticizes official discourses that hypocritically decried foreign meddling in the country even as they supported internal empire. Nope's discourse reflects the insanity of a political movement that believed it had to exploit to be truly modern, and, more subversively, it shows that these modernity-driven projects validated systems of oppression that would never allow the country an equal position in the international, global hierarchy. His fictitious account communicates many of the strongest grievances of the student movements of the 1960s. If anything, 1960s Mexico was more oppressive than even Centroméjico's reigning Party; Nope is placed in an insane asylum in large part due to his subversive discourse. His punishment seems especially light when compared to the fate that "dangerous" critics of the postrevolutionary regime suffered at the hands of state-sponsored violence in places like Tlatelolco.

Conclusion

Official postrevolutionary discourses began to lose their appeal by the 1960s. The state employed numerous strategies to control the narrative on national modernity; most of the time it did this by sponsoring (and policing the discourse of) B-movies and other forms of officialist art. On other occasions, however, it resorted to violence in order to enforce its claims to modernity. My juxtaposition of El Santo's cinema with Carlos Olvera's countercultural novel *Mejicanos en el espacio* sheds light on the attitudes that permeated Mexican society during the 1960s and into the 1970s. Both the novel and the films concur that 1960s and 1970s Mexico engaged in projects of internal empire, but they disagree about whether or not this practice was moral. The tension between la Onda and state-sponsored cinema certainly extended beyond SF, but this genre proved especially adept at negotiating discourses of modernity. If there is any one common moral denominator between *Mejicanos* and Mexploitation, it is that both assert Mexico's right to exist autonomously from external imperialists. While Santo's films validated programs of internal empire, they rarely asserted Mexico's right to become an international colonial power. Rather, they opted for a live-and-let-live approach to global politics. At the end of *Santo contra la invasión de los marcianos*, for example, the luchador, after having killed the invading Martian forces, destroys the invaders' spaceship because he knows that humanity would use any technology on the vessel for ill. Rather than transform his country into Earth's hegemonic imperial superpower, the luchador opts to rid the planet of this tempting technology of domination. This suggests that officialist thinkers and directors justified internal imperialism in large part because they viewed the domestication of the

Amerindian as an acceptable form of nation-building rather than immoral, colonial, or even militarist. *Mejicanos* deconstructs this distinction by positing an intimate relationship between internal and external imperialism. As they challenged the most cherished ideals of the postrevolutionary state, Onda novels like *Mejicanos* popularized new ways to consider national identity and politics. Under these circumstances, the prestige of officialist representations of mexicanidad began to ebb.

Conclusion

The Legacy of the Modernization of the Body Today

At the end of his book *Naciones intelectuales: Las fundaciones de la modernidad literaria mexicana (1917–1959)*, Ignacio M. Sánchez Prado argues, "The framework of imaginaries and identities developed during the years of the Revolution—both with the encouragement of the government of the Revolution and in the reproduction of its ideologies in the field of cultural production—continues to be the starting point in contemporary Mexican studies" ["La fábrica de imaginarios e identidades que se desarrolló durante los años del gobierno de la Revolución, tanto con el fomento del Estado como en la reproducción de sus ideologías en espacios del campo de producción cultural, sigue siendo el punto de partida en los estudios mexicanos actuales."] (239). As I have argued throughout this book, one of the key components of officialist literary and cultural production was the assertion that the state could modernize the indigenous masses by fusing their bodies with technology. It should come as no surprise, then, that the technologically hybrid body would continue to interface with national politics and identity in the twenty-first century. As my experience at the *lavandería*—which I narrated at the beginning of this book—shows, many people still view indigeneity as primitive by definition. People rarely discuss mestizaje openly in contemporary society, but racial hybridity continues to function as an omnipresent yet invisible counterpoint to the indigenous. Much of this is due to the officialist artists and letrados who produced nationalist discourses with the aim of building and articulating a viable, twentieth-century nation-state. They enjoyed so much success in decreeing "proper" articulations of race that their literature and art continue to inform ideas of national identity decades after they completed their work.

The residual effects of postrevolutionary official mestizaje on Mexican society become especially clear in major urban centers that facilitate the continued presence of state-sponsored art, literature, and culture. On a normal day, a resident of Mexico City may go to the headquarters of the Secretaría de Educación Pública and view the murals of Diego Rivera. While there, she may decide to take a photograph with the life-size statue of José Vasconcelos standing at the base of the stairs. When she goes to the Parque de Chapultepec, several vendors will try to sell her the masks of El Santo, Blue Demon, Mil Máscaras, and many other luchadores. If she refuses (or accepts), these same people may offer to sell her a pirated copy of *Santo contra las mujeres vampiro*. As she flips through the channels on her television after returning home, she will almost certainly come across movies from the Golden Age; indeed, she may see one directed by Emilio Fernández and starring Pedro Armendáriz alongside María Félix or Dolores del Río. The state may not commission intellectuals and artists to produce a shared national identity anymore, but the works of those who went before continue to shape how present-day Mexicans interpret their national heritage. This continued relevance means that intellectuals have a duty to discuss twentieth-century cultural nationalism if they wish to understand and explain present-day attitudes and conditions within the country.

My book adds to discussions that contemporary scholars like Joshua Lund and Pedro Ángel Palou have recently approached in their own studies. Both critics have positioned discourses of racial hybridity within postrevolutionary (and even postindependence in the case of Lund) constructs of modernity. Their excellent studies show how literary and cultural production helped construct and negotiate a racialized national identity throughout the twentieth century, and they suggest that the effects of mestizo normativity continue to ripple throughout the nation to this day. My own focus on the body has uncovered numerous strategies that postrevolutionary state actors employed to assimilate indigenous peoples. Modernity became, at its core, an embodied condition. Racial, genetic, cultural, and technological hybridity represented different incarnations of an official mestizaje that understood race to mean something more than a characteristic inherited at birth. Officialist thinkers ranging from letrados like Vasconcelos and Gamio to artists and filmmakers like Emilio Fernández and the muralists held that people could modernize their bodies and assimilate to the state through technological hybridity. Given the prominence of the diverse voices that championed state-sanctioned racial doctrines—and particularly since their work permeated the nation's intellectual, artistic, and popular sectors—it is of no surprise that twentieth-century representations of racial and technological hybridity remain very much alive in the popular imaginary.

The continued relevance of these postrevolutionary discourses of race and technology is especially striking because the state shifted its racial and ideational priorities with the adoption of neoliberal policies in the 1980s and 1990s. Beyond further institutionalizing a preference for technocratic political leaders over broadly educated intellectuals, this political and economic shift prescribed a more hands-off approach from the government regarding literary and cultural production. This was especially the case regarding film, where "the Secretaría de Hacienda y Crédito Público (SHCP) . . . surveyed a project of *desincorporación*—that is, of extricating COTSA [Compañía Operadora de Teatros S. A.] and film exhibition from the umbrella of government funding and management" (Sánchez Prado, *Screening*). Cinema had provided one of the last media through which the state could promulgate official discourses, but the new political climate born out of the 1989 Washington Consensus—and intensified with the passage of NAFTA in 1994—largely erased the medium as a means for dictating statist ideologies.[1] This did not mean that the national cinema became a bastion of progressive ideals; as Sánchez Prado observes, the quest for profits led the industry to "manifest regressive political positions and problematic representations of race, class, and gender" (*Screening*).[2] In recent years, the state has continued to intervene in certain aspects of film production—in 2015, for example, the government reserved the right to amend elements of Sony Pictures' James Bond movie, *Spectre* (Partlow)—but the fact remains that the decision to privatize the film industry sounded the death knell of Mexican cultural nationalism. As the government limited its role in sponsoring cultural production, it became difficult for it to use art for didactic purposes.

The state's diminished role in promoting official doctrines by funding cultural production has not coincided with a similar disappearance of technological hybridity from discourses of modernity. Indeed, the technologized body remains a powerful force in the national imaginary. Whether a eugenically evolved mestizo, a medically enhanced technological hybrid, or one of its various articulations in Onda literature and Mexploitation cinema, the fusion of the body with technology disrupts and reconstructs the reigning paradigms of race, gender, and even nation. Studies on cyborg and posthuman articulations of Mexican identity, then, become especially pertinent as they show the problematic relationship between technology and corporeal privileges tied to race and gender. As we look at the discursive role that the technologized body plays in modernity-driven contexts like postrevolutionary Mexico, it becomes clear that scientific discourse exists as a Foucauldian technology of power whose interpretation and implementation necessarily interfaces with the established hierarchies of racial and gender privilege.

The connection between racial identity and technological privilege continues into twenty-first-century Mexico, where people from indigenous communities continue to lack the amenities that their mestizo counterparts enjoy. This fact became especially clear on October 2, 2013, when Irma López Aurelio, a nine-months-pregnant indigenous woman from Jalapa de Díaz, Oaxaca, arrived at the local medical clinic and requested emergency medical assistance. After workers refused to attend to her, she gave birth on her own in a grassy patio on the public clinic's grounds (NTR). What was truly remarkable about this case was, unfortunately, not its singularity (in June 2014 the reporter Pedro Matías found that at least thirteen indigenous women had given birth under similar circumstances that year in Oaxaca alone) but the fact that Eloy Pacheco López, a nearby witness, photographed the ordeal and posted the images to his Facebook page.[3] The picture captures López Aurelio squatting over the grass as her newborn child, still connected to her body through the umbilical cord, lies on the ground. This powerful image went viral almost immediately, and bloggers and activists the world over soon decried the negligence that had allowed the event to occur ("Mexicana"). By October 4, the story had appeared in newspapers throughout the country, and the Oaxacan secretary of health, Germán Tenorio Vasconcelos, extended an official apology to the new mother through his personal blog. He later announced that he would investigate the facility's director, Adrián René Cruz Cabrera, who was absent on the day that López Aurelio gave birth.[4] Cruz Cabrera later claimed that, because he lived over an hour and a half away from the clinic, he was unable to go every day; he had been requesting another medic for the facility for several years, but the state had ignored him (SDP Noticias). After López Aurelio's story went viral, state officials approved the requests for more staff at the clinic. In a separate case, government officials determined that López Aurelio's experience, while unfortunate, was not the result of negligence.[5]

López Aurelio provides a paradigmatic example of the lower-quality health care available to Mexico's indigenous population. Because it was a clinic rather than a hospital, the institution did not have to have medical doctors on site; rather it could have nurses and volunteers. The clinic was poorly equipped to provide services to its primarily indigenous patrons; many reporters conjectured that the mother had been unable to communicate with nurses and staff due to linguistic barriers (NTR). Such assertions fed into the idea that the Mexican health care system continued to favor those who had assimilated to mestizo society. Part of the linguistic struggle reflected practicality; it remained difficult to find medics and nurses who were fluent in languages like Náhuatl and Zapoteco. Nevertheless, it also underscored the fact that the current health care system in Mexico "creat[es] incentives that maintain or increase inequity rather than channeling public resources to the most pressing needs" (Barraza-Lloréns et al. 49). Two studies from the first decade of the twenty-first century highlight the unequal access to prenatal care for indigenous women as compared to their mestiza peers. Sarah L. Barber et al. note that the infant mortality rate in indigenous communities is "54 deaths per 1,000 live births—twice that of the rest of the country" (Barber et al. w311), while Mariana Barraza-Lloréns et al. report that the maternal mortality rate among indigenous women in Guerrero "is 28.3 per 10,000 live births, compared with the national rate of 5.1 per 10,000 live births" (48–49).[6] Given that systemic factors lead Mexican health centers to favor mestizo actors over their Amerindian counterparts, the perpetually poor condition of indigenous health care (particularly in rural areas) has become a self-fulfilling prophecy.

In contrast to the 1940s, when Lamarckian paradigms led state officials to believe that medicine could alter the national genome, contemporary actors simply view medicine as a technology that can help people to mitigate the effects of injury and disease. Medicine can improve an individual's life, but it no longer carries the eugenic overtones of decades past.[7] That said, the country continues to assert the need to extend medical care to the indigenous population. Julio Frenk, who served as secretary of health during the administration of Vicente Fox, identified equitable access to health care as one of the most pressing needs facing Mexico in the twenty-first century (Frenk et. al 1670). The bureaucrat's reasons for extending health care reverberated with those of his postrevolutionary forebears. Where 1940s medical policies aimed to assimilate rural Mexicans to a mestizo order to produce national modernity, research cited by Frenk et al. suggested that the stability of the nation's democracy depended on equality of health care (1670). In both cases, the primary justification for improving indigenous health care had less to do with helping Amerindian individuals than it did with maintaining the stability of the mestizo state. Due to this approach, it should come as no surprise that access to medical care continues to reflect a person's ties to cultural mestizaje. Medicine still functions as a modern good that health facilities more successfully direct toward "modern," mestizo consumers. Indeed, indigenous people greatly improve their access to health care as they assimilate to the dominant culture.

The ideologies that underpinned midcentury rural health and hygiene projects continue to shape national politics into the present. By refusing her care, the clinic cast López Aurelio as medically and technologically bare. It is perhaps ironic, then, that it was her image, captured and posted across ultramodern social media, that ultimately denounced—and denaturalized—the clinic's (in)actions. Other women later gave birth under similar circumstances, but now medics and nurses knew they could be held accountable if this occurred under their watch. Given this fact, López Aurelio's experience can help us compare and contrast the nature of the technologically hybrid body of postrevolutionary cultural nationalism to that depicted in the early twenty-first century. Postrevolutionary officials aimed to produce a new nation-state by imagining a modernized, national body from the top down. As such, they took great pains to imagine and articulate appropriate types of technological and racial hybridity. The cyborg body was not a site of resistance but a strategy for amending the postrevolutionary biopolitics in a way that could incorporate the indigenous population into the nation-state. The end goal, then, was to grow economically and achieve Western-style modernity. Amerindian culture sat at the heart of these practices, but the state ignored the input of the very indigenous peoples whom it aimed to assimilate. In López Aurelio's case, the photograph was uploaded to testify against the failings of a public institution. The photo's very existence shows that technology, beyond being a tool for top-down domination, can also play a role in resistant, grassroots activism. In contrast to the status quo of past decades, the state can no longer simply ignore its indigenous citizens by asserting their supposedly tenuous ties to modernity. As indigenous Mexicans use technology in sophisticated ways to voice their grievances against those in power, they can assert their own role in a modern yet indigenous society. Unlike in the postrevolutionary period, when technological hybridity played a conservative, homogenizing role in the national imaginary, the tension—and even slippage—between technological bareness and hybridity produces a problematic, resistant entity in the neoliberal society of the early twenty-first century.

In a 2016 article, I theorized this new articulation of the technologically hybrid, cyborg subject of Mexican literature and culture as *robo sacer*: a cyborg articulation of Giorgio Agamben's homo sacer. Like Agamben's theorization, the robo sacer is a dehumanized, marginal human being whose life does not receive equal protection under the law ("*Robo Sacer*" 16). This condition emerges from an array of institutionalized states of exception such as the transnational flows of bodies, capital, technology, and labor; however, one key component of robo sacer identity is the way in which those in power signal certain individuals as less than human due to their relationship—or the lack thereof—with technology. The most interesting aspect of robo sacer subjectivity is not that foreign—or local—technologies dehumanize certain individuals; rather, it is that the oppressed can use the very technologies that relegate them to the periphery to denaturalize the constructs of race, gender, and capital that facilitate their marginalization. Perhaps the most striking example of robo sacer resistance in Mexico occurred on January 1, 1994, when the Zapatista army took over the city of San Cristobal de las Casas. The rebels selected this as the date to rise up in arms because it coincided with the implementation of NAFTA, an agreement that eased trade restrictions among Mexico, the United States, and Canada, but threatened to displace and ignore indigenous peoples who could not compete in an open market. The indigenous rebels lost the military confrontation, but they won the hearts of intellectuals and activists both domestically and internationally through their adept use of internet technology. Robo sacer resistance can clearly be used to check an oppressive government's actions, but it remains to be seen the extent to which marginalized people can foment systemic change through the subversive use of technology and to what extent this practice simply allows people to express their outrage. I have not been able to adequately engage this figure in *Mestizo Modernity: Race, Technology, and the Body in Postrevolutionary Mexico* because it lies outside the scope of my project. But the role of the technologized body in contemporary Mexico merits closer study. Many Mexican and Mexican American / Chicano authors and cultural producers have engaged this concept directly, a fact that suggests that any discussion of the liberatory role of robo sacer resistance in Mexico must of necessity engage fiction and creative works.

The prominent role of literary and cultural production in contemporary theorizations of the technologically hybrid body should come as no surprise given the role of various media in developing similar concepts in the postrevolutionary period. At the same time, many of the underlying racial ideologies of the early and mid-twentieth century run against the grain of more recent work. Because postrevolutionary artists and letrados favored mixed-race identity over indigenous, Afro-Mexican, and even Anglo-Saxon/European cultures, they interpreted the scientifically and technologically modified body in ways that buoyed discourses of racial hybridity. When posthuman entities appeared in officialist art and literature, they demonized external imperialists—be they Europeans, North Americans, Australians, or the aliens of Mexploitation—while they exalted the hegemony and sovereignty of (mestizo) Mexico. State officials rarely imagined the Amerindian populations as enemies per se, but they did view these communities as a hindrance to national progress. As such, officialist thinkers confronted the "threats" of indigeneity through paternalistic works that generally essentialized native cultures and knowing. For this reason, representations of the posthuman tended to justify mestizo interventions in indigenous communities that sought to resolve the "Indian Problem" without dialoguing with the very people they aimed to uplift. Because official discourses held that the inevitable conversion of Mexico's native population into mestizos was the key element of national progress, officialist artists imbued their posthuman creations with messianic qualities. Nevertheless, the domineering attitudes that informed official mestizaje—whose implementation in society would relegate indigenous peoples and cultures to the periphery—lurked beneath the surface of their apparent benignity.

It is for this reason that, while I recognize Donna Haraway's argument that cyborg identity can greatly amend the performative identities of the body, I stop short of espousing the notion that technologized bodies eliminate constructs of race and gender. Instead, the posthuman figures that I have considered frequently reinforce notions of race and gender even as they articulate these aspects of corporeal identity in ways that go against previously held, prerevolutionary notions of performativity. Rather than usher in a utopian (post)humanity that exists free from the biases of contemporary humanity, it seems more precise to argue that technological hybridity provided a new means for imagining and organizing economies and societies around the national (mestizo) body. It is for this reason that a study of the posthuman in postrevolutionary Mexico elucidates the modernity-driven projects of racial miscegenation that lasted through the 1970s and into the 1980s. Postrevolutionary artists and thinkers constantly returned to the technologically hybrid body to discuss official mestizaje. Given this fact, far from existing on the fringe of Mexican studies, posthumanism should take up greater prominence in the field. The converse is also true; as posthuman theory explains certain aspects of postrevolutionary cultural nationalism, the singularities of the Mexican context signal new ways of thinking about posthuman theory in general. One of the most salient findings of this project is that official representations of posthuman bodies interfaced with the reigning paradigms of race, gender, and nation, yet they were hardly liberatory from a social justice point of view. On the one hand, this observation undercuts much of the optimism that many early cyborg theorists like Haraway attributed to the technologized body. On the other hand, it seems self-evident that the simple act of amending performative aspects of the body is not necessarily liberatory. That said, it is important to note that state-sponsored artists tended to see themselves as champions—not oppressors—of the masses. Emilio "El Indio" Fernández, for example, dreamed of a world free from caciques who took advantage of and abused the nation's Amerindians. However, as he imagined a mestizo utopia, he necessarily silenced indigenous voices, and his discourse contributed to the continued oppression of indigenous peoples and societies. Similar observations hold true regarding José Vasconcelos, the muralists, and even El Santo.

Discourses of technological and racial hybridity appeared across a wide array of political ideologies, but in each case they produced a problematic understanding of indigenous Mexico. My book has shown that the postrevolutionary conflation of racial hybridity with modernity reached across ideological lines. Figures like José Vasconcelos, Manuel Gamio, Emilio "El Indio" Fernández, Diego Rivera, José Clemente Orozco, and David Alfaro Siqueiros certainly did not share the same political persuasions—indeed, even rightists like Vasconcelos and Gamio held at times irreconcilable worldviews. Yet all of them engaged the technologically hybrid body at some level, ascribing it a utopian, even spiritual value that would usher in indigenous "redemption" through mestizaje. Despite—or perhaps because of—this optimism, postrevolutionary thinkers often favored programs of internal empire. This led to a palpable ambivalence as the very people who championed indigenista projects were the most vocal opponents of foreign incursions into Mexican territory. No example of state-sponsored cultural production surpasses the hypocrisy inherent to ambivalent projects of internal empire more than the films of El Santo, whose work represented one of the last incarnations of state-supported representations of mexicanidad.

The fact that Mexican artists and directors created a homegrown, posthuman, mestizo superhero who could defend his country against both indigenous and imperial threats is especially interesting as we consider how posthuman identities constructed and reflected midcentury thought. The notion of internal colonialism as a form of imitation rings especially clearly in chapter 4, but it is a key, underlying theme in chapters 1–3 as well. Vasconcelos, the muralists, and Fernández were highly critical of U.S. attempts to intervene within their country's borders even as they attempted to incorporate indigenous Mexico through coerced assimilation. Given this fact, one could argue that, beyond putting forward their competing representations of the posthuman, postrevolutionary Mexican artists and intellectuals also frequently employed morally ambivalent discourses of colonial mimicry. This finding, while perhaps unsurprising, underscores the fact that posthuman and technologically hybrid identities can be at times enslaving. In the end, statist attempts to mark indigenous and female bodies with technology reflected a desire to de-Indianize the population and transform it—both genetically and culturally—into a mestizo entity.

In no place was the desire to incorporate the indigenous masses more visible than in the muralist movement, which largely set the tone for the expressions of cultural nationalism that followed. Certainly, the main protagonists of the movement were hardly monolithic. Diego Rivera, José Clemente Orozco, and David Alfaro Siqueiros all ascribed to some form of Marxist thought, but they differed from each other ideologically—at times violently—in many ways. Rivera, for example, was an unapologetic Trotskyite, while Siqueiros sided with Stalin after Lenin's death. When Trotsky found hospice in Rivera's home after Stalin took power, Siqueiros, on orders from Moscow, orchestrated a failed assassination attempt on the former Soviet leader (Fulton 69–71). Not surprisingly, the political differences between these figures extended beyond the brand of Marxism that each preferred and into how they conceived the ideal articulation of mestizo subjectivity. Each muralist afforded indigenous Mexico a slightly different role within the modern state. Rivera espoused—and largely constructed—postrevolutionary ideals of indigenismo. In his works, Amerindian peasants and proletarians took power by seizing control of the (high-tech) modes of production within their country while at the same time demonstrating a supposedly autochthonous and indigenous approach to technology. For his part, Orozco emphasized notions of hispanismo that tended to justify the conquering, European component of mestizo identity (Rochfort

46; Swarthout 75–76). The muralists were not the only people who used the visual arts to construct and critique the national body politics; artists like Frida Kahlo challenged gendered discourses of power through self-portraits that emphasized female ties to both (medical) technology and nature. Muralism may have set the standard for didactic, official discourses, but geographical limitations confined its ability to reach people living beyond the urban center. It was for this reason that the state invested in film as another mouthpiece of official ideals.

Not all postrevolutionary artists and letrados—or politicians for that matter—agreed with every aspect of state-sponsored representations of official mestizaje. Most dissented from the official line from time to time, and their rebuttals showed up in their cultural production. For example, Dolores Tierney reminds us that much of "El Indio's" cinema undermines officialist notions of Mexican national identity (*Emilio Fernández* 2–3). That said, a belief in the modernizing effect of technology on the body united postrevolutionary thinkers (both mestizo and criollo) from all over the political spectrum. Each artist imagined the technologized body in ways that reverberated with his or her own worldview, but they all produced surprisingly coherent versions of a technologically hybrid mestizaje and modernity. Perhaps the most surprising fact about these representations of posthumanity is the fact that none of the cultural producers of this study was privy to the work of Donna Haraway. Indeed, with the possible exception of Olvera and El Santo, none of these artists had even heard of a cybernetic organism, because the scientific community had not yet coined the term. Nevertheless, these thinkers' work clearly shows that the juxtaposition of technology with the body reconstituted how society interpellated racial and gender identities onto individuals. Viewed in this light, my book contributes to current debates of posthumanism and Latin American studies by inviting students and scholars to consider the effects of technological hybridity in societies that predate the earliest academic theorizations of cyborg identity.

Most studies of Latin American cyborg identity focus on literary and cultural production from the late twentieth and early twenty-first centuries (Brown, *Cyborgs*; Hoeg 95–107).[8] As I noted in chapter 3, Jerry Hoeg imagines a cyber-mestiza that resists rigid interpellations of the body and thus undermines traditional notions of performativity (99). J. Andrew Brown's book *Cyborgs in Latin America* theorizes the Spanish American cyborg body as a site for negotiating both the traumas inherent to postdictatorial society and the continued oppression of the neoliberal order. Both studies of the posthuman differ from mine in that they consider literature and cultural production from throughout post-neoliberal Latin America. Given that their focus on the cyborg deals almost entirely with recent literature, their theorizations fit more neatly within the framework of the robo sacer that I discussed earlier in this chapter than with the entity that official thinkers invoked for nation-building projects. Certainly, there are differences between the cyborgs that Brown and Hoeg discuss and the robo sacer; neither critic explicitly views the cyborg through a biopolitical lens, for example. That said, the resistant nature of technological hybridity remains at the core of their work. In the end, these studies deal less with notions of race construction and more with the cyborg body's ability to resist and undermine traditional structures of power. The focus on a region rather than a single nation-state facilitates both critics' attempts to broadly theorize the role of cyborg identity in constructing twenty-first-century human being in Latin America. My own focus on Mexico complements these earlier studies as it allows us to view the role of the cyborg body across space and time in constructing racial and gender identities in a single country.

My focus on Mexico has allowed me to flesh out similarities in the thought of people whose work seems antithetical at first glance. It would have been difficult to show that the discursive significance of the technologized body reverberated across the thought of figures from all over the political spectrum if I had not focused on a single country. Nevertheless, because Mexico is only one of many Latin American nation-states that underwent social upheaval in the twentieth century, this focus also by necessity ignores how discourses of technological hybridity may have played out in other parts of the region. Latin America's turbulent twentieth century included a revolution in Cuba, decades of terrorism and violence in Colombia and Peru, and military dictatorships in the Southern Cone, Central America, and the Caribbean. Given this shared trauma and the need for national reconciliation, a focus on state-sponsored representations of the technologized body may also shed light on the nature of twentieth-century nationhood and modernity throughout Latin America. The postrevolutionary Mexican government aimed to incorporate indigenous bodies into the modern, mestizo state to ameliorate class and race-based grievances. The similarities among these cases suggest that other Latin American countries may have also used the technologized body for nation-building. My theorizations may even inform approaches beyond Latin America and illuminate conditions in other developing countries that have faced the dilemma of embracing Westernized modernity or maintaining their cultural heritage. It would be interesting to see what insights a study on race formation and cyborg identity may provide within other contexts both inside and beyond Latin America. Mexico is not alone in negotiating such difficult concepts as modernity, race, and equality.

While these suggestions for further research signal fascinating avenues of study for future projects, the primary focus of the present study has been on how state officials within Mexico used the technologized body as a tool for nation-building. This study has shown that, as scientific and technological discourses interact with and are inscribed upon the body, their union creates new structures of performativity that affect the day-to-day lives of those who live within a given society. As postrevolutionary artists and letrados employed posthuman discourses in their work, they suggested new strategies for modernization. Within the Mexican context, notions of modernity became inextricably tied to official mestizaje, which in turn evoked both eugenics and technological hybridity. This focus on scientific discourse as a technology of power sheds light on the ways in which discourses of domination can be presented as supposedly unbiased, self-evident "truths." Although the articulation and the ramifications of the technologized body change depending on the context, this entity almost always signals the possibility of domination or liberation. The solution, of course, is not to become antiscientific; instead, it is to critically gauge all forms of knowledge, especially those that project an aura of self-evident infallibility. As the Mexican case indicates, technology and science are not oppressive of their own accord; they take on a domineering nature only when those in power articulate them in ways that oppress marginalized peoples and cultures.

In the coming years, Mexican society will face new challenges as innovations in the sciences, technology, and medicine change the way that people—both within the country and beyond—lead their lives. As these new technologies are inscribed upon the national body, they will necessarily interact with and amend the country's identitarian discourses by interfacing with the reigning biopolitics. Viewed alongside this reality, it becomes especially necessary that more people consider the ways in which science constructs agency within Mexico (and beyond). Science and technology, for better and for worse, are forever enshrined in contemporary society. Authors, artists, playwrights, and film directors will continue to imagine—at times deliberately, and at others unconsciously—how the juxtaposition of the body with technology informs human being in a specific historical moment. The future may remain to be written, but as this study shows, one thing is certain: the technologically hybrid body will, in its myriad forms, continue to provide avenues from which to (re)consider notions of race, gender, and national citizenship in Mexico.

Notes

Introduction: (Re)Constructing the Racialized Body through Technology

1. All translations are mine unless otherwise indicated.

2. For further studies that tie mestizo identity to modernity, see Pedro Ángel Palou (13–37), Mary K. Vaughan and Stephen E. Lewis (1–20), and Kelley R. Swarthout (52–66).

3. Beyond the categories of *indígena*, criollo, and mestizo, Mexico has also inherited a vibrant culture from people of African descent. See Bobby Vaughn (118–33).

4. Throughout this study I use the term "race formation" rather than "racial formation."

5. Nineteenth-century constructs of mestizaje tended to emphasize ties to Europe and to ignore the country's indigenous and African heritage. See Lomnitz (*Exits from the Labyrinth* 262–80) and Thomas B. Irving (xii).

6. For discussions on how the state employed people of indigenous descent in its attempts to carry out projects of education and medicine in indigenous communities (particularly in Chiapas), see Laurent Corbeil (60) and William Robert Holland (214).

7. We should note that the modernism that García Canclini refers to has nothing to do with *modernismo*, a literary movement that spanned from the late nineteenth century into the twentieth century.

8. I use the term technological hybridity to denote the process of fusing the body with technology in its myriad forms: factory work, medicine, industrial agriculture, education, and so forth. In many ways, technological hybridity is synonymous with cyborg identity; both emerge from the juxtaposition of the body with technology, and as I explain later in this chapter, both amend the reigning body politics.

9. Racial hybridity here refers to reproduction between indigenous and mestizo/criollo parents.

10. While I do not mention it here, gender hybridity appears in many Mexican works. Of particular interest is the art of Frida Kahlo, which deconstructs rigid divisions of masculinity and femininity.

11. As Rick A. López points out, this inferiority complex extended to mestizo society as well: "The worthiness of the European side of this equation [national identity] seemed self-evident. But the indigenous side still needed validation" (36).

12. Alan Knight asserts that revolutionary discourse was more class-based than racial ("Racism" 76). He further argues that any assertion of the Revolution as the moment when indigenous Mexico achieved consciousness comes in retrospect.

13. According to Henry C. Schmidt, terms like mexicanidad, *lo mexicano*, "Mexicanness," and "Mexicanism" are used in an attempt to create a cohesive nation-state. Generally speaking, these terms extend a privileged position to Mexico's indigenous history (and resulting mestizaje) as a counterpoint to European influences (*Roots* 34–37). During the postrevolutionary period, the search for *lo mexicano* became a strategy not only for opposing Europe, but also for "keep[ing] the reaction on its guard" (68). See also Joseph and Henderson (9) and Alexandra Stern (2–4).

14. For a discussion of the role of radio in constructing a postrevolutionary consciousness, see Justin Castro (105–95) and Elena Jackson Albarrán (129–74).

15. Mary K. Vaughan and Stephen E. Lewis's edited volume *The Eagle and the Virgin: Nation and Cultural Revolution in Mexico, 1920–1940* contains numerous essays that discuss different ways in which the state manipulated popular culture to propagate myths of mestizaje through cultural nationalism.

16. Ruben Flores recognizes the legitimate criticisms of *indigenismo* but also argues that "rather than simply being a colonialist discourse through which to control Indians by orientalizing them," the movement also provided a means for critiquing state overreach, particularly regarding its shortcomings vis-à-vis the indigenous population (85).

17. The shifts within the Mexican literary community from 1917 to 1959 compose the subject matter of Sánchez Prado's book *Naciones intelectuales: Las fundaciones de la modernidad literaria mexicana (1917–1959)*.

18. Broadly educated individuals ceded their privileged position in government to specially trained technocrats in the 1960s. However, these new leaders often showed an even greater commitment than their forbears to positing mixed-race—or, perhaps more precisely, nonindigenous—identity as the "authentic" articulation of mexicanidad. Dolores Pla Burgat demonstrates this fact when she notes that the postrevolutionary government used linguistic and cultural indicators—and even self-identification—to identify citizens as Amerindian until the 1960s. After seizing power in the 1970s, however, state technocrats changed the self-identification policies and chose to count only those people who spoke indigenous languages as anything other than mestizo/criollo. By doing this, the state drastically lowered the official count of Amerindians living within its borders despite the fact that its demographic composition had changed very little.

19. Within the philosophical realm, the thinker Andrés Molina Enríquez had already written *Grandes problemas nacionales*, a book that both discussed the social obstacles to Mexican progress and also posited the eventual "triumph" of mestizaje both in Mexico and throughout the world.

20. Thomas S. Kuhn defines science as a process in which falsifiable observations are organized into paradigms (*Structure* 10–11). Because these paradigms are ultimately human constructs, the cultural factors within a specific society necessarily affect how scientific knowledge is transmitted, articulated, and executed ("Objectivity" 387).

21. A debate raged within scientific circles in postrevolutionary Mexico about whether to adopt a paradigm of Mendelian or Lamarckian genetics. Nancy Leys Stepan cites José Rulfo as the first scientist to bring a Mendelian approach to national genetics during the 1930s and 1940s (57). What is more, she notes that Mexico was the only Latin American country to legalize sterilizations (albeit briefly), but this was as much an affront to the political clout of the Catholic Church as it was a profession of eugenic beliefs (112–13).

22. Andy Clark furthers Gray's assertion when he states that cyborg identity—which he terms as "cognitive hybridization"—is nothing new. Instead, he traces the "cognitive fossil trail" at least as far back as language acquisition (4), a fact that suggests that humans have been cyborgs since prehistoric times.

23. In chapter 2 I discuss readings by Chris Hables Gray and J. Andrew Brown that view Diego Rivera's *Pan-American Unity* from a posthuman angle.

24. Although Potter traces the "technified muse" across the twentieth century, she notes that it reappears in Mexican narrative in dramatic fashion near the end of the twentieth century. This reflects the fact that estridentista literature—though not necessarily art—was largely erased from the national consciousness until the 1980s. See Rashkin and Zurián (309–33).

25. Williams argues that Agamben's "metaphysics of sovereign exceptionality" fails to account for the "historical specificity" of the postrevolutionary period (10).

26. Although Haraway proclaims a cyborgian end to biopolitics, her own writing has proven foundational in the work of the Italian biopolitical theorist Roberto Esposito.

27. Jennifer Parker-Starbuck notes other intersectionalities of discourses that contribute to cyborg identities such as those "of popular culture, science, technology, medicine, and other fields" (7).

28. Significantly, Anzaldúa's U.S. appropriation of Vasconcelian thought was much more inclusive than its forbear, so mestizo discourses in the United States tend to lack the imperial nature inherent to its articulation within Mexico.

29. For in-depth discussions of how the mythic union of la Malinche with Cortés has affected Mexican understandings of race and sexuality, see Sandra M. Cypess (*Malinche* 1–14; *Uncivil Wars* 31), Octavio Paz (*Labyrinth of Solitude* 65–88), Jean Franco (*Plotting Women* xviii–xix, 131–32), and Gerald Martin (8–13).

30. Bartra questions this narrative when he refers to the cosmic race as "a pathetic mascarade [sic] of sentimental *machismo*" (*Cage* 104). He later asks, "What future can a country have when its national conscience seems to capsize tragically in the stormy waters of progress and modernization?" (*Cage* 104).

31. For Robert Doede, transhumanism is the self-conscious effort of humanity to transcend *Homo sapiens* (225).

Chapter 1. Science and the (Meta)Physical Body: A Critique of Positivism in the Vasconcelian Utopia

1. Fell's book *José Vasconcelos: Los años del águila* discusses Vasconcelos's cultural missions in rigorous detail. See also Joaquín Cárdenas Noriega (59–99).

2. Vasconcelos created numerous political enemies during his time in the government. See John Skirius (92–109).

3. While I focus primarily on the thinker's relationship with the indigenous population in this chapter, Vasconcelos was equally racist against blacks. For a discussion of Vasconcelos's racism against Afro-Mexicans, see Marco Polo Hernández (70–74).

4. Henry C. Schmidt ("Power and Sensibility" 178) states that positivism remained in force in rural areas following the Revolution; however, urban centers began to repudiate it during these years.

5. Hoeg builds on the work of Antonio Benítez Rojo, who asserts an "over there" within Caribbean tradition that can be either repressive or liberating. Whereas Benítez Rojo refers principally to racial identities (290), Hoeg extends the definition to explain science's problematic role in Vasconcelian thought.

6. Acosta Rico notes that Vasconcelos turns to ancient Greece in an attempt to emphasize his metaphysical preoccupations over the positivistic (22–24). Hernán G. H. Taboada, however, disagrees, noting that much of Vasconcelos's aesthetics resulted from his time in Asia, which was another region with a great mestizo tradition (112).

7. Zum Felde mentions in passing that Vasconcelos included science in the curriculum, but he never reconciles this with the thinker's antipositivism.

8. Tace Hedrick notes that Vasconcelos and Gamio often worked together, with the latter becoming undersecretary of the SEP (39–40). Ana María Alonso also asserts a great deal of ideological common ground between them (466–69).

9. For a list of scholars who link Vasconcelos to early Latin Americanism, see Ignacio M. Sánchez Prado ("Mestizaje" 381–97), Ana María Introna (97–125), Germán Posada 379–81, Carlos Real de Azúa (23), and Zea (*Precursores* 118).

10. The threat of Anglo-Saxon imperialism was a major element in Vasconcelos's early writings. See Regina Crespo (252–54) and Fernando Vizcaíno ("Repensando" 196–98). Indeed, Vasconcelos argued in his book ¿Qué es el comunismo? (1936) that the Spanish Republic would have ushered in the ultimate destruction of the Anglo-Saxon race and the exaltation of Hispanic society if it had not been impeded by the communist elements in their ranks (91–92).

11. Monsiváis sees Vasconcelos as a figure who began on the left—he was one of Madero's biggest supporters—but who would ultimately "exalt" fascist regimes following his devastating electoral defeat in 1929 ("Notas" 356).

12. For an in-depth discussion on how Vasconcelos's failed presidential run wore him down, see John W. Sherman (23) and José Joaquín Blanco (146–68).

13. One of the principal features of Vasconcelos's cultural missions was the plays—generally European—that actors from Mexico City would take to rural, indigenous parts of the country. Indeed, authors like Elena Garro eventually wrote plays like *La dama boba* (1968) that metatheatrically criticized the paternalistic nature of these dramatic representations. My article "Imaginando comunidades en tensión: Elena Garro y el indigenismo" discusses this play in depth.

14. Given that Satan regrets destroying Jesus (35–37), his animosity toward Jehovah may foreshadow Vasconcelos's later anti-Semitism. See Héctor Orestes Águilar (154–56) and Miriam Jerade Dana (274).

15. Depending on his political inclinations on a given day, Vasconcelos would either ignore the indigenous component of Mexican identity (*Breve historia*) or accentuate it (*Indología*). See Ilán Stavans (4, 14) and Marilyn Grace Miller (40–44).

16. Vasconcelos's espousal of platonic views of the body caused him to adopt fascist ideals later in life. In his essay "La B-H" ["The Hydrogen Bomb"], for example, he asserts that he would prefer to see humanity annihilated through nuclear war than for the world to adopt a Soviet-style "slavery" (970).

17. Beyond their allusions to posthuman theory, the oppositional fates of the Anglo-Saxon and mestizo worlds invoke the binary of "Lo absoluto," and "La nada," the two Bergsonian poles of human experience (Vasconcelos, "Bergson" 243–47).

Chapter 2. Painting *Mestizaje* in a New Light: Racial, Technological, and Cultural Hybridity in the Murals of Diego Rivera and José Clemente Orozco

1. Horacio Legrás documents the attempts of Vasconcelos and his Ateneo colleagues to construct an ethical state. See "El Ateneo y los orígenes del estado ético en México."

2. For in-depth studies on Vasconcelos's ties to the muralist movement, see David Craven (*Art and Revolution* 34–37), Leonard Folgarait (16–20), Desmond Rochfort (23), Elisa García Barragán (94–98), Juan Diego Caballero Oliver (11–12), Stephen Polcari (38), Cecilia Belej (6), Indira Sánchez-López (68), and Ida Rodríguez Prampolini (178–80).

3. Numerous studies have discussed at length how Mexican visual culture became the preferred means for discussing and promulgating discourses of mexicanidad. See Theresa Avila (220–22), John Lear (237–43), Rochfort (20–21), Mary K. Coffey (*How a Revolutionary Art* 1–24), and Octavio Paz (*Labyrinth of Solitude* 151–56).

4. The muralists were such important cultural icons that their work appears in cultural histories directed even at children throughout the world. For a few examples, see Sheila Wood Foard (*The Great Hispanic Heritage*) and James Olés (*Diego Rivera, David Alfaro Siqueiros, José Clemente Orozco*).

5. Rivera did not participate in this particular event, but he later expressed his indebtedness to Murillo in his autobiography, *My Art, My Life* (47–49).

6. Samuel Ramos notes Rivera's invocation of the "authentic" national landscape (*Diego Rivera* 13), and a quick inspection of the works of other muralists—particularly Orozco—shows that the same holds true for them. Chapter 3 discusses the cinematography of Gabriel Figueroa, a cameraman who credited the muralists with inspiring his work.

7. According to Robin Adèle Greeley ("Muralism" 19), the muralist movement took a decidedly left turn after Vasconcelos left power.

8. There were limits to the artistic freedom that Vasconcelos was willing to grant. As Leticia López Orozco notes, he destroyed the murals of Gerardo Murillo (257).

9. New generations of scholars have been less critical of Rivera's willingness to work with political rivals than were his contemporaries. Rochfort claims that the artist used his platform within the government to support socialist policy without antagonizing Mexican leaders (51). Alberto Híjar Serrano argues that "even his skids to the Right" were pragmatic moves that allowed him to continue to uphold his socialist aesthetic (638).

10. Rochfort cements the apparent separation of racial and technological discourse in Rivera and Orozco's work by dedicating one chapter to their racial ideals (83–120) and another to their approach to technology (121–60). Interestingly, he never discusses how these ideals were intertwined.

11. Fearing he would offend U.S. puritanical attitudes if he included genitalia on his nudes, for example, Orozco painted the protagonist of his mural *Prometheus* at Pomona College in Los Angeles (1930) as a eunuch (Cordero Reiman 116–17).

12. Many critics have noted that Mexican muralism played a foundational role in twentieth-century Latin American art (Traba, *Art of Latin America*; Lombán 15; Goldman 123–26; Carpita 435–45; Jaimes 19), mainstream U.S. art (Polcari 37–39; Olés 1–7; Dickerman 22; Pitol 188), and Chicano/a art (Daniel D. Arreola 410; Goldman 126–31). Many recent studies have shown how Mexican muralism reached beyond the Western Hemisphere to places like

Sweden (Falkman 389–93) and even Japan (Kato 247–54). See López Orozco (262–67) for an in-depth discussion about the cross-pollination that occurred among artists throughout the world as a result of the muralist movement.

13. The success of the murals in explaining national identity was imperfect, especially at first, because the art-viewing public misunderstood and rejected the murals due to their purported ugliness (Romera Velasco 421).

14. For a comparison and contrast of Mexican *estridentismo* with futurism, see Elissa Rashkin (*Stridentist* 2–4).

15. For a short list of recent studies that tend to conflate muralist aesthetics with indigenismo, see Anna Indych-López (*Muralism without Walls* 2), Guzmán Urrero (20), Itzel Rodríguez Mortellaro (51–59), and Carlos Alberto Gámez R. and Diego Quintero (83–84).

16. For a discussion on the problematic tendency to conflate Rivera's work and words with the muralist movement in general, see Coffey ("State Ritual" 349–50). Not all critics view the muralist movement as solely indigenista. Swarthout asserts that Orozco's work was hispanista, while several others have argued that it is a struggle to place him as either indigenista or hispanista (Rochfort 30; Reyes Palma 222–23; Mandel 48–50). Writing at the height of the muralist movement, MacKinley Helm stated that Orozco's principal motivation was quality art, regardless of ideology (*Modern Mexican Painters* 82). Itzel Rodríguez even asserts a certain level of indigenismo in Orozco's U.S. mural *Épica de la civilización americana* (1932–1934). However, this mural is less a treatise on racial miscegenation and more a tragic history about the series of conquests that have plagued the Americas since pre-Columbian times, and it suggests that Amerindians deserved to be conquered due to the practice of human sacrifice.

17. Greeley argues that much of the diversity of political opinions in the murals resulted from neglect from state leaders. See "Muralism and the State" (22–23).

18. Orozco followed Dr. Atl into war, siding with Carranza (Olés 38), where he witnessed the executions of many zapatistas (Charlot 149–50). Thus Orozco—unlike many postrevolutionary intellectuals—not only participated in the armed conflict, but he did so for the most conservative revolutionary faction. See Joyce Waddell Bailey (79, 85) and Jean Charlot (149–50).

19. For a list of critics who view the *Hombre en llamas* series as Orozco's seminal work, see David W. Scott ("Prometheus Revisited" 27), Desmond Rochfort (99), Roderic Ai Camp (69), Juan Carlos Lombán (18), Stephen Polcari (45), and John Palmer Leeper (xxiii).

20. Baas's argument is especially pertinent to the *Hombre en llamas* series because, as Coffey points out ("Angels" 191–92), Orozco's Dartmouth murals served as the inspiration for the later *Hombre en llamas* series.

21. Rivera's most controversial mural was his work at the Rockefeller Center, where he included an homage to Vladimir Lenin that his patrons summarily destroyed. The artist repainted the mural at the Palacio de Bellas Artes as *El hombre controlador del universo*, and he severely criticized both Stalin and the Rockefellers. See Dora Apel (58; see also 57–71) and William Richardson (55–57).

22. One of Rivera's greatest innovations was to paint murals on portable platforms (Aviram and Albertson 126–28), which made it possible to transport them to different venues. Even so, his artwork remained largely confined to a single space; certainly, it could never reach people in rural sectors of Mexico or the United States.

23. There is obviously a degree of overlap between his work in both countries. Anna In-

dych-López, for example, discusses indigenista imageries in his U.S. painting *Guerrero indio* (1931) ("Plates" 52), while at the same time noting his technological imageries in his SEP murals ("Technology" 283–99). However, she does not attempt to reconcile Rivera's technophilia with his indigenismo.

24. The painter constantly included his many lovers in his art. See Dina Comisarenco Mirkin ("Diosas y madres" 192) and Alberto Híjar Serrano (639).

25. Chapters 3 and 4 deal more explicitly with programs of internal empire in Mexico.

26. The charge that the state failed to extend medical care to the masses was certainly not universal among officialist literary and cultural producers. As we shall see in chapter 3, Emilio Fernández celebrated state medical projects that purportedly modernized indigenous Mexicans.

Chapter 3. Emilio Fernández, Gabriel Figueroa, and the Race for Mexico's Body: Immunization and Lamarckian Genetics

1. For a list of studies that link the director and cinematographer to the muralist movement, see Daniel Chávez ("Alta modernidad" 163), Carlos García Benítez ("Construcción"), Emilio García Riera (*Emilio* 108–9), Evan Lieberman and Kerry Hegarty (33), John Mraz (107–8, 110), Daniel Cuitláhuac Peña Rodríguez and Vicente Castellanos (2–3), and Gloria Tuñón ("Emilio Fernández" 185).

2. Numerous scholars have noted the formal elements of Golden Age Mexican film that separated it from Hollywood. See Charles Ramírez-Berg ("Figueroa's Skies" 28–30; "Cinematic Invention" 15–17), Lieberman and Hegarty (35–48), and Héctor Villarreal ("La cinematografía" 4). It is somewhat ironic, then, that the Mexican national cinema also depended on U.S. markets—particularly Latino viewers in the United States—for its commercial success. See Maricruz Castro Ricalde and Robert McKee Irwin (265).

3. A document I uncovered in the SEP archives shows that Mexican officials consciously emulated fascist Italy's propaganda in their own attempt to construct a national identity (Secretaría de Educación Pública [México] 1–2).

4. For a list of scholars who view Fernández as a purveyor of statist doctrines, see Mraz (107–8), Carl J. Mora (78), Erica Segre (87–94), Ernesto R. Acevedo-Muñoz (24–25), and Liz Consuelo Rangel (63).

5. While *María Candelaria* and *Río Escondido* were filmed within only four years of each other, official versions of mexicanidad shifted greatly during these years. See Anne Doremus (376, 396).

6. For readings about Porfirian and postrevolutionary hygiene and medicine campaigns, see Ana María Kapelusz-Poppi ("Rural Health" 261–67), Claudia Agostoni (461), and María Rosa Gudiño-Cejudo, Laura Magaña-Valladares, and Mauricio Hernández Ávila (84).

7. Rural teachers often functioned as the primary disseminators of hygienic practices. See Alan Knight ("Popular Culture" 413).

8. Of Fernández's films, several critics classify only *María Candelaria*, *La perla*, and *Maclovia* as indigenista (Tierney 75; Martínez Gómez 271). Nevertheless, *Río Escondido* is perhaps Fernández's most indigenista film of all because it explicitly preaches indigenous redemption through modernization and assimilation.

9. See chapter 2 for a more in-depth discussion on how Agamben's thought applies to postrevolutionary constructs of official mestizaje.

10. Gray bases many of his concerns on now-discredited evidence that seemed to link vaccinations to health problems like autism. Nevertheless, his underlying argument about the tension between individual liberty and the common good remains largely unscathed. For a study refuting the supposed connection between autism and vaccinations, see Kreesten Meldgaard Madsen et al. (1477–84).

11. Claudia Agostoni notes that many state-funded medics struggled to vaccinate an indigenous population that did not want medication (463–65); to extend hygiene throughout the country, they turned to both force and persuasion—an end it often achieved through state-sponsored film.

12. According to Fernando Mino Gracia, Diego Rivera severely criticized Fernández for postulating an indigenous population with bourgeois values; however, the artist probably erred on the side of essentialization (122). That said, Fernández aimed to produce mythic, and not necessarily "true," representations of Mexican indigeneity.

13. Ana M. López argues that, far from opening new spaces for female performativity, Félix's type-cast characters are "simply the vampiresque flip-side of the saintly mothers of the family melodramas" (450).

14. Sandra M. Cypess reminds us that the trope of la Malinche pertains to all Mexican women regardless of race (*Malinche* 155). The film, then, emphasizes that Mercedes's "primitive" status results not from her racial identity, but from her supposedly deviant gender performativity.

15. Benito Juárez's preference for mestizaje influenced his policy decisions. As James D. Cockcroft notes, the president aligned himself with the mixed-race and criollo bourgeoisie over the indigenous peasants and proletariat (80–81).

16. Several scholars have documented state attempts to teach healthy cooking. See Oresta López Pérez (259–61) and Sandra Aguilar Rodríguez ("Cooking" 182; "Alimentando" 29–33).

17. José Juan's love interest is named Beatriz in *Enamorada* and María Dolores in *The Torch*. I choose to call her Miss Peñafiel in this study to emphasize her marital status and because she acts in much the same way in both films.

18. According to García Riera (*Emilio* 193), *Enamorada* held its own against the highly successful *Cantinflas: Soy un prófugo* in the Mexican box office.

19. Miss Peñafiel's North American fiancé is an engineer named Eduardo Roberts in *Enamorada* and a medic named Edward Roberts in *The Torch*. In both cases, the character represents U.S. scientific prowess and the money that accompanies it.

20. Doris Sommer views heterosexual romantic relationships in Latin American fiction as allegories for nation-building, modernization, and the reconciliation of disparate sectors of society (30–51).

21. Perhaps due to misgivings about how the U.S. public would react to a movie that glorified the man who infamously invaded New Mexico, the director never films José Juan as a *villista* in *The Torch*.

22. Robert McCaa disagrees that influenza caused more deaths than any other factor during the decade of the Revolution, and he argues instead that the rampant violence amplified the virus's effect (395).

23. Certainly, the *federales* and the carrancistas were two very different groups. However,

the film's focus on tempering the demands of the zapatistas implicitly buoys those who eventually came to power.

Chapter 4. Colonizing Resistance: Liminal Imperiality in the Cinema of El Santo and in Carlos Olvera's *Mejicanos en el espacio*

1. Poniatowska's testimonial book, *La noche de Tlatelolco* (1971), speaks out against the state for ordering the murders.

2. For an extensive discussion of PRI abuses of power between the 1950s and 1970s, see Gareth Williams (118–24).

3. Many critics are now asserting that PRI-sponsored state violence is not something from the past; indeed, Jacqueline E. Bixler notes certain similarities between Tlatelolco and the 2014 massacre of forty-three unarmed students in Ayotzinapa (203–4).

4. Mexploitation is a term used to denote Mexican exploitation cinema, which is known for its low budgets and weak aesthetics. Many of these movies were dubbed into English and exported to the United States, where to this day they enjoy a cult status as entertaining "bad" movies (Syder and Tierney 50; Greene 1–3). In this chapter I use the terms "*Mexploitation*" and "lucha libre cinema" interchangeably.

5. Not everyone agrees with Sánchez Prado's negative characterization of *Mejicanos*; Ramón López Castro (122–24), for example, lauds the film as an entertaining and timely addition to Mexico's SF tradition.

6. Mexploitation was certainly not the only cinematic movement to follow the Golden Age. Some directors, like Luis Buñuel, severely criticized the postrevolutionary state. See Acevedo-Muñoz.

7. See Andrew Syder and Dolores Tierney (42), Tiziana Bertaccini (88–89), Jorge del Pozo Marx (185–86), and Carlos Monsiváis ("De lucha libre" 6).

8. Not surprisingly, Mexploitation cinema became heavily associated with "naco" tropes and imageries. See Adán Avalos (189).

9. According to Rafael Aviña ("Ring"), Wolf Rufinskis was the most well-known unmasked wrestler to star in Mexploitation films.

10. The original Frankenstein appears in Mary Shelley's novel of the same name, but the character probably made its way into Mexploitation cinema by way of Hollywood.

11. The original Spanish uses the term "mezcla de sangres," which means "mixture of blood" (Vasconcelos, *Raza* 16).

12. Armando Bartra notes that El Santo often asserted ties to the Virgin of Guadalupe in his *fotomontajes* (63). His invocation of the Virgin became less obvious as he transitioned to film, but the idea of divine intervention runs across his cinema.

13. For a discussion of cyborg superheroes in the U.S. tradition, see Mark Oelhert (219–32).

14. We have already identified Irving Frankenstein as a European scientist who uses his knowledge to enslave innocent (mestizo) Mexicans. See also *Santo y Blue Demon contra los monstruos*.

15. Andrew Syder and Dolores Tierney note that the Aztec mummy posed a mystical threat in other Mexploitation films, such as *Las luchadoras contra la momia azteca* and *La momia azteca contra el robot humano* (39–40).

16. Patricia Cabrera López argues that *Mejicanos en el espacio* is one of two novels that Diógenes published in 1968 that was not overtly leftist (149). Her observation alludes to the fact that there was a heterogeneous opposition to the 1960s PRI that stretched across the political spectrum.

17. La Onda's irreverent, playful, and combative style has inspired a great deal of scholarship. For a brief list of important studies on la Onda, see Jean Franco (*Decline and Fall* 196–200), María Isela Chiu-Olivares (13–16), and Pedro Ángel Palou and Brian L. Price (*De perfiles: José Agustín ante la crítica*).

18. Beyond *Mejicanos en el espacio*, other works from la Onda, particularly José Agustín's *Abolición de la propiedad* (1969), use a science-fiction-esque narrative to challenge the dogmas of the state.

19. Gabriel Trujillo Muñoz identifies forty-three twentieth-century SF texts from Mexico that preceded *Mejicanos* (*Crónica* 271–73). The majority of these works are short stories, but a few of them are novels. In most cases, the authors were probably not aware of the fact that they were writing SF because that term did not exist until the 1930s.

20. To this day, the spelling "Méjico" is common throughout Spain.

21. In this section of the chapter, I use the term "Party" to refer to the political entity that controls Centroméjico, while the term PRI refers to the twentieth century Partido Revolucionario Institucional. Furthermore, I capitalize the term to emphasize the single-party nature of Centromexican politics.

22. Castellanos's texts that most masterfully show the nuance within the social hierarchies of Chiapas are her novel *Balún Canán* (1957) and her collection of short stories *Ciudad Real* (1960).

23. Demographic information from the United States and Mexico seems to uphold the imaginary of U.S. extermination of Native Americans and that of eventual miscegenation in Mexico. According to the CIA's *World Factbook*, Mexico is 60 percent mestizo and 30 percent indigenous, while the United States is approximately 1 percent Amerindian. That said, these numbers are misleading because mestizaje does not fit into the U.S. racial imaginary; as such, many people self-identify as white despite having indigenous ancestry. This artificially lowers the number of people counted as being of Native American descent in the United States.

24. Convergence is "the process whereby organisms not closely related (not monophyletic) independently evolve similar traits as a result of having to adapt to similar environments or ecological niches." See *Science Daily*.

Conclusion: The Legacy of the Modernization of the Body Today

1. Duncan Wood notes a disturbing relationship between the television station Televisa and the ruling PRI in recent years (98). Given this fact, one could conceivably look at certain telenovelas and even the news media as major distributors of official, pro-PRI discourses. Of course, the PRI was an opposition party—at least to the executive branch—during the first two administrations of the twenty-first century. As such, the collaboration between the PRI and Televisa cannot be classified as officialist until at least the election of Enrique Peña Nieto in 2012.

2. The state still subsidizes films, but it generally does so with fewer demands from directors than were imposed in previous epochs. Luis Estrada's *El infierno* (2010), for example, received government moneys, but it satirized the pomp associated with the bicentennial with a scathing rebuke of the country's handling of the drug war. See Sánchez Prado (*Screening*).

3. Journalists have cited many cases where indigenous women gave birth on hospital grounds (Briseño; "Otra mujer"; Pérez Alfonso).

4. See Quadratín/El Universal.

5. See El Piñero de la Cuenca.

6. The study further notes that indigenous women enjoy lower access to prenatal care than their mestiza counterparts, even after controlling for socioeconomic status. See Barber et al. (w318–19).

7. One could argue that the decision to withhold health care from indigenous mothers during childbirth represents a form of unconscious eugenics because the health care system allocates greater resources to the successful birth of mestizo children.

8. Several recent dissertations engage with the cyborg body. For examples, see Hernán Manuel García's "La globalización desfigurada o la post-globalización imaginada: La estética cyberpunk (post)mexicana" (2012), Sara Anne Potter's "Disturbing Muses: Gender, Technology and Resistance in Mexican Avant-Garde Cultures" (2013), Stephen Christopher Tobin's "Visual Dystopias from Mexico's Speculative Fiction: 1993–2008" (2015), and Alexander P. Shafer's "Queering Bodies: Aliens, Cyborgs, and Spacemen in Mexican and Argentine Science Fiction" (2017). Of these dissertations, only Potter's engages with notions of technological hybridity prior to the 1960s.

Works Cited

Acevedo-Muñoz, Ernesto R. *Buñuel and Mexico: The Crisis of National Cinema.* Berkeley: University of California Press, 2003.
Acosta, Abraham. *Thresholds of Illiteracy: Theory, Latin America, and the Crisis of Resistance.* New York: Fordham UP, 2014.
Acosta Rico, Fabián. *El pensamiento político de José Vasconcelos.* Guadalajara: Secretaría de Cultura de Jalisco, 2004.
Affron, Matthew. "Modern Art and Mexico, 1910–1950." In *Paint the Revolution: Mexican Modernism, 1910–1950*, ed. Matthew Affron, Mark A. Castro, Dafne Cruz Porchini, and Renato González Mello, 1–9. Philadelphia: Philadelphia Museum of Art, 2016.
Agamben, Giorgio. 1995. *Homo Sacer: Sovereign Power and Bare Life.* Trans. Daniel Heller-Roazen. Stanford: Stanford UP, 1998.
Agostoni, Claudia. "Strategies, Actors, Promises and Fears in the Smallpox Vaccinations Campaigns in Mexico: From the Porfiriato to the Post-revolution (1880–1940)." *Ciência & Saúde Coletiva* 16, no. 2 (2011): 459–70.
Aguilar-Moreno, Manuel, and Erika Cabrera. *Diego Rivera: A Biography.* Westport, CT: Greenwood, 2011.
Aguilar Rodríguez, Sandra. "Alimentando a la nación: Género y nutrición en México (1940–1960)." *Revista de Estudios Sociales* 29 (2008): 28–41.
———. "Cooking Modernity: Nutrition Policies, Class, and Gender in 1940s and 1950s Mexico." *The Americas* 64, no. 2 (2007): 177–205.
Agustín, José. *Abolición de la propiedad.* Mexico City: Editorial Joaquín Mortíz, 1969.
Albarrán, Elena Jackson. *Seen and Heard in Mexico: Children and Revolutionary Cultural Nationalism.* Lincoln: University of Nebraska Press, 2014.
Alonso, Ana María. "Conforming Disconformity: 'Mestizaje,' Hybridity, and the Aesthetics of Mexican Nationalism." *Cultural Anthropology* 19, no. 4 (2004): 459–90.
Alonso, Carlos J. *The Burden of Modernity: The Rhetoric of Cultural Discourse in Latin America.* New York: Oxford UP, 1998.
Anderson, Benedict. *Imagined Communities: Reflections on the Origin and Spread of Nationalism.* 2nd ed. New York: Verso, 1991.
Anreus, Alejandro. "*Los Tres Grandes*: Ideologies and Styles." In *Mexican Muralism: A Critical History*, ed. Alejandro Anreus, Robin Adèle Greeley, and Leonard Folgarait, 27–55. Berkeley: University of California Press, 2012.

Antebi, Susan. "Prometheus Re-bound: Disability, Contingency and the Aesthetics of Hygiene in Post-revolutionary Mexico." *Arizona Journal of Hispanic Cultural Studies* 17 (2013): 163–80.

Anzaldúa, Gloria. *Borderlands/La frontera: The New Mestiza*. San Francisco: Aunt Lute, 1987.

Apel, Dora. "Diego Rivera and the Left: The Destruction and Recreation of the Rockefeller Center Mural." *Left History* 6, no. 1 (1999): 57–75.

Aréchiga Córdoba, Ernesto. "'Dictadura sanitaria,' educación y propaganda higiénica en el México Revolucionario, 1917–1934." *Dynamis* 25 (2005): 117–43.

———. "Educación, propaganda o 'dictadura sanitaria': Estrategias discursivas de hygiene y salubridad públicas en el México posrevolucionario, 1917–1945." *Estudios de Historia Moderna y Contemporánea de México* 33 (2007): 57–88.

Arquin, Florence. *Diego Rivera: The Shaping of an Artist (1889–1921)*. Norman: Oklahoma UP, 1971.

Arreola, Daniel D. "Mexican American Exterior Murals." *American Geographical Society* 74, no. 4 (1984): 409–24.

Arreola Martínez, Betsabé. "José Vasconcelos: El caudillo cultural de la nación." *Casa del tiempo* 25 (2010): 4–10.

Avalos, Adán. "The *Naco* in Mexican Film: *La banda del carro rojo*, Border Cinema, and Migrant Audiences." In *Latsploitation, Exploitation Cinemas, and Latin America*, ed. Victoria Ruétalo and Dolores Tierney, 185–200. New York: Routledge, 2009.

Avelar, Idelber. *The Untimely Present: Postdictatorial Latin American Fiction and the Task of Mourning*. Durham: Duke UP, 1999.

Avila, Theresa. "Art and Revolution in Mexico: Introduction." *Third Text* 28, no. 3 (2014): 219–22.

Aviña, Rafael. "Del ring a la pantalla." *Somos: El Santo, vida, obra y milagros* 9 (1999).

———. "Santo el enmascarado de plata." *Cinémás d'Amérique latine* 19 (2011): 25–38.

Aviram, Anny, and Cynthia Albertson. "Agrarian Leader Zapata: Creative Process and Technique." In *Diego Rivera: Murals for the Museum of Modern Art*, ed. Leah Dickerman and Anna Indych-López, 125–35. New York: Museum of Modern Art, 2009.

Ayala Blanco, Jorge. *La búsqueda del cine mexicano*. Vol. 2. Mexico City: UNAM, 1974.

Azuela, Alicia. *Arte y poder: Renacimiento artístico y revolución social México, 1910–1945*. Mexico City: FCE, 2005.

———. "*El Machete* and *Frente a Frente*: Art Committed to Social Justice in Mexico." *Art Journal* 52, no. 1 (1993): 82–87.

Baas, Jacquelynn. "*The Epic of American Civilization*: The Mural at Dartmouth College (1932–34)." In *José Clemente Orozco in the United States, 1927–1934*, ed. Renato Gonzalez Mello and Diane Miliotes, 142–85. New York: W.W. Norton, 2002.

Bailey, Joyce Waddell. "José Clemente Orozco (1883–1949): Formative Years in the Narrative Graphic Tradition." *Latin American Research Review* 15, no. 3 (1980): 73–93.

Balsamo, Anne M. "Reading Cyborgs, Writing Feminism." In *The Gendered Cyborg: A Reader*, ed. Gill Kirkup, Linda Janes, Kath Woodward, and Fiona Hovenden, 148–58. London: Routledge, 2000.

Barber, Sarah L., Stefano M. Bertozzi, and Paul J. Gertler. "Variations in Prenatal Care Quality for the Rural Poor in Mexico." *Health Affairs* 26, no. 3 (2007): w310–w323.

Bargellini, Clara. "Diego Rivera en Italia." *Anales del instituto de investigaciones estéticas* 66 (1995): 85–136.
Barquero, Andrea A. "Plantas sanadoras: Pasado, presente y future." *Revista QuímicaViva* 2, no. 6 (2007): 53–69.
Barraza-Lloréns, Mariana, Stefano Bertozzi, Eduardo González-Pier, and Juan Pablo Gutiérrez. "Addressing Inequity in Health and Health Care in Mexico." *Health Affairs* 21, no. 3 (2002): 47–56.
Barthes, Roland. *Mythologies*. Trans. Annette Lavers. New York: Hill and Wang, 1954–1956.
Bartra, Armando. "Las viñetas del apocalipsis." *Luna Córnea* 27, no. 1 (2004): 46–63.
Bartra, Roger. *The Cage of Melancholy*. Trans. Chrisopher J. Hall. New Brunswick, NJ: Rutgers UP, 1992.
———. *Cerebro y libertad: Ensayo sobre la moral, el juego y el determinismo*. Mexico City: FCE, 2013. Kindle.
Basave Benítez, Agustín F. *México mestizo*. Mexico City: FCE, 1992.
Belej, Cecilia. "La conquista en el muralismo mexicano: Representaciones de las matanzas de indígenas." *Intersticios* 8, no. 1 (2014): 249–62.
Belnap, Jeffrey. "Diego Rivera's Greater America: Pan-American Patronage, Indigenism, and H.P." *Cultural Critique* 63 (2006): 61–98.
Benítez Rojo, Antonio. *La isla que se repite: El caribe y la perspectiva posmoderna*. Hanover: Ediciones del Norte, 1989.
Benjamin, Thomas. "Rebuilding the Nation." In *The Oxford History of Mexico*, ed. Michael C. Meyer and William H. Beezley, 467–502. New York: Oxford UP, 2000.
Benjamin, Walter. "Theses on the Philosophy of History." In *Critical Theory since 1965*, ed. Hazard Adams and Leroy Searle, 680–85. Tallahassee: Florida State UP, 1986.
Bernal, Rafael. *Su nombre era muerte*. Mexico City: Editorial JUS, 1947.
Bertaccini, Tiziana. *Ficción y realidad del héroe popular*. Mexico City: Universidad Iberoamericana, 2001.
Bhabha, Homi K. "Of Mimicry and Man: The Ambivalence of Colonial Discourse." *Discipleship: A Special Issue on Psychoanalysis* 28 (1984): 125–33.
Billings, Molly. "The Influenza Pandemic of 1918." Stanford: Virus.Stanford.Edu, 1997. https://virus.stanford.edu/uda/.
Bixler, Jacqueline E. "Archiving Amnesia: Tlatelolco and the Artfulness of Memory." In *Modern Mexican Culture: Critical Foundations*, ed. Stuart A. Day, 203–18. Tucson: University of Arizona Press, 2017.
Blanco, José Joaquín. *Se llamaba Vasconcelos: Una evocación crítica*. Mexico City: FCE, 1977.
Bliss, Katherine E. "For the Health of the Nation: Gender and the Cultural Politics of Social Hygiene in Revolutionary Mexico." In *The Eagle and the Virgin*, ed. Vaughan and Lewis, 196–218.
———. "The Science of Redemption: Syphilis, Sexual Promiscuity, and Reformism in Revolutionary Mexico City." *Hispanic American Historical Review* 79, no. 1 (1999): 1–40.
Bonfil Batalla, Guillermo. *México profundo: Una civilización negada*. Mexico City: SEP. CIESAS, 1987.
———. "The Problem of National Culture." In *The Mexico Reader: History, Culture, Politics*. 3rd ed., ed. Gilbert M. Joseph and Timothy J. Anderson, 28–32. Durham: Duke UP, 2005.

Brading, David A. "Manuel Gamio and Official Indigenismo in Mexico." *Bulletin of Latin American Research* 7, no. 1 (1988): 75–89.

Breton, André, and Diego Rivera. *Manifesto for an Independent Revolutionary Art*, 1938. https://www.marxists.org/subject/art/lit_crit/works/rivera/manifesto.htm.

Brewster, Keith. "Caciquismo in Rural Mexico during the 1920s: The Case of Gabriel Barrios." *Journal of Latin American Studies* 28, no. 1 (1996): 105–28.

Briseño, Patricia. "Mujer da a luz en el patio del Hospital de Huajapan, León." *Esquema*, Mar. 7, 2014. http://www.excelsior.com.mx/nacional/2014/03/07/947519.

Brooks, Rodney A. *Flesh and Machines: How Robots Will Change Us*. New York: Pantheon, 2002.

Brown, J. Andrew. *Cyborgs in Latin America*. New York: Palgrave Macmillan, 2010.

———. "Cyborgs, Post-punk, and the Neobaroque: Ricardo Piglia's *La ciudad ausente*." *Comparative Literature* 61, no. 3 (2009): 316–26.

Brown, J. Andrew, and M. Elizabeth Ginway. Introduction to *Latin American Science Fiction: Theory and Practice*, ed. M. Elizabeth Ginway and J. Andrew Brown, 1–15. New York: Palgrave Macmillan, 2012.

Bruno-Jofré, Rosa, and Carlos Martínez Valle. "Ruralizando a Dewey: El amigo americano, la colonización interna y la escuela de la acción en el México posrevolucionario (1921–1940)." *Encuentros sobre educación* 10 (2009): 43–64.

Butler, Judith. *Gender Trouble: Feminism and the Subversion of Identity*. New York: Routledge, 1999.

Caballero Oliver, Juan Diego. "El muralismo mexicano." *Revista Atticus* 15 (2011): 11–23.

Cabello C., Felipe. "Diego Rivera: Gran maestro y un didáctico y lúcido historiador de la medicina." *Revista Médica de Chile* 142 (2014): 1458–66.

Cabrera López, Patricia. *Una inquietud de amanecer: Literatura política en México, 1962–1987*. Mexico City: Plaza y Valdés, 2006.

Camp, Roderic Ai. "An Image of Mexican Intellectuals: Some Preliminary Observations." *Mexican Studies* 1, no. 1 (1985): 61–82.

Campbell, Timothy. "Translator's Introduction: *Bíos*, Immunity, Life: The Thought of Roberto Esposito." In *Bíos: Biopolitics and Philosophy*. Trans. Timothy Campbell. Minneapolis: University of Minnesota Press, 2008, vii–xlii.

Cañedo, Diego. *El réferi cuenta nueve*. Mexico City: Editorial Cultura, 1943.

Cárdenas Noriega, Joaquín. *José Vasconcelos: Caudillo cultural*. Mexico City: Consejo Nacional para la Cultura y las Artes, 2008.

Cardona, René, dir. *Las luchadoras contra la momia azteca*. Calderón, 1964. DVD.

Carmona, Fernando, Guillermo Montaño, Jorge Carrión, and Alonso Aguilar. *El milagro mexicano*. Mexico City: Editorial Nuestro Tiempo, 1970.

Carpita, Marcelo. "Muralismo en América: Actitud y revolución a través de la solidaridad." *Crónicas* 15/16 (2008): 435–45.

Carro, Nelson. *El cine de luchadores*. Mexico City: Rosette, 1984.

Carter, Warren. "Painting the Revolution: State, Politics, and Ideology in Mexican Muralism." *Third Text* 28, no. 3 (2014): 282–91.

Caso, Alfonso. "Definición del indio y de lo indio." *América Indígena* 8, no. 4 (1948): 145–81.

Castellanos, Rosario. *Balún Canán*. Mexico City: FCE, 2007. First published 1957.

———. *Ciudad Real*. Mexico City: Punto de Lectura, 2010. First published 1960.

———. "Otra vez Sor Juana." In *Obras II: Poesía, teatro y ensayo*, comp. Eduardo Mejía. Mexico City: FCE, 1998.

Castro, Justin. *Radio in Revolution: Wireless Technology and State Power in Mexico, 1897–1938*. Lincoln: University of Nebraska Press, 2016.

Castro Ricalde, Maricruz, and Robert McKee Irwin. *El cine mexicano "se impone": Mercados internacionales y penetración cultural en la época dorada*. Mexico City: UNAM, 2011.

Central Intelligence Agency. "Mexico." World Factbook. Accessed Oct. 16, 2013. https://www.cia.gov/library/publications/the-world-factbook/geos/mx.html.

———. "United States." World Factbook. Accessed Oct. 16, 2013. https://www.cia.gov/library/publications/the-world-factbook/geos/us.html.

Charlot, Jean. "Orozco's Stylistic Evolution." *College Art Association* 9, no. 2 (1949–1950): 148–57.

Chávez, Daniel. "La alta modernidad visual y la intermedialidad de la historieta en México." *Hispanic Research Journal* 8, no. 2 (2007): 155–69.

———. "The Eagle and the Serpent on the Screen." *Latin American Research Review* 45, no. 3 (2010): 115–41.

Chevalier de Lamarck, Jean-Baptiste Pierre Antoine de Monet. *Zoological Philosophy*. Trans. Ian Johnston. Creative Commons 2.5, 2009. Accessed Feb. 21, 2018. http://johnstoniatexts.x10host.com/lamarck/lamarcktofc.htm.

Chiu-Olivares, María Isela. *La novela mexicana contemporánea (1960–1980)*. Madrid: Editorial Pliegos, 1990.

Cisneros, Odile. "Futurism and Cubism in the Early Poetics of Mexican *Estridentismo* and Brazilian *Modernismo*." *International Yearbook of Futurism Studies* 7 (2017): 206–31.

Clark, Andy. *Natural-Born Cyborgs: Minds, Technologies, and the Future of Human Intelligence*. Oxford: Oxford UP, 2003.

Clark, Andy, and David Chalmers. *Supersizing the Mind: Embodiment, Action, and Cognitive Extension*. Oxford: Oxford UP, 2008.

Clendinnen, Inga. "'Fierce and Unnatural Cruelty': Cortés and the Conquest of Mexico." *Representations* 33 (1991): 65–100.

Clynes, Manfred E., and Nathan S. Kline. 1960. "Cyborgs and Space." In *The Cyborg Handbook*, ed. Chris Hables Gray, Heidi J. Figueroa-Sarriera, and Steven Mentor, 29–33. New York: Routledge, 1995.

Cochran, Gregory, and Henry Harpending. *The 10,000 Year Explosion: How Civilization Accelerated Human Evolution*. New York: Basic Books, 2009.

Cockcroft, James D. *Mexico: Class Formation, Capital Accumulation, and the State*. New York: Monthly Review, 1983.

Coe, Andrew. "Slugfests del Sur." *Film Comment* 23, no. 4 (1987): 27–30.

Coester, Alfred. "México or Méjico?" *Hispania* 8, no. 2 (1925): 109–16.

Coffey, Mary K. "'All Mexico on a Wall': Diego Rivera's Murals at the Ministry of Public Education." In *Mexican Muralism: A Critical History*, ed. Alejandro Anreus, Robin Adèle Greeley, and Leonard Folgarait, 56–74. Berkeley: University of California Press, 2012.

———. "Angels and Prostitutes: José Clemente Orozco's 'Catharsis' and the Politics of Female Allegory in 1930s Mexico." *New Centennial Review* 4, no. 2 (2004): 185–217.

———. *How a Revolutionary Art Became Official Culture: Murals, Museums, and the Mexican State*. Durham: Duke UP, 2012.

———. "Promethean Labor: Orozco and the Gendering of American Art." In *José Clemente Orozco: Prometheus*, ed. Marjorie L. Harth, 63–77. Pomona, CA: Pomona College Museum of Art, 2001.

———. "State Ritual, Mass Politics, or Mythopoesis? The Many Modalities of Mexican Muralism, 1929–1950." In *Paint the Revolution: Mexican Modernism, 1910–1950*, ed. Matthew Affron, Mark A. Castro, Dafne Cruz Porchini, and Renato González Mello, 349–57. Philadelphia: Philadelphia Museum of Art, 2016.

Comaroff, John L., and Jean Comaroff. *Ethnicity, Inc*. Chicago: University of Chicago Press, 2009.

Comisarenco Mirkin, Dina. "Diosas y madres, el arquetipo femenino en Diego Rivera." *Athenea Digital* 10 (2010): 191–212.

———. "Donde caben dos caben tres: La intertextualidad en la fotografía y la pintura de Edward Weston, Tina Modotti y Diego Rivera." *ALED* 14, no. 1 (2014): 23–42.

Corbeil, Laurent. "El Instituto Nacional Indigenista en el municipio de Oxchuc, 1951–1971." *LiminaR* 11, no. 1 (2013): 57–72.

Cordero Reiman, Karen. "Prometheus Unraveled: Readings of and from the Body: Orozco's Pomona College Mural (1930)." In *José Clemente Orozco in the United States, 1927–1934*, ed. Renato Gonzalez Mello and Diane Miliotes, 98–117. New York: W.W. Norton, 2002.

Craven, David. *Art and Revolution in Latin America 1910–1990*. New Haven: Yale UP, 2002.

Crespo, Regina. *Itinerarios intelectuales: Vasconcelos, Lobato y sus proyectos para la nación*. Mexico City: Universidad Nacional Autónomo de México, 2004.

Cubadebate. "Mexicana da a luz frente a hospital que se negó a atenderla." *Cubadebate*, Oct. 7, 2013. http://www.cubadebate.cu/noticias/2013/10/07/mexicana-da-a-luz-frente-a-hospital-que-se-nego-a-atenderla/#.WfIFlmhSwps.

Cypess, Sandra M. *La Malinche in Mexican Literature from History to Myth*. Austin: University of Texas Press, 1991.

———. *Uncivil Wars: Elena Garro, Octavio Paz, and the Battle for Cultural Memory*. Austin: University of Texas Press, 2012.

Dalton, David S. "Educating Social Hierarchies in Rosario Castellanos's *Balún Canán*." *Chasqui* 43, no. 2 (2014): 150–60.

———. "Imaginando comunidades en tensión: Elena Garro y el indigenismo." *Nocturnario* 13 (2016). http://nocturnario.com.mx/revista/elena-garro-indigenismo/.

———. "*Robo Sacer*: 'Bare Life' and Cyborg Labor beyond the Border in Alex Rivera's *Sleep Dealer*." *Hispanic Studies Review* 1 (2016): 15–29.

Daniel, G. Reginald. *More than Black? Multiracial Identity and the New Racial Order*. Philadelphia: Temple UP, 2002.

Deanda Camacho, Elena. "*María Candelaria* y *Oficio de tinieblas*: La mujer indígena en el México del siglo XX." *Semiosis* 8, no. 13 (2011): 69–84.

De Beer, Gabriella. *José Vasconcelos and His World*. New York: Las Américas, 1966.

De la Mora, Sergio. *Cinemachismo*. Austin: University of Texas Press, 2006.

Del Pozo Marx, Jorge. "Máscara contra cabellera . . ." In *Nos vemos en el cine*, 183–211. Guadalajara: Gobierno del Estado de Jalisco, 2007.

Dendle, Peter. "The Zombie as Barometer of Cultural Anxiety." In *Monsters and the Monstrous: Myths and Metaphors of Enduring Evil*, ed. Niall Scott, 45–54. Amsterdam: Rodopi, 2007.
De Reuse, Willem J. "Mariano Rojas and His 'Manual de la lengua náhuatl' (1927)." In *Análisislingüístico: Enfoques sincrónico, diacrónico e interdisciplinario*, ed. Rosa María Ortiz Ciscomani, 225–46. Hermosillo: Universidad de Sonora, 2010.
Dever, Susan. *Celluloid Nationalism and Other Melodramas: From Post-revolutionary Mexico to fin de siglo Mexamérica*. Albany: State University of New York Press, 2003.
Díaz Arciniega, Víctor. *Querella por la cultura "revolucionaria" (1925)*, 2nd ed. Mexico City: FCE, 2010.
Dickerman, Leah. "Leftist Circuits." In *Diego Rivera: Murals for the Museum of Modern Art*, ed. Leah Dickerman and Anna Indych-López, 12–47. New York: Museum of Modern Art, 2009.
Doede, Robert. "Technologies and Species Transitions: Polanyi, on a Path to Posthumanity?" *Bulletin of Science, Technology and Society* 31, no. 3 (2011): 225–35.
Doremus, Anne. "Indigenism, Mestizaje, and National Identity in Mexico during the 1940s and the 1950s." *Mexican Studies* 17, no. 2 (2001): 375–402.
Downs, Linda Bank. *Diego Rivera: The Detroit Industry Murals*. New York: Museum of Modern Art, 2011.
Drake, Susan Wiebe. "María Félix: The Last Great Mexican Film Diva; The Representation of Women in Mexican Film, 1940–1970." PhD diss., Ohio State University, 2005.
Duarte Sánchez, María Estela. "Science and Medicine: Marvelous Color." In *Diego Rivera: The Complete Murals*, ed. Luis-Martín Lozano and Juan Rafael Coronel Rivera, 514–17. Hong Kong: Taschen, 2008.
Echavarría, Salvador. *Orozco: Hospicio Cabañas*. Guadalajara: Planeación y Promoción, 1959.
Eder, Rita. "Against the Lacoon: Orozco and History Painting." In *José Clemente Orozco in the United States, 1927–1934*, ed. Renato Gonzalez Mello and Diane Miliotes, 230–43. New York: W.W. Norton, 2002.
Ellis, Keith. "Concerning the Question of Influence." *Hispania* 55, no. 2 (1972): 340–42.
El Piñero de la Cuenca. "No hay negligencia, fue evento fortuito, dice Comisión de Arbitraje Médico sobre mujer que dio a luz en jardinera." *El Piñero de la Cuenca*, Oct. 30, 2013. http://archivo.elpinerodelacuenca.com.mx/index.php/oaxaca/64098-no-hay-negligencia-fue-evento-fortuito-dice-comision-de-arbitraje-medico-sobre-mujer-que-dio-a-luz-en-jardinera.
Esposito, Roberto. *Bíos: Biopolitics and Philosophy*. Trans. Timothy Campbell. Minneapolis: Minneapolis UP, 2008.
Estrada, Luis, dir. *El infierno*. Bandidos Films, 2010. DVD.
Fajardo Ortiz, Guillermo, and Rey Arturo Salcedo Álvarez. "Semblanza del México anterior a la creación del hospital 20 de noviembre." *Revista de Especialidades Médico-Quirúrgicas* 16, no. 1 (2011): S9–S19.
Falkman, Johan. "Los murales de Trelleborg: Muerte, política y religión; Influencias del muralismo mexicano en un pintor sueco." *Crónicas* 15/16 (2008): 388–95.
Favre, Henri. *El indigenismo*. Mexico City: FCE, 1997.
Feder, Elena. "Engendering the Nation, Nationalizing the Sacred: Guadalupismo and the Cin-

ematic (Re)Formation of Mexican Consciousness." In *National Identities and Sociopolitical Changes in Latin America*, ed. Mercedes F. Durán-Cogan and Antonio Gómez-Moriana, 229–68. New York: Routledge, 2001.

Fein, Seth. "From Collaboration to Containment: Hollywood and the International Political Economy of Mexican Cinema after the Second World War." In *Mexico's Cinema: A Century of Film and Filmmakers*, ed. Joanne Hershfield and David R. Maciel, 123–63. Wilmington: Scholarly Resources, 1999.

Félix, María. *Todas mis guerras: Una raya en el agua*. Mexico City: Sanborns, 2000.

Fell, Claude. "El ideario literario de José Vasconcelos." *NRFH* 42, no. 2 (1994): 549–62.

———. *José Vasconcelos: Los años del águila*. Mexico City: UNAM, 1989.

Feria, María Fernanda, and Rosa María Lince Campillo. "Arte y grupos de poder: El muralismo y la ruptura." *Estudios Políticos* 21 (2010). http://www.redalyc.org/pdf/4264/426439542004.pdf.

Fernández, Emilio, dir. *Enamorada*. Performances by María Félix and Pedro Armendáriz. CLASA, 1946. DVD.

———. *Maclovia*. Performances by María Félix and Pedro Armendáriz. Filmex, 1948. DVD.

———. *María Candelaria*. Performances by Dolores del Río and Pedro Armendáriz. CLASA, 1943. DVD.

———. *Río Escondido*. Performance by María Félix. CLASA, 1947. DVD.

———. *The Torch*. Performances by Paulette Goddard and Pedro Armendáriz. Alpha Video, 1950. DVD.

Fernández Delgado, Miguel Ángel. "An X-Ray of Mexican Science Fiction Films." In *El futuro más acá: Cine mexicano de ciencia ficción*, ed. Itala Schmelz, 131–48. Mexico City: CONACULTA, 2006.

Fernández Retamar, Roberto. 1972. *Calibán: Apuntes sobre la cultura de nuestra América*. 2nd ed. Mexico City: Diógesis, 1974.

Fernández Reyes, Álvaro A. *Santo, el Enmascarado de Plata: Mito y realidad de un héroe mexicano moderno*. Zamora: D.R. El colegio de Michoacán, 2004.

Flisser, Ana. "La medicina en México hacia el siglo XX." *Historia y filosofía de la medicina* 145, no. 4 (2009): 353–56.

Flores, Ruben. *Backroads Pragmatists: Mexico's Melting Pot and Civil Rights in the United States*. Philadelphia: University of Pennsylvania Press, 2014.

Flores, Tatiana. *Mexico's Revolutionary Avant-Gardes: From Estridentismo to ¡30-30!* New Haven: Yale UP, 2013.

———. "Murales Estridentes: Tensions and Affiliations between *Estridentismo* and Early Muralism." In *Mexican Muralism: A Critical History*, ed. Alejandro Anreus, Robin Adèle Greeley, and Leonard Folgarait, 108–24. Berkeley: University of California Press, 2012.

Foard, Sheila Wood, and Diego Rivera. *Diego Rivera*. Philadelphia: Chelsea House, 2003.

Folgarait, Leonard. *Mural Painting and Social Revolution in Mexico, 1920–1940: Art of the New Order*. Cambridge: Cambridge UP, 1998.

Foster, David William. *Para una lectura semiótica del ensayo latinoamericano: Textos Representativos*. Madrid: Porrúa, 1983.

Foucault, Michel. "The Birth of Biopolitics." In *The Essential Foucault*, ed. Paul Rabinow and Nikolas Rose, 202–7. New York: New Press, 1994.

———. "The Birth of Social Medicine." In *The Essential Foucault*, ed. Paul Rabinow and Nikolas Rose, 319–37. New York: New Press, 1994.

———. "Madness and Society." In *The Essential Foucault*, ed. Paul Rabinow and Nikolas Rose, 370–77. New York: New Press, 2003.

———. "Technologies of the Self." In *The Essential Foucault*, ed. Paul Rabinow and Nikolas Rose, 145–69. New York: New Press, 2003.

Francis, Henry S. "*The Wounded Soldier* by Orozco." *Bulletin of the Cleveland Museum of Art* 42, no. 4 (1955): 61–63.

Franco, Jean. *The Decline and Fall of the Lettered City: Latin America in the Cold War*. Cambridge: Harvard UP, 2002. Nook.

———. *Plotting Women: Gender and Representation in Mexico*. New York: Columbia UP, 1988.

Frenk, Julio, Jaime Spúlveda, Octavio Gómez-Dantés, and Felicia Knaul. "Evidence-Based Health Policy: Three Generations of Reform in Mexico." *Lancet* 362, no. 9396 (Nov. 15, 2003): 1667–71.

Fuentes, Rocío. "José Vasconcelos y las políticas del mestizaje en la educación." In *De Atahuallpa a Cuauhtémoc: Los nacionalismos de Benjamín Carrión y José Vasconcelos*, ed. Juan Carlos Grijalva and Michael Handelsman, 115–46. Quito: Instituto Internacional de Literatura Iberoamericana, 2014.

Fulton, Christopher. "Siqueiros against the Myth: Paeans to Cuauhtémoc, Last of the Aztec Emperors." *Oxford Art Journal* 32, no. 1 (2009): 67–93.

Gallardo Muñoz, Juan. *Diego Rivera*. Madrid: Dastin, 2003.

Gallo, Ruben. "Maples Arce, Marinetti and Khlebnikov: The Mexican Estridentistas in Dialogue with Italian and Russian Futurisms." *Revista Canadiense de Estudios Hispánicos* 31, no. 2 (2007): 309–24.

———. *Mexican Modernity: The Avant Garde and the Technological Revolution*. Boston: MIT Press, 2005.

Gámez R., Carlos Alberto, and Diego Quintero. *Papel Político Estudiantil* 1 (2005): 81–86.

Gamio, Manuel. *Forjando patria: Pro nacionalismo*. Mexico City: Porrúa, 1916.

———. *Hacia un México nuevo: Problemas sociales*. Mexico City: México, 1935.

García, Hernán Manuel. "La globalización desfigurada o la post-globalización imaginada: La estética cyberpunk (post)mexicana." PhD diss., University of Kansas, 2011.

García Barragán, Elisa. "El muralismo mexicano." In *Iberoamérica y Extremadura: Memoria de un vínculo*, ed. Fernando Durán Ayanegui, 91–120. Extremadura: Centro Extremeño de Estudios y Cooperación con Iberoamérica, 2010.

García Benítez, Carlos. "Construcción, entronización y degradación de los símbolos de la identidad nacional en el cine mexicano contemporáneo." *Nuevo Mundo Mundos Nuevos*, 2013. http://nuevomundo.revues.org/65708.

———. "La identidad nacional mexicana desde la lente del cine mexicano contemporáneo." *Nuevo Mundo Mundos Nuevos*, 2010. http://nuevomundo.revues.org/58346.

García Blizzard, Mónica del Carmen. "The Indigenismos of Mexican Cinema before and through the Golden Age: Ethnographic Spectacle, 'Whiteness,' and Spiritual Otherness." PhD diss., Ohio State University, 2016.

García Canclini, Néstor. *Hybrid Cultures: Strategies for Entering and Leaving Modernity*, trans.

Christopher L. Chiappari and Silvia L. López. Minneapolis: University of Minnesota Press, 1995.

Garciadiego, Javier. "Vasconcelos y libros 'clásicos.'" In *De Atahuallpa a Cuauhtémoc: Los nacionalismos de Benjamín Carrión y José Vasconcelos*, ed. Juan Carlos Grijalva and Michael Handelsman, 179–99. Quito: Instituto Internacional de Literatura Iberoamericana, 2014.

García-García, José Manuel. "El humor en la novela mexicana, 1964–1989." PhD diss., University of Kansas, 1991.

García Riera, Emilio. *Emilio Fernández, 1904–1986*. Guadalajara: University of Guadalajara, 1987.

———. *México visto por el cine extranjero, 1941–1969*. Vol. 4. Mexico City: Centro de Capacitación Cinematográfico, 1988.

Garrido, Luis. *José Vasconcelos*. Mexico City: UNAM, 1963.

Gillingham, Paul. "Maximino's Bulls: Popular Protest after the Mexican Revolution 1940–1952." *Past & Present* 206, no. 1 (2010): 175–211.

Giordano, Jaime A. "Notas sobre Vasconcelos y el ensayo del siglo veinte." *Hispanic Review* 41, no. 3 (1973): 541–54.

Goldman, Shifra M. "Mexican Muralism: Its Social-Educative Roles in Latin America and the United States." *Aztlán* 13, no. 1–2 (1982): 111–33.

González, Jennifer. "Envisioning Cyborg Bodies: Notes from Current Research." In *The Gendered Cyborg: A Reader*, ed. Gill Kirkup, Linda Janes, Kath Woodward, and Fiona Hovenden, 58–73. London: Routledge, 2000.

González Ambriz, Marco, Jose Luis Ortega Torres, Octavio Serra, and Rodrigo Vidal Tamayo. *Mostrología del cine mexicano*. Mexico City: Conaculta, 2015.

González Mello, Renato. "Orozco in the United States: An Essay on the History of Ideas." In *José Clemente Orozco in the United States*, ed. Renato González Mello and Diane Miliotes, 22–61. New York: W.W. Norton, 2002.

Gracia, Fernando Mino. "Los indios que forjaron una patria: Comunidades indígenas y el mito nacional; El caso de María Candelaria." *Montajes* 1 (2012): 107–33.

Graham, Elaine L. *Representations of the Post/Human: Monsters, Aliens, and Others in Popular Culture*. New Brunswick, NJ: Rutgers UP, 2002.

Gray, Chris Hables. *Cyborg Citizen: Politics in the Posthuman Age*. New York: Routledge, 2001.

———. "An Interview with Manfred Clynes." In *The Cyborg Handbook*, ed. Chris Hables Gray, Heidi J. Figueroa-Sarriera, and Steven Mentor, 43–54. New York: Routledge, 1995.

Greeley, Robin Adèle. "Muralism and the State in Post-revolution Mexico, 1920–1970." In *Mexican Muralism: A Critical History*, ed. Alejandro Anreus, Robin Adèle Greeley, and Leonard Folgarait, 13–36. Berkeley: University of California Press, 2012.

———. "Witnessing Revolution, Forging a Nation." In *Paint the Revolution: Mexican Modernism, 1910–1950*, ed. Matthew Affron, Mark A. Castro, Dafne Cruz Porchini, and Renato González Mello, 263–69. Philadelphia: Philadelphia Museum of Art, 2016.

Greene, Doyle. *Mexploitation Cinema: A Critical History of Mexican Vampire, Wrestler, Ape-Man and Similar Films, 1957–1977*. Jefferson, NC: McFarland, 2005.

Grenier, Yvon. "The Politics of Art and Literature in Latin America." *Canadian Journal of Latin American and Caribbean Studies* 31, no. 62 (2006): 245–58.

Grijalva, Juan Carlos. "Introducción: Vasconcelos/Carrión, una democratización restringida." In *De Atahuallpa a Cuauhtémoc: Los nacionalismos de Benjamín Carrión y José Vasconcelos*, ed. Juan Carlos Grijalva and Michael Handelsman, 7–28. Quito: Instituto Internacional de Literatura Iberoamericana, 2014.

———. "Vasconcelos o la búsqueda de la Atlántida: Exotismo, arqueología y utopía del mestizaje en *La raza cósmica*." *Revista de Crítica Literaria Latinoamericana* 30, no. 60 (2004): 333–49.

Gruzinski, Serge. *The Mestizo Mind: The Intellectual Dynamics of Colonization and Globalization*. New York: Routledge, 2002.

Gudiño-Cejudo, María Rosa, Laura Magaña-Valladares, and Mauricio Hernández Ávila. "La Escuela de Salud Pública de México: Su fundación y primera época, 1922–1945." *Salud Pública de México* 55, no. 1 (2013): 81–91.

Hale, Charles A. *The Transformation of Liberalism in Late Nineteenth-Century Mexico*. Princeton: Princeton UP, 1989.

Hamill, Pete. *Diego Rivera*. New York: Harry N. Abrams, 1999.

Handelsman, Michael. "Visiones del mestizaje en *Indología* de José Vasconcelos y *Atahuallpa* de Benjamín Carrión." In *De Atahuallpa a Cuauhtémoc: Los nacionalismos de Benjamín Carrión y José Vasconcelos*, ed. Juan Carlos Grijalva and Michael Handelsman, 31–57. Quito: Instituto Internacional de Literatura Iberoamericana, 2014.

Haraway, Donna. *Simians, Cyborgs, and Women: The Reinvention of Nature*. London: Free Association of Books, 1991.

Hassig, Ross. *Mexico and the Spanish Conquest*. 2nd ed. Norman: University of Oklahoma Press, 2006.

Hayes, Joy Elizabeth. "National Imaginings on the Air: Radio in Mexico: 1920–1950." In *The Eagle and the Virgin*, ed. Vaughan and Lewis, 243–58.

Hayles, N. Katherine. *How We Became Posthuman: Virtual Bodies in Cybernetics, Literature, and Informatics*. Chicago: University of Chicago Press, 1999. Kindle.

———. "The Life Cycle of Cyborgs: Writing the Posthuman." In *The Cyborg Handbook*, ed. Chris Hables Gray, Heidi J. Figueroa-Sarriera, and Steven Mentor, 321–35. New York: Routledge, 1995.

Hedrick, Tace. *Mestizo Modernism: Race, Nation, and Identity in Latin American Culture, 1900–1940*. New Brunswick, NJ: Rutgers UP, 2003.

Hegel, Georg Wilhelm Friedrich. *Lectures of the Philosophy of the Spirit*. Trans. Robert R. Williams. London: Oxford UP, 2007.

Helm, MacKinley. *Man of Fire J.C. Orozco: An Interpretive Memoir*. Boston: Institute of Contemporary Art, 1953.

———. *Modern Mexican Painters*. New York: Harper & Brothers, 1941.

Hemingway, Andrew. "American Communists View Mexican Muralism: Critical and Artistic Responses." *Crónicas* 8/9 (2001): 13–42.

Hernández, Marco Polo. "The 'Afro-Mexican' and the Revolution: Making Afro-Mexicans Invisible through the Ideology of *Mestizaje* in *La raza cósmica*." *PALARA* 4, no. 4 (2000): 59–83.

Herrera-Sobek, María. "Social Protest, Folklore, and Feminist Ideology in Chicana Prose and Poetry." In *Folklore, Literature, and Cultural Theory: Collected Essays*, ed. Cathy Lynn Preston, 102–16. New York: Garland, 1995.

Hershfield, Joanne. *Mexican Cinema/Mexican Woman, 1940–1950*. Tucson: University of Arizona Press, 1996.

———. "Screening the Nation." In *The Eagle and the Virgin*, ed. Vaughan and Lewis, 259–78.

Higgins, Ceridwen Rhiannon. "Pulling Focus: New Perspectives on the Work of Gabriel Figueroa." PhD diss., Durham University, 2007.

Híjar Serrano, Alberto. "The Latin American Left and the Contribution of Diego Rivera to National Liberation." Trans. Dylan A. T. Minor. *Third Text* 19, no. 6 (2005): 637–46.

Hill, Matthew J. K. "The *Indigenismo* of Emilio 'El Indio' Fernández: Myth, *Mestizaje*, and Modern Mexico." MA thesis, Brigham Young University, 2009.

Hoeg, Jerry. *Science, Technology, and Latin American Narrative in the Twentieth Century and Beyond*. Bethlehem, PA: Lehigh UP, 2000.

Holland, William Robert. 1962. *Medicina maya en los altos de Chiapas: Un estudio del cambio socio-cultural*. Trans. Daniel Cazés. Mexico City: Instituto Nacional Indigenista, 1989.

Hoyos Galvis, Jairo Antonio. "Los cuerpos de María Félix: La incoherencia, el pacto y el monstruo." Talk given at Counter Stories of Greater Mexico, Cornell University, Ithaca, NY, Mar. 22, 2014.

Illescas Nájera, Francisco. "¿Hasta qué punto fue el Santo, 'El Enmascarado de Plata', definido por la ascendente cultura popular mexicana del siglo XX?" *En-claves del pensamiento* 6, no. 12 (2012): 49–66.

Indych-López, Anna. "Mural Gambits: Mexican Muralism in the United States and the 'Portable' Fresco." *Art Bulletin* 89, no. 2 (2007): 287–305.

———. *Muralism without Walls: Rivera, Orozco, and Siqueiros in the United States, 1927–1940*. Pittsburgh: University of Pittsburgh Press, 2009.

———. "Plates." In *Diego Rivera: Murals for the Museum of Modern Art*, ed. Leah Dickerman and Anna Indych-López, 52–119. New York: Museum of Modern Art, 2009.

———. "Technology, Labor, and Realism: Diego Rivera's Secretaría de Educación Pública Murals." In *Technology and Culture in Twentieth-Century Mexico*, ed. Araceli Tinajero and J. Brian Freeman, 283–301. Tuscaloosa: University of Alabama Press, 2013.

Introna, Ana María. "Vasconcelos americanista." Universidad Nacional de Cuyo, 1989. http://bdigital.uncu.edu.ar/objetos_digitales/4028/05-vol-06-introna.pdf.

Irving, Thomas B. Introduction to *Profile of Man and Culture in Mexico*, i–xix. Trans. Peter G. Earle. New York: McGraw-Hill, 1963.

Jaén, Didier T. Introduction to *The Cosmic Race: A Bilingual Edition*, ix–xxxiii. Baltimore: Johns Hopkins UP, 1997.

Jaimes, Héctor. *El muralismo mexicano desde un filtro filosófico: La relación entre la estética marxista y el muralismo*. Mexico City: Plaza y Valdés, 2012.

Janzen, Rebecca. *The National Body in Mexican Literature: Collective Challenges to Biopolitical Control*. New York: Palgrave Macmillan, 2015.

Jerade Dana, Miriam. "Antisemitismo en Vasconcelos: Antiamericanismo, nacionalismo y misticismo estético." *Mexican Studies* 31, no. 2 (2015): 248–86.

Joseph, Gilbert M., and Timothy J. Henderson. "The Search for 'Lo mexicano.'" In *The Mexico Reader: History, Culture, Politics*, ed. Gilbert M. Joseph and Timothy J. Henderson, 9–10. Durham: Duke UP, 2002.

Kapelusz-Poppi, Ana María. "Physician Activists and Development of Rural Health in Post-revolutionary Mexico." *Radical History Review* 80 (2001): 35–50.

———. "Rural Health and State Construction in Post-revolutionary Mexico: The Nicolaita Project for Rural Medical Services." *The Americas* 58, no. 2 (2001): 261–83.

Karttunen, Frances. "Rethinking Malinche." In *Indian Women of Early Mexico*, ed. Susan Schroeder, Stephanie Vood, and Robert Stephen Haskett, 291–312. Norman: University of Oklahoma, 1997.

Kato, Kauro. "Acercamiento a la influencia del movimiento muralista mexicano en el arte contemporáneo de Japón." *Crónicas* 13 (2008): 237–64.

Kettenman, Andrea. *Rivera*. Köln: Taschen, 2000.

Kirkup, Gill. "Introduction to Part One." In *The Gendered Cyborg: A Reader*, ed. Gill Kirkup, Linda Janes, Kath Woodward, and Fiona Hovenden, 3–10. London: Routledge, 2000.

Klich, Lynda. "Mexico Estridentista." In *Paint the Revolution: Mexican Modernism, 1910–1950*, ed. Matthew Affron, Mark A. Castro, Dafne Cruz Porchini, and Renato González Mello, 301–9. Philadelphia: Philadelphia Museum of Art, 2016.

Klor de Alva, J. Jorge. "The Postcolonialization of the (Latin) American Experience: A Reconsideration of 'Colonialism,' 'Postcolonialism,' and '*Mestizaje*.'" In *After Colonialism: Imperial Histories and Postcolonial Displacements*, ed. Gyan Prakash, 241–75. Princeton: Princeton UP, 1995.

Knight, Alan. "Popular Culture and the Revolutionary State in Mexico 1910–1940." *Hispanic American Historical Review* 74, no. 3 (1994): 339–444.

———. "Racism, Revolution, and *Indigenismo*: Mexico, 1910–1940." In *The Idea of Race in Latin America, 1870–1940*, ed. Richard Graham, 71–113. Austin: University of Texas Press, 1990.

Krauze, Enrique. *Caras de la historia*. Mexico City: Cuadernos de Joaquín Mortiz, 1983.

Kuhn, Thomas S. "Objectivity, Value Judgment, and Theory Choice." In *Critical Theory since 1965*, ed. Hazard Adams and Leroy Searle, 383–93. Tallahassee: Florida State UP, 1986.

———. *The Structure of Scientific Revolutions*. 3rd ed. Chicago: University of Chicago Press, 1996.

Kuznesof, Elizabeth Anne. "Ethnic and Gender Influence on 'Spanish' Creole Society in Colonial Spanish America." *Colonial Latin American Review* 4, no. 1 (1995): 153–76.

Landau, Ellen G. "Performing the Self and Other: Portraits and Self-Portraits by Diego Rivera and Frida Kahlo." *Crónicas* 10/11 (2006): 15–32.

Laraway, David. "Teenage Zombie Wasteland: Suburbia and the Apocalypse in Mike Wilson's *Zombie* and Edmundo Paz Soldán's *Los vivos y los muertos*." In *Latin American Science Fiction: Theory and Practice*, ed. M. Elizabeth Ginway and J. Andrew Brown, 133–51. New York: Palgrave Macmillan, 2012.

Lauro, Sarah Juliet, and Karen Embry. "A Zombie Manifesto: The Nonhuman Condition in the Era of Advanced Capitalism." *boundary2* 35, no. 1 (2008): 85–108.

Lear, John. "Representing Workers, the Workers Represented: Artists, Unions and Print Production in the Mexican Revolution." *Third Text* 28, no. 3 (2014): 235–55.

Lee, Anthony W. *Painting on the Left: Diego Rivera, Radical Politics, and San Francisco's Public Murals*. Berkeley: University of California Press, 1999.

Leeper, John Palmer. Introduction to *José Clemente: An Autobiography*, xvii–xxii. New York: Dover Press, 2011.

Legrás, Horacio. *Culture and Revolution: Violence, Modernity, and the Making of Modern Mexico*. Austin: University of Texas Press, 2017.

———. "El Ateneo y los orígenes del estado ético en México." *Latin American Research Review* 38, no. 2 (2003): 34–60.

Levi, Heather. *The World of Lucha Libre: Secrets, Revelations, and Mexican National Identity*, Durham: Duke UP, 2008. Kindle.

Levitas, Ruth. *The Method of Utopia*. New York: Palgrave Macmillan, 2013.

Lieberman, Evan. "Mask and Masculinity: Culture, Modernity, and Gender Identity in the Mexican Lucha Libre Films of El Santo." *Studies in Hispanic Cinemas* 6, no. 1 (2009): 3–17.

Lieberman, Evan, and Kerry Hegarty. "Authors of the Image: Cinematographers Gabriel Figueroa and Gregg Toland." *Journal of Film and Video* 62, nos. 1/2 (2010): 31–51.

Lomas, David. "Remedy or Poison? Diego Rivera, Medicine and Technology." *Oxford Art Journal* 30, no. 3 (2007): 454–83.

Lombán, Juan Carlos. "El muralismo mexicano." *Revista Atticus* 15 (2011): 15–19.

Lomnitz, Claudio. *Death and the Idea of Mexico*. New York: Zone Books, 2005.

———. *Deep Mexico, Silent Mexico: An Anthropology of Nationalism*. Minneapolis: University of Minnesota Press, 2001.

———. *Exits from the Labyrinth: Culture and Ideology in the Mexican National Space*. Berkeley: University of California Press, 1992.

López, Ana M. "Tears and Desire: Women and Melodrama in the 'Old' Mexican Cinema." In *The Latin American Cultural Studies Reader*, ed. Ana del Sarto, Alicia Ríos, and Abril Trigo, 441–58. Durham: Duke UP, 2004.

López, Rick A. "The Noche Mexicana and the Exhibition of Popular Arts: Two Ways of Exalting Indianness." In *The Eagle and the Virgin*, ed. Vaughan and Lewis, 23–42.

López-Beltrán, Carlos, and Vivette García Deister. "Scientific Approaches to the Mexican Mestizo." *História, Ciências, Saúde-Manguinhos* 20, no. 2 (2013): 391–410.

López Castro, Ramón. *Expedición a la ciencia ficción mexicana*. Mexico City: Lectorum, 2001.

López Orozco, Leticia. "The Revolution, Vanguard Artists, and Mural Painting." Trans. Andrea Guendelman and Theresa Avila. *Third Text* 28, no. 3 (2014): 256–68.

López Pérez, Oresta. "De libros elegantes a folletos rústicos: Lecturas y conocimientos de hygiene y enseñanzas domésticas para las mujeres rurales mexicanas." *Educação Unisonos* 14, no. 3 (2010): 255–62.

Lozano, Luis-Martín. "From Bad Government to Liberated Land." In *Diego Rivera: The Complete Murals*, ed. Luis-Martín Lozano and Juan Rafael Coronel Rivera, 136–43. Hong Kong: Taschen, 2008.

———. "From Carnival to Pan-American Unity: Two Murals in the Struggle against Fascism." In *Diego Rivera: The Complete Murals*, ed. Luis-Martín Lozano and Juan Rafael Coronel Rivera, 388–91. Hong Kong: Taschen, 2008.

Lund, Joshua. *The Impure Imagination: Toward a Critical Hybridity in Latin American Writing*. Minneapolis: University of Minnesota Press, 2006.

———. *The Mestizo State: Reading Race in Modern Mexico*. Minneapolis: University of Minnesota Press, 2012.

Lykke, Nina. "Between Monsters, Goddesses and Cyborgs: Feminist Confrontations with Science." In *The Gendered Cyborg: A Reader*, ed. Gill Kirkup, Linda Janes, Kath Woodward, and Finda Hovenden, 76–87.

Lynch, James B., Jr. "Orozco's House of Tears." *Journal of Inter-American Studies* 3, no. 3 (1961): 367–83.

Machado, Fernando. "Orozco: El mural de la escalera del antiguo Colegio de San Idelfonso." *Crónicas* 10/11 (2006): 63–72.

Madsen, Kreesten Meldgaard, Anders Hviid, Mogens Vestergaard, Diana Schendel, Jan Wohlfahrt, Poul Thorsen, Jorn Olsen, and Mads Melbye. "A Population-Based Study of Measles, Mumps, and Rubella Vaccination and Autism." *New England Journal of Medicine* 347, no. 19 (2002): 1477–82.

Mahieux, Viviana. "De ceja a ceja: Retos nacionales y espejismos sexuales en *Enamorada* de Emilio Fernández." *Delaware Review of Latin American Studies* 7, no. 1 (2006). http://udspace.udel.edu/bitstream/handle/19716/19562/Vo17-1Mahieux.pdf?sequence=1&isAllowed=y.

Mandel, Claudia. "Muralismo mexicano: Arte público/identidad/memoria colectiva." *Revista Exena* 30, no. 61 (2007): 37–54.

Maples Arce, Manuel. *Actual No. 1: Hoja de vanguardia comprimido estridentista*. 1921. http://artespoeticas.librodenotas.com/artes/1571/manifiesto-estridentista-1921.

Marentes, Luis A. *José Vasconcelos and the Writing of the Mexican Revolution*. New York: Twayne, 2000.

Marinetti, Filippo Tommaso. 1909. *I manifesti del futurismo: Prima serie*. Florence: Lacerba, 1914.

Martin, Gerald. *Journeys through the Labyrinth: Latin American Fiction in the Twentieth Century*. London: Verso, 1989.

Martínez Gómez, Raciel D. "Cine, etnicidad, migración y discurso de la representación." *Versión* 14 (2005): 265–88.

Matías, Pedro. "Otra mujer oaxaqueña da a luz en el baño de hospital; van 13." *Proceso*, June, 16, 2014. http://www.proceso.com.mx/374847/otra-mujer-oaxaquena-da-a-luz-en-bano-de-hospital-van-13.

Mayo Clinic. "Smallpox: Treatments and Drugs." Accessed Feb. 21, 2018. https://www.mayoclinic.org/diseases-conditions/smallpox/diagnosis-treatment/drc-20353032.

McAllister, Elizabeth. "Slaves, Cannibals, and Infected Hyper-whites: The Race and Religion of Zombies." *Anthropological Quarterly* 85 (2012): 457–86.

McCaa, Robert. "Missing Millions: The Human Cost of the Mexican Revolution." *Mexican Studies* 19, no. 2 (2003): 367–400.

McIntosh, Daniel. "Human, Transhuman, Posthuman: Implication of Evolution-by-Design for Human Security." *Journal of Human Security* 4, no. 3 (2008): 4–20.

McKay, John. "On Rivera's 'Detroit Industry': Community beyond Knowledge." *Legal Spaces* 9 (2005): 125–56.

McMeekin, Dorothy. *Science and Creativity in the Detroit Murals/Ciencia y creatividad en los murals de Detroit*. East Lansing: Michigan State UP, 1985.

Mijangos Díaz, Eduardo, and Alexandra López Torres. "El problema del indigenismo en el debate intelectual posrevolucionario." *Signos Históricos* 25 (2011): 42–67.

Miller, Frank. "*Enamorada*." *Turner Classic Movies*. http://www.tcm.com/this-month/article/93554%7Co/Enamorada.html.

Miller, Marilyn Grace. *Rise and Fall of the Cosmic Race: The Cult of Mestizaje in Latin America.* University of Texas Press, 2004.

Miner, Dylan A. T. "*El renegado comunista*: Diego Rivera, La Liga de Obreros y Campesinos and Mexican Repatriation in Detroit." *Third Text* 19, no. 6 (2005): 647–60.

Mitchell, Renae L. "Fernández and Cinematic Propaganda in the U.S. and Mexico." *CLCWeb* 13, no. 4 (2011): 2–9. http://docs.lib.purdue.edu/cgi/viewcontent.cgi?article=1825&context=clcweb.

Modenessi, Alfredo Michel. "Looking for Mr. GoodWill in 'Rancho Grande' and Beyond: The 'Ghostly' Presence of Shakespeare in Mexican Cinema." *Revista Alicantina de Estudios Ingleses* 25 (2012): 97–112. https://rua.ua.es/dspace/bitstream/10045/27449/1/RAEI_25_08.pdf.

Molina Enríquez, Andrés. *Grandes problemas nacionales.* Mexico City: Imprenta de A. Carranza e hijos, 1909.

Monsiváis, Carlos. "De lucha libre como Olimpo enmascarado." In *Espectacular de Lucha Libre,* ed. Lourdes Grobet, Alfonso Morales, Gustavo Fuentes, and Juan Manuel Aurrecoechea, 6. Mexico City: Trilce Ediciones, 2005.

———. "Diego Rivera: Creador de públicos." In *Diego Rivera hoy: Simposio sobre el artista en el centenario de su natilicio,* 117–28. 1986. http://www.estudioshistoricos.inah.gob.mx/revistaHistorias/wp-content/uploads/historias_13_117-128.pdf.

———. *Los rituales del caos.* Mexico City: Ediciones Era, 1995. Kindle.

———. "Mythologies." In *Mexican Cinema,* ed. Paul Antonio Paranaguá, trans. Ana M. López, 117–27. London: British Film Institute, 1995.

———. "Notas sobre la cultura mexicana en el siglo XX." In *Historia general de México.* Vol. 4. Mexico City: El Colegio de México, 1976, 305–476.

Mora, Carl J. *Mexican Cinema: Reflections of a Society, 1896–2004.* 3rd ed. Jefferson, NC: McFarland, 2005.

Morales, Alfonso. "Missiles and Marionettes." In *El futuro más acá: Cine mexicano de ciencia ficción,* ed. Itala Schmelz, 171–85. Mexico City: CONACULTA, 2006.

Moraña, Mabel. "The Boom of the Subaltern." In *The Latin American Cultural Studies Reader,* ed. Ana del Sarto, Alicia Ríos, and Abril Trigo, 643–54. Durham: Duke UP, 2004.

Mraz, John. *Looking for Mexico: Modern Visual Culture and National Identity.* Durham: Duke UP, 2009. Kindle.

Naam, Ramez. *More Than Human: Embracing the Promise of Biological Enhancement.* New York: Broadway, 2005.

Nahmad Rodríguez, Ana Daniela. "Las representaciones indígenas y la pugna por las imágenes: México y Bolivia a través del cine y el video." *Latinoamérica* 45 (2007): 105–30.

Negrete, Tania, and Héctor Orozco. "From the Countryside to the Capital . . . and from the Capital to Space." In *El futuro más acá: Cine mexicano de ciencia ficción,* ed. Itala Schmelz, 187–200. Mexico City: CONACULTA, 2006.

Nervo, Amado. "Nueva escuela literaria." *Boletín de Instrucción Pública: Órgano de la Secretaría del Ramo* 12, no. 4 (1909): 929–35.

Neumeyer, Alfred. "Orozco's Mission." *College Art Journal* 10, no. 2 (1951): 121–30.

Niblo, Stephen R. *Mexico in the 1940s: Modernity, Politics, and Corruption.* Wilmington, DE: SR Books, 1999.

Noble, Andrea. *Mexican National Cinema*. London: Routledge, 2005.
Noble, David Cook. *Born to Die: Disease and New World Conquest, 1492–1650*. Cambridge: Cambridge UP, 1998.
NTR. "Investigarán en Oaxaca caso de mujer que dio a luz en patio." *NTR: Periodismo Crítico*, Oct. 4, 2013. http://ntrzacatecas.com/2013/10/04/investigaran-en-oaxaca-caso-de-mujer-que-dio-a-luz-en-patio/.
Ocasio, Rafael. "La apropiación de María Félix del icónico personaje en *Doña Bárbara* de Rómulo Gallegos." *Romance Quarterly* 57, no. 4 (2010): 273–85.
O'Connell, Joanna. *Prospero's Daughter: The Prose of Rosario Castellanos*. Austin: University of Texas Press, 1995.
Oelhert, Mark. "From Captain America to Wolverine: Cyborgs in Comic Books, Alternative Images of Cybernetic Heroes and Villains." In *The Cyborg Handbook*, ed. Chris Hables Gray, Heidi J. Figueroa-Sarriera, and Steven Mentor, 219–32. New York: Routledge, 1995.
Olés, James. *Diego Rivera, David Alfaro Siqueiros, José Clemente Orozco*. New York: Museum of Modern Art, 2011.
Oleszkiewicz, Malgorzata. "Los cultos marianos nacionales en América: Guadalupe/Tonantzin y Aparecida/Iemanjá." *Revista Iberoamericana* 64, no. 182–83 (1998): 241–52.
Olvera, Carlos. *Mejicanos en el espacio*. Mexico City: Ed. Diógenes, 1968.
Omi, Michael, and Howard Winant. *Racial Formation in the United States: From the 1960s to the 1990s*. 2nd ed. New York: Routledge, 1994.
Orestes Águilar, Héctor. "Ese olvidado nazi mexicano de nombre José Vasconcelos." *Coincidencias y Divergencias* 8, no. 30 (2007): 148–57.
Orozco, José Clemente. *Catarsis*. Mural. Palacio de Bellas Artes, Mexico City. 1934.
———. *Cortés y la Malinche*. Mural. Colegio San Ildefonso, Mexico City. 1926.
———. *José Clemente Orozco: An Autobiography*. Mineola: Dover Press, 2001.
———. *La conquista española de México: Cortés triunfante*. Mural. Hospicio Cabañas, Guadalajara. 1938–39.
———. *La conquista española de México: El caballo mecánico*. Mural. Hospicio Cabañas, Guadalajara. 1938–39.
———. *La conquista española de México: El franciscano*. Mural. Hospicio Cabañas, Guadalajara. 1938–39.
———. *Prometheus*. Mural. Pomona College, Claremont, CA. 1930.
Ortega, Gema. "Writing and Hybridity: Identity, Dialogics, and Women's Narratives in the Americas." PhD diss., University of Illinois at Urbana-Champaign, 2011.
Ortiz Bullé Goyri, Alejandro. "El teatro indigenista mexicano de los años veinte: ¿Orígenes del teatro popular mexicano actual?" *Latin American Theatre Review* 37, no. 1 (2003): 75–93.
"Otra mujer oaxaqueña da a luz en acceso a hospital." *Diario Cambio*, Nov. 5, 2013. http://www.diariocambio.com.mx/2013/nacional/item/33380-otra-mujer-oaxaquena-da-a-luz-en-acceso-a-hospital.
Pacheco, Adriana. "El salón de baile en la Época de Oro del cine mexicano: Espacio de conflicto entre el estado laico y la sociedad católica." *Chasqui* 42, no. 2 (2013): 31–46.
Palou, Pedro Ángel. *El fracaso del mestizo*. Mexico City: Paidós, 2014.

Palou, Pedro Ángel, and Brian L. Price. *De perfiles: José Agustín ante la crítica*. Special edition, *Revista de Literatura Mexicana Contemporánea* 22, no. 69 (2016).

Paranaguá, Paulo Antonio. "María Félix: Image, Myth, and Enigma." *Studies in Latin American Popular Culture* 17 (1998).

Parker-Starbuck, Jennifer. *Cyborg Theatre: Corporeal/Technological Intersections in Multimedia Performance*. New York: Palgrave Macmillan, 2011.

Partlow, Joshua. "Mexico Wanted James Bond, but Only if the Country Looked as Good as He Does." *Washington Post*, Mar. 12, 2015. https://www.washingtonpost.com/news/worldviews/wp/2015/03/12/mexico-wanted-james-bond-but-only-if-the-country-looked-as-good-as-he-does/?utm_term=.4abd5bba17db.

Paul, Diane B. *Controlling Human Heredity: 1865 to the Present*. Atlantic Highlands: Humanities Press, 1995.

Paz, Octavio. 1950. "Antivíspera: *Taller*." In *Obras completas*. Vol. 4, *Generaciones y semblanzas*, 94–112. Mexico City: FCE, 1994.

———. *The Labyrinth of Solitude. The Other Mexico. Return to the Labyrinth of Solitude. Mexico and the United States. The Philanthropic Ogre*. Trans. Lysander Kemp, Yara Milos, and Rachel Phillips Belash. New York: Grove, 1985.

Peña Rodríguez, Daniel Cuitláhuac, and Vicente Castellanos. "Imitación entre pintura y cine: *El réquiem* de Orozco recreado por Gabriel Figueroa." *Razón y palabra* 71 (2010): 1–12.

Pérez Alfonso, Jorge. "Otra mujer da a luz en baño de un hospital en Oaxaca; le negaron atención." *La Jornada*, June 15, 2014. http://semanal.jornada.com.mx/ultimas/2014/06/15/otra-mujer-da-a-luz-en-el-bano-de-un-hospital-en-oaxaca-luego-de-que-le-negaran-atencion-7420.html.

Pierce, Gretchen. "Fighting Bacteria, the Bible, and the Bottle: Projects to Create New Men, Women, and Children, 1910–1940." In *A Companion to Mexican History and Culture*, ed. William H. Beezley, 505–17. Oxford: Blackwell Press, 2011.

Pitol, Sergio. "De cómo Diego Rivera volvió a inventar el mundo." *Crónicas* 10/11 (2008): 186–94.

Pizarro, Ana. "Divas de los cincuenta: María Félix." *Alpha* 28 (2009): 183–96.

Pla Brugat, Dolores. "Más desindianización que mestizaje: Una relectura de los censos generales de población." *Dimensión Antropológica* 18, no. 53 (2011): 69–91.

Podalsky, Laura. "Disjointed Frames: Melodrama, Nationalism, and Representation in 1950s Mexico." *Studies in Latin American Popular Culture* 12 (1993).

Polcari, Stephen. "Orozco and Pollock. Epic Transfigurations." *American Art* 6, no. 3 (1992): 36–58.

Poniatowska, Elena. *La noche de Tlatelolco*. Mexico City: ERA, 1971.

Portillo, Rafael, dir. *La momia azteca contra el robot humano*. CLASA, 1957. DVD.

Posada, Germán. "La idea de América en Vasconcelos." *Historia Mexicana* 12, no. 3 (1963): 379–403.

Potter, Sara Anne. "Disturbing Muses: Gender, Technology and Resistance in Mexican Avant-Garde Cultures." PhD diss., Washington University, 2013.

Prashad, Vijay. *Everybody Was Kung Fu Fighting: Afro-Asian Connections and the Myth of Cultural Purity*. Boston: Beacon, 2001.

Pratt, Dale. "La mente en la cueva: El yo del Otro prehistórico." *Ometeca* 17 (2012): 15–34.

Preston, Julia, and Samuel Dillon. *Opening Mexico: The Making of a Democracy*. New York: Farrar, Straus and Giroux, 2004.
Price, Brian L. *Cult of Defeat in Mexico's Historical Fiction: Failure, Trauma, and Loss*. New York: Palgrave Macmillan, 2012.
Puig Casauranc, José Manuel. "Departamento de psicopedagogia e hygiene." *Memoria que indica el estado que guarda el ramo de educación pública* 11 (1925): 157–67.
Quadratín/El Universal. "Mujer da a luz en patio de hospital por falta de atención." *Quadratín/ El Universal*, Oct. 4, 2013.
Quijano, Aníbal. "Coloniality of Power, Eurocentrism, and Latin America." Trans. Michael Ennis. *Nepantla* 1, no. 3 (2000): 533–80.
Quintanilla, Susana. *Nosotros: La juventud del Ateneo de México*. Mexico City: Tusquetts, 2008.
Rabasa, José. *Without History: Subaltern Studies, the Zapatista Insurgency, and the Specter of History*. Pittsburgh: University of Pittsburgh Press, 2012.
Rama, Ángel. *The Lettered City*. Trans. John Charles Chasteen. Durham: Duke UP, 1996.
Ramírez-Berg, Charles. "The Cinematic Invention of Mexico: The Poetics and Politics of the Fernández-Figueroa Style." In *The Mexican Cinema Project*, ed. Chon A. Noriega and Steven Ricci, 13–24. Los Angeles: UCLA Film and Television Archive, 1994.
———. "Figueroa's Skies and Oblique Perspective: Notes on the Development of the Classical Mexican Style." *Spectator* 13, no. 1 (1992): 24–41.
Ramos, Samuel. *Diego Rivera*. Mexico City: UNAM, 1986.
———. *Profile of Man and Culture in Mexico*. Trans. Peter G. Earle. New York: McGraw-Hill, 1963.
Rangel, Liz Consuelo. "*La ley de Herodes (1999)* vs. *Río Escondido (1947)*: La desmitificación de la Revolución Mexicana." *Divergencias* 4, no. 1 (2006): 61–68.
Ransome, Arthur. *The Crisis in Russia*. Nov. 1920. https://www.marxists.org/history/archive/ransome/works/crisis/ch06.htm.
Rashkin, Elissa J. *The Stridentist Movement in Mexico: The Avant-Garde and Culture Change in the 1920s*. Lanham: Lexington Books, 2009.
Rashkin, Elissa J., and Carla Zurián. "The Estridentista Movement in Mexico: A Poetics of the Ephemeral." *International Yearbook of Futurism Studies* 7 (2017): 309–33.
Real de Azúa, Carlos. *José Vasconcelos: La Revolución y sus bemoles*. Montevideo: Universidad de la República, 1967.
Reed, Alma. *Orozco*. New York: Oxford UP, 1956.
Reyes Palma, Francisco. "Mural Devices." In *José Clemente Orozco in the United States, 1927–1934*, ed. Renato Gonzalez Mello and Diane Miliotes, 216–29. New York: W.W. Norton, 2002.
Richardson, William. "The Dilemmas of a Communist Artist: Diego Rivera in Moscow, 1927–1928." *Mexican Studies* 3, no. 1 (1987): 49–69.
Rieder, John. *Colonialism and the Emergence of Science Fiction*. Middletown, CT: Wesleyan UP, 2008.
Rivera, Diego. *El hombre controlador del universo*. Mural. Palacio de Bellas Artes, Mexico City. 1934.
———. *Guerrero indio*. Mural. Museum of Modern Art, New York. 1931.

———. *Historia de la medicina en México: El pueblo en demanda de salud*. Mural. Hospital La Raza, Mexico City. 1954.
———. *Mecanización de la tierra*. Mural. Secretaría de Educación Publica, Mexico City. 1926.
———. *México a través de los siglos*. Mural. Palacio Nacional, Mexico City. 1935.
———. *Pan-American Unity*. Mural. City College of San Francisco. 1940.
———. "The Revolutionary Spirit in Modern Art." *Modern Quarterly* 6, no. 3 (1932): 51–57.
———. *Vaccination*. Mural. Detroit Institute of Arts, Detroit. 1932.
Rivera, Diego, and Gladys March. *My Art, My Life: An Autobiography*. New York: Citadel, 1960.
Rochfort, Desmond. *Mexican Muralists: Orozco, Rivera, Siqueiros*. London: Laurence King, 1993.
Rodó, José Enrique. 1900. *Ariel*. Barcelona: Red Ed., 2011. Nook.
Rodríguez, Ileana. "Hegemonía y dominio: Subalternidad, un significado flotante." *Teorías sin disciplina*. 1998. http://www.ensayistas.org/critica/teoria/castro/rodriguez.htm.
Rodríguez, José María. "Federalización de la salubridad." In *50 Discursos doctrinales en el congreso constituyente de la Revolución Mexicana*, 309–22. Mexico City: Instituto Nacional de Estudios Históricos de la Revolución Mexicana, 1967.
Rodríguez Mortellaro, Itzel. "Arte nacionalista e indigenismo en México en el siglo XX: El renacimiento de la mitología indígena antigua en el movimiento muralista." *Vestigios de un mismo mundo* 3 (2010): 51–68.
Rodríguez Prampolini, Ida. "Diego Rivera ilustrador de la Historia Patria." *Crónicas* 10/11 (2008): 176–85.
Romanell, Patrick. "Bergson in Mexico: A Tribute to José Vasconcelos." *Philosophy and Phenomenological Research* 21, no. 4 (1961): 501–13.
Romera Velasco, José Antonio. "La ciudad como lienzo: Diego Rivera y el muralismo mexicano." *Actas I Jornadas Internacionales Arte y Ciudad* 1 (2011): 419–31. http://www.arteyciudad.com/libros/actasprimerasjornadas/.
Rubenstein, Anne. "El Santo's Strange Career." In *The Mexico Reader: History, Culture, Politics*, ed. Gilbert M. Joseph and Timothy J. Henderson, 570–78. Durham: Duke UP, 2002.
Ruétalo, Victoria, and Dolores Tierney. "Introduction: Reinventing the Frame—Exploitation and Latin America." In *Latsploitation, Exploitation Cinemas, and Latin America*, ed. Victoria Ruétalo and Dolores Tierney, 1–13. New York: Routledge, 2009.
Ruitenberg, Claudia W. "Art, Politics, and the Pedagogical Relation." *Studies in Philosophy and Education* 30 (2011): 211–23.
Sacoto, Antonio. *El indio en el ensayo de la América española*. New York: Las Américas, 1971.
Said, Edward. *Orientalism*. New York: Penguin, 2003.
Sánchez-López, Indira. "Representaciones y expresiones de lo mexicano en los muralistas de la primera generación." *Contribuciones desde Coatepec* 12, no. 24 (2013): 67–83.
Sánchez Prado, Ignacio M. "El mestizaje en el corazón de la utopía: *La raza cósmica* entre Aztlán y América Latina." *Revista Canadiense de Estudios Hispánicos* 33, no. 2 (2009): 381–404.
———. "Ending the World with Words: Bernardo Fernández (BEF) and the Institutionalization of Science Fiction in Mexico." In *Latin American Science Fiction: Theory and Practice*, ed. M. Elizabeth Ginway and J. Andrew Brown, 111–32. New York: Palgrave Macmillan, 2012.

———. *Naciones intelectuales: Las fundaciones de la modernidad literaria Mexicana (1917–1959)*. West Lafayette: Purdue UP, 2009.
———. *Screening Neoliberalism: Transforming Mexican Cinema 1988–2012*. Nashville: Vanderbilt UP, 2014. Kindle.
Sánchez Vázquez, Adolfo. "Diego Rivera: Painting and Partisanship." Trans. David Craven. *Third Text* 28, no. 3 (2014): 269–70.
Sandoval, Chela. "New Sciences: Cyborg Feminism and the Methodology of the Oppressed." In *The Cyborg Handbook*, ed. Chris Hables Gray, Heidi J. Figueroa-Sarriera, and Steven Mentor, 407–22. New York: Routledge, 1995.
Santiago, Silviano. *Latin American Literature: The Space in Between*. Buffalo: Council on International Studies, State University of New York, 1973.
El Santo: El Enmascarado de Plata, performance. *El hacha diabólica*. Dir. José Díaz Morales. Fílmica Vergara—Cinecomisiones, 1964. DVD.
———. *Las momias de Guanajuato*. Dir. Federico Curiel. Películas Latinoamericanas, 1970. DVD.
———. *La venganza de la momia*. Dir. René Cardona. Cinematográfica Calderón, 1970. DVD.
———. *Santo contra la hija de Frankenstein*. Dir. Miguel M. Delgado. Cinematográfica Calderón, 1971. DVD.
———. *Santo contra la invasión de los marcianos*. Dir. Alfred B. Crevenna. Producciones Cinemátograficas, 1966. DVD.
———. *Santo contra la magia negra*. Dir. Alfredo B. Crevenna. Películas Latinoamericanas—Cinematográfica Flama, 1972. DVD.
———. *Santo contra las mujeres vampiro*. Dir. Alfonso Corona Blake. Churubusco, 1962. DVD.
———. *Santo contra los zombies*. Dir. Benito Alazraki. Filmadora Panamericana, 1961. DVD.
———. *Santo y Blue Demon contra el doctor Frankenstein*. Dir. Miguel M. Delgado. Cinematográfica Calderón—Santo, 1973. DVD.
———. *Santo y Blue Demon contra los monstruos*. Dir. Gilberto Martínez Solares. Cinematográfica Calderón, 1969. DVD.
———. *Santo y Mantequilla Nápoles en la venganza de la Llorona*. Dir. Miguel M. Delgado. Cinematográfica Calderón, 1974. DVD.
Scarano, Mónica E. "La escritura de José Vasconcelos: Diseño de un modelo cultural." *Texto Crítico* 40–41 (1989): 139–49.
Schell, Patience A. "Nationalizing Children through Schools and Hygiene: Porfirian and Revolutionary Mexico City." *The Americas* 60, no. 4 (2004): 559–87.
Schmidt, Henry C. "Power and Sensibility: Toward a Typology of Mexican Intellectuals and Intellectual Life, 1910–1920." In *Los intelectuales y el poder en México*, 173–88. Los Angeles: University of California Press, 1991.
———. *The Roots of Lo Mexicano*. College Station: Texas A&M UP, 1978.
Schwarz, Roberto. *Misplaced Ideas: Essays on Brazilian Culture*. London: Verso, 1992.
Science Daily. "Convergent Evolution." *Science Daily*. Accessed Feb. 21, 2018. https://www.sciencedaily.com/terms/convergent_evolution.htm.
Scott, David W. "Orozco's Prometheus: Summation, Transition, Innovation." *College Art Journal* 17, no. 1 (1957): 2–18.

———. "Prometheus Revisited." In *José Clemente Orozco: Prometheus*, ed. Marjorie L. Harth, 27–45. Pomona, CA: Pomona College Museum of Art, 2001.
Scott, James C. *Domination and the Arts of Resistance: Hidden Transcripts*. New Haven: Yale UP, 1990.
Scott, Robert L. "Diego Rivera at Rockefeller Center: Fresco Painting and Rhetoric." *Western Journal of Speech Communication* 41 (1977): 70–82.
SDP Noticias. "Irma fue necesaria para que nos mandarin un médico, dice responsible de clínica en Oaxaca." *SDPNoticias.com*, Oct. 9, 2013. https://www.sdpnoticias.com/local/oaxaca/2013/10/09/irma-fue-necesaria-para-que-nos-mandaran-un-medico-dice-responsable-de-clinica-en-oaxaca.
Secretaría de Educación Pública (México). *Ideas generales para el establecimiento de la cinematografía educativa en México*, Dec. 1, 1934, 1–2. Archivonomía de la Secretaría de Educación Pública, Avenida Wilfrido Massieu, esquina Eje Central.
Segre, Erica. "Visualizing Mexico: The Interplay of Mexican Graphic Arts and Film in the 1930s and 1940s." *Hispanic Research Journal* 1, no. 1 (2000): 87–95.
Sergei, Vittorio. "Mexico, Railway Workers' Struggle, 1957–1960." In *International Encyclopedia of Revolution and Protest*, ed. Immanuel Ness, 2295–97. Oxford: Blackwell Press, 2009.
Shafer, Alexander P. "Queering Bodies: Aliens, Cyborgs, and Spacemen in Mexican and Argentine Science Fiction." PhD diss., University of California Riverside, 2017.
Sherman, John W. *The Mexican Right: The End of Revolutionary Reform, 1929–1940*. Westport, CT: Praeger, 1997.
Skirius, John. *José Vasconcelos y la cruzada de 1929*. Mexico City: Siglo Veintiuno Editores, 1982.
Smith, Anthony D. "Nacionalismo e indigenismo: La búsqueda de un pasado auténtico." *Estudios Interdisciplinarios de América latina y el caribe* 1, no. 2 (1990). http://www7.tau.ac.il/ojs/index.php/eial/article/view/1297/1323.
Smith, Benjamin T. "Towards a Typology of Rural Responses to Healthcare in Mexico, 1920–1960." *Endeavor* 37, no. 1 (2012): 39–46.
Sobrevilla, David. "Transculturación y heterogeneidad: Avatares de dos categorías literarias en América Latina." *Revista de Crítica Literaria Latinoamericana* 54 (2001): 21–33.
Sommer, Doris. *Foundational Fictions: The National Romances of Latin America*. Berkeley: University of California Press, 1991.
Sosa Ramos, Anastacio. "El humanismo iberoamericano de José Vasconcelos." In *Humanismo mexicano del siglo XX*. Vol. 1, 135–54. Toluca: UAEM, 2004.
Spencer, Herbert. 1851. *Social Statics*. London: George Woodfall and Son, 1851.
Spitta, Silvia. "Of Brown Buffaloes, Cockroaches and Others: *Mestizaje* North and South of the Río Bravo." *Revista de Estudios Hispánicos* 35, no. 2 (2001): 333–47.
Spitta, Silvia, and Lois Parkinson Zamora. "Introduction: The Americas, Otherwise." *Comparative Literature* 61, no. 3 (2009): 189–208.
Spivak, Gayatri Chakravorty. "Can the Subaltern Speak?" In *Marxism and the Interpretation of Culture*, ed. Carry Nelson and Lawrence Grossberg, 271–313. Urbana: University of Illinois Press, 1988.
Stavans, Ilán. "The Prophet of Race." In *José Vasconcelos: The Prophet of Race*, ed. Ilán Stavans, 1–44. New Brunswick, NJ: Rutgers UP, 2011.

Steinberg, Samuel. *Photopoetics at Tlatelolco: Afterimages of Mexico, 1968*. Austin: University of Texas Press, 2016.
Sten, María. *Cuando Orestes muere en Veracruz*. Mexico City: FCE, 2003.
Stepan, Nancy Leys. *"The Hour of Eugenics": Race, Gender, and Nation in Latin America*. Ithaca: Cornell UP, 1991.
Stern, Alexandra Minna. "Mestizophilia, Biotypology, and Eugenics in Post-revolutionary Mexico: Towards a History of Science and the State, 1920–1960." Working Paper Series 4, 1999, 1–21. https://clas.uchicago.edu/sites/clas.uchicago.edu/files/uploads/stern1999.pdf.
Stern, Steven J. *The Secret History of Gender: Women, Men, and Power in Late Colonial Mexico*. Chapel Hill: University of North Carolina Press, 1995.
Suárez y López Guazo, Laura Luz. *Eugenesia y racismo en México*. Mexico City: UNAM, 2005.
———. "Evolucionismo, mejoramiento racial y medicina legal." In *La ética y los avances recientes de la ciencia y la técnica*, ed. Fernando Sancén Contreras, 25–49. Mexico City: Universidad Autónoma Metropolitana, 2005.
Swarthout, Kelly R. *"Assimilating the Primitive": Parallel Dialogues on Racial Miscegenation in Revolutionary Mexico*. New York: Peter Lang, 2004.
Syder, Andrew, and Dolores Tierney. "Importation/Mexploitation: or, How a Crime-Fighting, Vampire-Slaying Mexican Wrestler Almost Found Himself in an Italian Sword-and-Sandals Epic." In *Horror International*, ed. Steven Jay Schneider and Tony Williams, 33–55. Detroit: Wayne State Press, 2005.
Tabernero Holgado, Carlos, and Enrique Perdiguero-Gil. "Cinema and the Collective Dimensions of Disease." *Revista de medicina y cine* 7, no. 2 (2011). http://revistas.usal.es/index.php/medicina_y_cine/article/view/13767/14140.
Taboada, Hernán G. H. "Oriente y mundo clásico en José Vasconcelos." *Cuyo* 24 (2007): 103–19.
Taibo, Paco Ignacio. *El Indio Fernández: El cine por mis pistolas*. Mexico City: Joaquín Mortiz, 1986.
Taylor, Analisa. "Malinche and Matriarchal Utopia: Gendered Visions of Indigeneity in Mexico." *Signs* 31, no. 3 (2006): 815–40.
Taylor, Julie, and George Yúdice. "*Mestizaje* and the Inversion of Social Darwinism in Spanish American Fiction." In *Literary Cultures of Latin America: A Comparative History*. Vol. 3, *Latin American Literary Culture: Subject to History*, ed. Mario J. Valdés and Djelal Kadir, 310–19. Oxford: Oxford UP, 2004.
Tibol, Raquel. *Diego Rivera: Luces y sombras*. Mexico City: Lumen, 2007.
———. *José Clemente Orozco: Una vida para el arte; Breve historia documental*. Mexico City: FCE, 1984.
Tierney, Dolores. *Emilio Fernández: Pictures in the Margins*. Manchester: Manchester UP, 2007.
Tobin, Stephen Christopher. "Visual Dystopias from Mexico's Speculative Fiction: 1993–2008." PhD diss., Ohio State University, 2015.
Toledo-Pereyra, Luis H. "Diego Rivera and His Extraordinary Art of Medicine and Surgery." *Journal of Investigative Surgery* 20, no. 3 (2007): 139–43.
Townsend, Sarah J. "The Unfinished Art of Theatre: Avante-Garde Intellectuals and Mass Publics in Mexico and Brazil." PhD diss., New York University, 2010.

Traba, Marta. *Art of Latin America, 1900–1980*. Baltimore: Johns Hopkins UP, 1994.
Trounson, K. E. "The Literature Reviewed." *Eugenics Review* 13 (1931): 236–41.
Trujillo Muñoz, Gabriel. *Biografías del futuro: La ciencia ficción mexicana y sus autores*. Mexicali: University Autónoma de Baja California, 2000.
———. *Los confines: Crónica de la ciencia ficción mexicana*. Mexico City: Grupo Ed. Vid, 1999.
Tuñón, Gloria. "Emilio Fernández: A Look behind the Bars." In *Mexican Cinema*, ed. Paulo Antonio Paranaguá, trans. Ana M. López, 179–92. London: British Film Institute, 1995.
———. "Femininity, 'Indigenismo,' and Nation: Film Representation by Emilio 'El Indio' Fernández." In *Sex in Revolution: Gender, Politics, and Power in Modern Mexico*, ed. Jocelyn Olcott, Mary Kay Vaughan, and Gabriela Cano, 81–96. Durham: Duke UP, 2006.
———. "Ritos y ritmos urbanos en el cine de Emilio Fernández." *Cahiers d'études romanes* 19 (2008). https://etudesromanes.revues.org/1983.
———. "Una escuela en celuloide: El cine de Emilio 'Indio' Fernández o la obsesión por la educación." *Historia Mexicana* 48, no. 2 (1998): 437–70.
U.S. National Library of Medicine. "Quinine." U.S. National Library of Medicine website. Accessed Feb. 22, 2018. https://www.ncbi.nlm.nih.gov/pubmedhealth/PMHT0011919/?report=details.
Ugalde Gómez, Nadia. "Diego Rivera's Historical Vision." In *Diego Rivera: The Complete Murals*, ed. Luis-Martín Lozano and Juan Rafael Coronel Rivera, 436–42. Hong Kong: Taschen, 2008.
Urías Horcasitas, Beatriz. "Degeneracionismo e higiene mental en el México posrevolucionario (1920–1940)." *FRENIA* 4, no. 2 (2004): 37–67.
Urrero, Guzmán. "El muralismo mexicano." *Revista Atticus* 15 (2011): 20–22.
Urzaiz, Eduardo. *Eugenia: Esbozo novelesco de costumbres futuras*. Mexico City: Premiá Editora de Libros, 1919.
Vargas, Luis Miguel. *Nostalgia: Ensayos sobre la novela en el Valle de Toluca, 1950–2000*. Toluca: Instituto Mexiquense de Cultura, 2006.
Vasconcelos, José. "Bergson en México." *Filosofía y letras* 2 (1941): 239–53.
———. *Breve historia de México*. Mexico City: Compañía Editorial Continental, 1978. First published 1956. https://archive.org/details/brevehistoriadem0000660mbp.
———. *The Cosmic Race: A Bilingual Edition*. Trans. Dider T. Jaén. Baltimore: Johns Hopkins UP, 1979.
———. *El monismo estético*. Mexico City: Tip Murguía, 1918.
———. *Indología: Una interpretación de la cultura ibero-americana*. Barcelona: Agencia Mundial de Librería, 1926.
———. "La B-H." In *El pensamiento de la reacción mexicana: Historia documental 1810–1962*, ed. Gaston García Cantú, 968–71. Mexico City: Empresas editoriales, 1965. First published 1957.
———. *La raza cósmica*. 5th ed. Mexico City: Ediciones Porrúa, 2010.
———. *Prometeo vencedor. Monismo estético*. Madrid: Editorial América, [1916?].
———. *¿Qué es el comunismo?* Mexico City: Ediciones Botas, 1936.
———. "The Race Problem in Latin America." In *José Vasconcelos: The Prophet of Race*, ed. Ilán Stavans, 91–111. New Brunswick, NJ: Rutgers UP, 2011.

Vaughan, Mary K., and Stephen E. Lewis. Introduction to *The Eagle and the Virgin*, ed. Vaughan and Lewis, 1–20.
Vaughan, Mary K., and Stephen E. Lewis, eds. *The Eagle and the Virgin: Nation and Cultural Revolution in Mexico, 1920–1940*. Durham: Duke UP, 2006.
Vaughn, Bobby. "Afro-Mexico: Blacks, Indígenas, Politics, and the Greater Diaspora." In *Neither Enemies nor Friends: Latinos, Blacks, Afro-Latinos*, ed. Anani Dzidzienyo and Suzanne Oboler, 117–36. New York: Palgrave Macmillan, 2005.
Velázquez, Marco, and Mary K. Vaughan. "*Mestizaje* and Musical Nationalism in México." In *The Eagle and the Virgin*, ed. Vaughan and Lewis, 95–118.
Villa Gómez, Adrián. "La biología en el muralismo de Diego Rivera." *Ciencias* 45 (1997): 24–30.
Villarreal, Héctor. "La cinematografía como industria de identidades." *Revista Digital Universitaria* 7, no. 9 (2006): 2–9.
———. "Simulacro, catarsis y espectáculo mediático en la lucha libre." *Razón y Palabra* 69 (2009). http://www.razonypalabra.org.mx/SIMULACRO%20CATARSIS%20Y%20 ESPECTACULO%20MEDIATICO%20EN%20LA%20LUCHA%20LIBRE.pdf.
Villegas, Abelardo. *Autognosis: El pensamiento mexicano en el siglo XX*. Mexico City: Instituto Panamericano de Geografía e Historia, 1985.
———. *La filosofía de lo mexicano*. Mexico City: FCE, 1960.
Villoro, Luis. *Los grandes momentos del indigenismo en México*. Mexico City: La Casa Chata, 1979.
Vizcaíno, Fernando. "Repensando el nacionalismo en Vasconcelos." *Argumentos* 26, no. 72 (2013): 193–216.
Volpi, Jorge. *La imaginación y el poder: Una historia intelectual de 1968*. Mexico City: Biblioteca Era, 1998.
Weil, Simone. *Gravity and Grace*. Trans. Arthur Wills. London: Routledge, 1999.
Wiggam, Albert E. *The Fruit of the Family Tree*. Indianapolis: Bobbs-Merrill, 1924.
Williams, Gareth. *The Mexican Exception: Sovereignty, Police, and Democracy*. New York: Palgrave Macmillan, 2011.
Wilt, David. "El Santo: The Case of a Mexican Multimedia Hero." In *Film and Comic Books*, ed. Ian Gordon, Mark Jancovich, and Matthew P. McAllister, 199–220. Jackson: UP of Mississippi, 2007.
Wolfe, Bertram D. *Diego Rivera: His Life and Times*. New York: Alfred A Knopf, 1939.
———. *The Fabulous Life of Diego Rivera*. New York: Stein and Day, 1963.
Wood, Duncan. "Mexico's Democratic Challenges." *Washington Quarterly* 35, no. 4 (2012): 93–104.
Yáñez, Viviana. "Historia de México en los murales de Diego Rivera del Palacio Nacional." *Universidad Nacional de Quilmes Fundación de Becas*, ed. Margarita Pierini, 90–110. Quilmes, Argentina: Universidad Nacional de Quilmes, 2006. Accessed Feb. 22, 2018. http://www.lab.unq.edu.ar/advf/documentos/4fe9cb6157891.pdf#page=90.
Zaramella, Enea. "Estridentismo and *Sonido Trece*: The Avant Garde in Post-revolutionary Mexico." *International Yearbook of Futurism Studies* 7 (2017): 3–28.
Zea, Leopoldo. *El positivismo en México*. Mexico City: FCE, 1943.

———. *Precursores del pensamiento latinoamericano contemporáneo*. Mexico City: SEP/Setentas, 1971.

———. "Vasconcelos y la utopía de *La raza cósmica*." *Cuadernos Americanos* 37, no. 1 (1993): 23–36.

Zolov, Eric. *Refried Elvis: The Rise of the Mexican Counterculture*. Berkeley: University of California Press, 1999.

Zum Felde, Alberto. *Índice crítico de la literatura hispanoamericana: Los ensayistas*. Mexico City: Editorial Guaranía, 1954.

Zylinska, Joanna. "'The Future . . . Is Monstrous': Prosthetics as Ethics." In *The Cyborg Experiments: The Extensions of the Body in the Media Age*, ed. Joanna Zylinska, 214–36. London: Continuum, 2002.

Index

Page locators in *italics* refer to illustrations.

Actual No. 1 manifesto, 63
"Aesthetic" ideal of racial hybridity, 31, 38, 39, 151–52
"Aesthetic monism," 35
Agamben, Giorgio: "bare life " notion, 65, 104, 106; on biopolitics, 21, 70, 71, 104
Agustín, José, 162
Albarrán, Elena Jackson, 88, 123–24
Alonso, Ana María, 7, 194n8
Alonso, Carlos, 2
Amerindian culture: cultural, linguistic, and self-identified indicators of, 192n18; "deindianization," 5; depicted in *Mejicanos en el espacio* (Olvera), 169–70; depicted in *Prometeo vencedor*, 41–42, 46–50; education programs for, 37–38; medicine and social immunization, 103–7, 138–39; postrevolutionary elimination of, 3–4, 178–79; U.S. extermination of, 169, 200n23. See also *Cortés y la Malinche* mural; Mestizaje
Anderson, Benedict, 100, 124
Angel: mechanized angel in *La conquista de México: Cortés triunfante* panel, 74, 75, 76–77; mechanized angel in *La conquista de México: El franciscano* panel, 77, 78, 79
Antebi, Susan, 3, 13
Arreola Martínez, Betsabé, 33
Assumption of social and political power by the masses, 9
Atom, organism, and consciousness, 52
Aured, Carlos, 158, 160
Australian character in *Prometeo vencedor*, 53–56

Aviña, Rafael, 146–47
Aztec beliefs in Rivera's murals, 84

Baas, Jacquelynn, 74
Barber, Sarah L., 181
"Bare life" notion, 65, 104, 106
Barquero, Andrea A., 93
Barraza-Lloréns, Mariana, 181
Barthes, Roland, 153
Bartra, Roger, 9, 19
Basave Benítez, Agustín F., 12–13
"Beingness," 174
Benjamin, Walter, 76–77
Bergson, Henri, 35
Bernal, Rafael, 162, 163
Bhabha, Homi K., 143
Biopolitics: biopolitical division of Amerindian and mestizo identities, 19–22; and *bios*, 21; in *Cortés y la Malinche* mural, 70–71; *Homo Sacer* (Agamben), 104; immunological role of the Catholic Church, 106–7; medicine and social immunization, 103–7, 138–39; in *The Torch* (film), 127–28
Body: attribution of indigenous "backwardness" to conditions of the body, 13; depictions of female bodies fused with technology, 3; female "technified muses," 17–18, 193n4; nationalistic depictions of, 3, 13. See also Cyborg identities
Bonfil Batalla, Guillermo, 5, 9
Borderlands (Anzaldúa), 23
Breton, André, 83
Breve historia de México (Vasconcelos), 53–54
Brooks, Rodney A., 174

Brown, J. Andrew: on cultural contexts and current cyborg theories, 22; depiction of ties between cyborgs and (neo)baroque in Latin America in *Pan-American Unity*, 84; on Latin American cyborg figures, 109, 187–88; on Latin American science fiction, 145; on masks and posthuman identities, 154
"Brown" mestizo, 5, 11
Butler, Judith, 22

Caciquismo, 100, 102, 108, 111–12, 118, 120, 123, 125
Calles, Plutarco Elías, 60
Cañedo, Diego, 163
Carranza, Venustiano, 63, 130
Carro, Nelson, 153
Carter, Warren, 66
Caso, Alfonso, 13
Castellanos, Rosario, 158
Catarsis mural, 72
Catholic Church, the: immunological role of, 106–7; the Virgin of Guadalupe, 107, 108, 110–11, 113, 117, 119, 125–26, 166, 199n12
Chalmers, David, 19
Chaplin, Charlie, 86
Charlot, Jean, 64, 82
Chávez, César, 167
"Chingones" and "chingados," 142, 152
Christ child in *Enamorada* (film), 134–35
Científicos, 4
Cinema: privatization of film industry, 179. See also Mexploitation cinema
Clark, Andy, 19
Coatlicue in *Pan-American Unity* mural, 83–86, 85, 88
Coe, Andrew, 146
Coffey, Mary K., 73
Cortés y la Malinche mural, 68, 69, 70–73, 74
The Cosmic Race essay: "aesthetic" ideal of racial hybridity, 38, 39; as allegory for human history, 41; ancient America as site of Atlantis, 43; assimilation as means to avoid annihilation, 74; depiction of Amerindians as "ugly women," 48, 50; festishization of racial miscegenation, 33–34, 44–45; mestizo identity in Mexico and postrevolutionary mixed-race dogmas, 31–32; and posthumanism, 32–33; race and anti-imperialism, 48–49; role of science in, 36–37; as science fiction, 39
Craven, David, 71, 88

Creation mural, 64
Criollo (white mestizo), 4, 11, 107–8
Cruz Cabrera, Adrián René, 180
Cultural missions, 11
Cyborg identities: biopolitical division of Amerindian and mestizo identities, 19–22; cultural contexts and current cyborg theories, 22; and cultural deconstruction of gender, 24; cultural nationalism as Foucauldian "technologies of the self," 18–19; "cybermestizas," 111, 187; cyborg Virgins in *María Candelaria* (film), 108–17; cyborg Virgins in *Río Escondido* (film), 117–27; deracialization of, 23; *estridentistas* and female "technified muses," 17–18, 193n24; in Latin America and postrevolutionary Mexico, 16–17, 187–88; in *Mejicanos en el espacio* (Olvera), 167–68, 171; in Mexploitation cinema, 151–52; mind as cyborg result of active externalism, 19; in *Pan-American Unity* mural, 84; protohumanism and postrevolutionary cultural production, 25–27; *robo sacer*, 183, 188; state-sanctioned immunization as forced cyborgization, 105, 198n10; technological hybridity and racial identity, 22–25
Cyborgs in Latin America (Brown), 187–88

Dalton, Margarita, 162
Darwinism, 35
Dawn of the Dead (film), 155
Deep Mexico (Lomnitz), 7–8
"Deindianization," 5
Delgado, Miguel M., 154
Del Río, Dolores, in *María Candelaria* (film), 107–9, 111–18, 120–21
Dever, Susan, 119, 127
Díaz, Porfirio, 59–60
Díaz Ordaz, Gustavo, 140, 141, 147
Dichotomy of classical spiritualism and Anglo-Saxon utilitarianism, 50
"Disturbing Muses" (article), 3
Doede, Robert, 25
Downs, Linda Bank, 92

Echeverría, Luis, 141, 146
El Ateneo de la Juventud, 34–35, 60
El ermitaño en el espacio (radio program), 164
El hacha diabólica (film), 153–54
El hombre en llamas frescoes, 73–81, 75, 78, 80; *La conquista de México: Cortés triunfante*

panel, 74, 75, 76–77; *La conquista de México: El caballo mecánico* panel, 79–81, *80*; *La conquista de México: El franciscano* panel, 77, *78*, 79
El Indio. *See* Fernández, Emilio "El Indio"
El réferi cuenta nueve (Cañedo), 163
El Santo films, 141–42, 146–61
Enamorada (film), 103, 128–30, 132–38
Environment, the brain, and consciousness, 19
Esposito, Roberto, 103–4
Estridentista movement, 63–64, 193, 193n24
Estridentistas (female "technified muses"), 17–18, 193n24
Eugenia (Urzaiz), 163
Eugenics: assimilation as patriotic act, 15; depicted in *Cortés y la Malinche* mural, 72–73; futurity of Mexican genetics, 14–15; juxtaposition of the body with technology, 15–16; Lamarckian genetics and modernization programs in Mexico, 13–14, 102–3; technological hybridity and racial identity, 24–25
Exits from the Labyrinth (Lomnitz), 4

Favre, Henry, 61
Félix, María, 100, 107, 119, 136
Fell, Claude, 39
Fernández, Emilio "El Indio": *Enamorada* (film), 128–30, 132–38; immunological role of the Catholic Church, 106–7; *María Candelaria* (film), 101–2, 107, 108–17; medicine and social immunization, 103–7, 138–39; *Río Escondido* (film), 100, 101–2, 107, 108, 117–27, 131–32; *The Torch* (film), 102–3, 127–33
Fernández Delgado, Miguel Ángel, 148
Ferrocarriles Nacionales railroad strike, 141
Figueroa, Gabriel, 100, 113–14, 117, 121, 126, 136, 138, 160
Film. *See* Mexploitation cinema
Flores, Tatiana, 63
Foucault, Michel: "Madness and Society" essay, 168–69; "technologies of the self," 18–19; views of social medicine, 91–92, 96
Franco, Jean, 129, 137
Futurist Manifesto (play), 63

Gallo, Rubén, 4, 12–13, 64
Gamio, Manuel, 13, 14–15, 37
García Blizzard, Mónica del Carmen, 112–13, 114–15
Garcia Canclini, Néstor, 5–6

García-García, José Manuel, 164, 166, 168
García Saldaña, Parménides, 162
Garrido, Luis, 52
"Gelasto-political literature," 164
Gender and performativity, 22
Gender Trouble (Butler), 22–23
Ginway, M. Elizabeth, 145
Giordano, Jaime A., 36
Goddard, Paulette, 86–87, 88, 128, 136
González, Jennifer, 22
González Ambriz, Marco, 145
Graham, Elaine L., 145
Gray, Chris Hables: cyborg theory in *Pan-American Unity* mural, 84; on state-sanctioned immunization as forced cyborgization, 105, 198n10; on technological modifications and cyborg imagery, 16
Greene, Doyle, 149, 150

Hale, Charles, 34, 35
Haraway, Donna: on cyborg identities and biopolitics, 21–22, 24, 168; on cyborg identities and performative traits, 16, 18, 54, 115–16, 184; "Cyborg Manifesto," 84; on cyborg Virgin figure, 109
Hayles, N. Katherine, 171
Health care: and anticlericalism, 106; medicine and social immunization, 103–7, 138–39
Herrera-Sobek, María, 158
Hidden transcript and mimicry, 144
Hill, Matthew J. K., 105
Hispanista form of mestizaje, 11
Historia de la medicina en México: El pueblo en demanda de la salud mural, 92–93, *94–95*, 96–98
Hoeg, Jerry, 36, 111, 187
Homo Sacer (Agamben), 104
Hospicio Cabañas, 73, 74, 81
Huerta, Rodolfo Guzmán (El Santo), 146–47, 151
Huesera, 114
Hybridity. *See* Technological hybridity

Ideological constructs of the "mestizo state," 1–2
"Imagined communities," 100
Immunization: "immunization paradigm," 103–4; medicine and social immunization, 103–7, 121–22, 138–39; state-sanctioned immunization as forced cyborgization, 105, 198n10

Indigeneity: assimilation as patriotic act, 15; defining characteristics of, 13; viewed as primitive and/or a form of disability, 1–3, 177. *See also* Amerindian culture; Mestizaje
Indigenista ("brown" mestizo), 5, 11
Introna, Ana María, 40
Irving, Thomas B., 9

Jaimes, Héctor, 59
Janzen, Rebecca: on biopolitics, 21; on depictions of sickly characters in literary works, 101; on racial miscegenation in *Prometeo vencedor*, 47; on representations of disability as reflections of state power, 3; on submission of weak individuals to state authority, 103; on Vasconcelos's utopian discourses, 38
Juárez, Benito, 124

Kahlo, Frida, 86
Karttunen, Frances, 68
King, Martin Luther, Jr., 167
Kirkup, Gill, 24
Klee, Paul, 77
Kuznesof, Elizabeth Anne, 173

La chingada, 86
La conquista de México: Cortés triunfante panel, 74, 75, 76–77
La conquista de México: El caballo mecánico panel, 79–81, *80*
La conquista de México: El franciscano panel, 77, *78*, 79
La Llorona in *Santo contra la venganza de la Llorona* (film), 157–58
La Malinche in *Cortés y la Malinche* mural, 68, 69, 70–73, 74
Lamarckian genetics and modernization programs in Mexico, 13–14, 102–3, 192n21
Landau, Ellen G., 86
La Onda literary movement, 12, 141–42, 162
Laraway, David, 155
Las momias de Guanajuato (film), 161
Latin American imitation of European cultures and political systems, 142–43
Latin Americanism movement, 38–39
La Vanguardia (newspaper), 63
La venganza de la momia (film), 157, 158–61
Leal, Fernando, 64

Legrás, Horacio, 9, 11
Letrados, 9–10
Levi, Heather, 147, 148, 161
Levitas, Ruth, 36–37
Leys Stepan, Nancy, 102
Lieberman, Evan A., 154, 157
Lomas, David, 84
Lomnitz, Claudio: on biopolitics, 20; *gringos no, gringas sí*, 86–87; on Mexican internal colonialism, 143
"Lo naco" and *lo mexicano*, 148, 161, 192n13
López Aurelio, Irma, 180–82
López Castro, Ramón, 166, 199n5
Lucha libre cinema. *See* Mexploitation cinema
Lund, Joshua, 1–2, 35, 178
Lykke, Nina, 109, 110

"Madness and Society" essay, 168–69
Maestra rural, 100, 108, 123, 127
Malcolm X, 167
Manifesto for an Independent Revolutionary Art (Rivera), 82–83
Maples Arce, Manuel, 64
María Candelaria (film), 101–2, 107, 108–17
Marinetti, Filippo Tommaso, 63
Martians: in *Mejicanos en el espacio* (Olvera), 167–75; in *Santo contra la invasión de los marcianos* (film), 148–50
Marxism as theoretical glue of Big Three muralists, 59
Masks and lucha libre wrestlers, 151, 153–54
Matehuala, San Luis Potosí, 1–2
Mecanización de la tierra mural, 87, 88–90
Mediation of nature by society in *Mecanización de la tierra* mural, 88
Medicine: indigenous health care, 93, 180–82; and "modernization" of primitive bodies, 101–3; and social immunization, 103–7, 138–39
Mejicanos en el espacio (Olvera): overview, 141–46, 161–62, 175–76; depiction of "Centroméjico" state, 163–75; and early twentieth century science fiction, 162–63; and Weil's oppressive structure of society, 164–65
Mendelian genetics, 14, 25, 102, 192n21
Mestizaje: as construct for homogeneity and unity, 7; *criollo* (white mestizo), 4, 11, 107–8; hybridity, eugenics, and postrevolution-

ary ideals of mestizaje, 3–5, 178; ideological "mestizo state" and "myth of modernity," 1–2; *indigenista* (brown mestizo), 11; mestizo imperialism, 8, 142–46; "mestizos in embryo," 105; modernization of indigenous Mexico via pro-mestizo propaganda, 15–16, 89; transformation of Amerindians into mestizos, 5. *See also* Mexploitation cinema

Mestizophilia, 9, 12–13

Mexicanidad: described, 192n13; in El Indio's films, 101, 187; officialist discourses of, 12–14

"Mexican Miracle," 12

México a través de los siglos mural, 118

Mexico's "sanitary dictatorship," 102

Mexploitation cinema: overview, 141–46, 175–76, 187, 199n4; *El hacha diabólica* (film), 153–54; *Las momias de Guanajuato* (film), 161; *La venganza de la momia* (film), 157, 158–61; *Mostrología del cine mexicano* (González Ambriz et al.), 145–46; *Santo contra la hija de Frankenstein* (film), 151–53; *Santo contra la invasión de los marcianos* (film), 148–50, 175; *Santo contra la venganza de la Llorona* (film), 157–58; *Santo contra los zombies* (film), 154, 155–57; *Santo y Blue Demon contra el doctor Frankenstein* (film), 151, 154–55

Mimicry: Latin American imitation of European cultures and political systems, 142–43; and mestizo colonialism, 143–45

Mitchell, Renae L., 116

Monclova, Coahuila, 1–2, 177

Monsters and the "Other," 145–46

Mora, Carl J., 118, 145

Morales, Alfonso, 157

Mostrología del cine mexicano (González Ambriz et al.), 145–46

Mraz, John, 130, 133–34

Mummies in *La venganza de la momia* (film), 157, 158–61

Muralist movement: overview, 28, 59–67, 98–99, 186–87, 196n16; beginnings of, 59–60; the "Big Three," 59; and cultural hybridity, 28, 67, 71, 83; and postrevolutionary government, 66–67; state censorship of muralists, 60–61; state funding for nationalist art, 11, 59–60. *See also* Siqueiros, David Alfaro

Murillo, Gerardo (Dr. Atl), 60

"Myth of modernity," 2

Naciones intelectuales (Sánchez Prado), 177

Náhuatl and "proper" Spanish spelling of México, 163–64

The National Body in Mexican Literature (Janzen), 3

Nationalist "communion" through education, 124

National reconciliation depicted in *Enamorada* (film), 129–30, 133–34

Nervo, Amado, 63

Neumeyer, Alfred, 74

Night of the Living Dead (film), 155

North American Free Trade Agreement (NAFTA), 2, 183

Nudity: in *Cortés y la Malinche* mural, 71; depictions of Amerindians as primitive, 26; nude painting of María Candelaria, 116; Orozco's depictions of, 65–66; Rivera's depictions of, 65–66

"Nueva escuela literaria" (article), 63

Obregón, Álvaro, 31, 130

Olvera, Carlos. See *Mejicanos en el espacio* (Olvera)

Olympic games, 1968, 140, 166

Omi, Michael, 2

Orozco, José Clemente: biopolitics in *La conquista de México: El caballo mecánico* panel, 79–81, *80*; *Catarsis* mural, 72; *Cortés y la Malinche* mural, 68, 69, 70–73, 74; on depictions of Amerindians as primitive, 26; depictions of nudity, 65–66; *El hombre en llamas* frescoes, 73–81, *75*, *78*, *80*; and futurism, 65–66; *La conquista de México: Cortés triunfante* panel, 74, *75*, 76–77; *La conquista de México: El caballo mecánico* panel, 79–81, *80*; *La conquista de México: El franciscano* panel, 77, *78*, 79; muralist movement overview, 28, 59–67, 98–99, 196n16; on murals as painted Bibles, 62–63; nonpolitical nature of work, 67–68; statist policy of official mestizaje, 58

Pacheco López, Eloy, 180

Palou, Pedro Ángel, 4–5

Pan-American Unity mural, 83–88, *85*

Partido Comunista Mexicano, 81–82

Partido Nacional Revolucionario (PNR), 11

Partido Revolucionario Institucional (PRI), 11, 130, 140–41, 145, 147–48, 162

Paz, Octavio: on "chingones" and "chingados," 142; on loss of prestige of official discourses after Tlatelolco massacre, 12; on relevance of Vasconcelos within Mexico, 32; on Russian futurists and the estridentistas, 64; on Vasconcelos's traditionalism, 36
Peña Nieto, Enrique, 141
Perdiguero-Gil, Enrique, 131
Physical sciences as aesthetic tool, 51–52
Pierce, Gretchen, 106
Pitol, Sergio, 83
Plaza de las Tres Culturas, 140
Podalsky, Laura, 116
Polcari, Stephen, 67
Poniatowska, Elena, 140
Positivist politics, 34, 35
Posthumanism: *The Cosmic Race* essay, 32–33; defining characteristics of, 25; in *Mejicanos en el espacio* (Olvera), 171–72; in Mexploitation cinema, 151–52; and postrevolutionary Mexican society, 17–18, 183–84, 187; in *Prometeo vencedor* (play), 39–46
Postrevolutionary landscapes in *Mecanización de la tierra* mural, 88
Postrevolutionary schools as secular churches, 123–24
Potter, Sara Anne, 64, 109, 193n24
Pratt, Dale, 26, 157–58
Price, Brian L., 53–54
Prometeo vencedor (play): domesticated outdoor space in, 45; female sexuality in, 45–50; infeasibility of staging, 41; mestizo identity as necessary component of progress and modernity, 32; as philosophical work, 40; posthumanism in, 39–46; role of technology in Vasconcelian utopia, 50–56
"Proper" Spanish spelling of México, 163–64
Protohumanism, 25–27, 157–58
Public transcript and mimicry, 143
Puig Casauranc, José Manuel, 60, 103–4

Quijano, Aníbal, 9

Race constructs in Mexico: body's central role in economic and societal privileges, 3; and contemporary theories of hybridity in Latin America, 5–7; creation of people rather than recognition of existing people, 9; eugenics and postrevolutionary ideals of mestizaje, 3–5; hybridity and modernity in Latin America, 5–7; ideological "mestizo state" and "myth of modernity," 1–2; indigeneity as a form of disability, 3; "internal colonialism" and mestizophilia, 7–8; key role of technology in, 29–30; racial formation theory, 2. *See also* Technological hybridity
Rama, Ángel, 9
Ramos, Samuel, 15–16, 89
Revueltas, Fermín, 64
Río Escondido (film), 100, 101–2, 107, 108, 117–27, 131–32
Rivera, Diego: *Creation* mural, 64; depictions of nudity, 65–66; engagement with local communities, 82; and futurism, 64, 65–66; *Historia de la medicina en México: El pueblo en demanda de la salud* mural, 92–93, 94–95, 96–98; *Manifesto for an Independent Revolutionary Art* (Rivera), 82–83; *Mecanización de la tierra* mural, 87, 88–90; *México a través de los siglos* mural, 118; muralist movement overview, 28, 59–67, 98–99; *Pan-American Unity* mural, 83–88, 85; statist policy of official mestizaje, 58; as *tlacuilo*, 63; use of cactus juice to dissolve paint pigments, 61–62; *Vaccination* mural, 90–92, 91, 97; viewed as Marxist, 81–82, 196n21
Robo sacer, 183, 188
Rodó, José Enrique, 38–39, 50
Rodríguez, José María, 102
Rudos, 148
Ruétalo, Victoria, 146
Ruitenberg, Claudia W., 82

Sainz, Gustavo, 162
Sánchez Prado, Ignacio M.: on Amerindian assimilation, 37; on *The Cosmic Race* as "utopian essay," 38; on Mexican science fiction, 145, 161–62; *Naciones intelectuales* (Sánchez Prado), 177; on race and anti-imperialism, 48, 49; on role of literature in the Mexican Revolution, 10
San Cristobal de las Casas, 183
Sandoval, Chela, 23
Santiago, Silviano, 8
Santo contra la hija de Frankenstein (film), 151–53
Santo contra la invasion de los marcianos (film), 148–50, 175
Santo contra la venganza de la Llorona (film), 157–58
Santo contra los zombies (film), 154, 155–57

Index   235

Santo y Blue Demon contra el doctor Frankenstein (film), 151, 154–55
Scarano, Mónica, 55–56
Schwarz, Roberto, 142–43
Science and the (meta)physical body: overview, 27–28, 57–58; "aesthetic" ideal of racial hybridity, 31; *The Cosmic Race* essay, 31–34, 36–37, 39; Kuhnian organization of observations into paradigms, 50–51, 192n20; role of technology in Vasconcelian utopia, 50–56; science as doctrine of modernity, 90–91. *See also* Vasconcelos, José
Scott, James C., 143–44
Secretariat of Public Education, 31, 32, 35–37, 55, 59, 61, 82, 101, 102, 115, 131–32, 178
Secretariat of Public Health, 102, 131–32
Sexuality: female sexuality in *Prometeo vencedor* (play), 45–50; in *Mejicanos en el espacio* (Olvera), 172–74
Shafer, Alexander P., 172
Sindicato Siqueiros, 67
Siqueiros, David Alfaro, 28, 59–67
Smith, Benjamin T., 106
Spanish flu depicted as community threat, 131
Spectre (film), 179
Spencer, Herbert, 32, 35
Spitta, Silvia, 39
Spivak, Gayatri Chakravorty, 172
State support of Mexploitation cinema, 146
Statist modernization of mestizaje, 4–5, 178
Steinberg, Samuel, 140–41
Sten, María, 40
Su nombre era muerte (Bernal), 163
Swarthout, Kelley R., 15

Tabernero Holgado, Carlos, 131
Talcuilo, 63
Taylor, Analisa, 71
"Technified muse," 109, 193n24
Technological hybridity: "aesthetic" ideal of racial hybridity, 31, 38, 39, 151–52; cultural hybridity and the muralist movement, 28, 67, 71, 83; cyborg Virgins in *María Candelaria* (film), 108–17; cyborg Virgins in *Río Escondido* (film), 117–27; described, 191n8; in El Indio's films, 100; in *Historia de la medicina en México: El pueblo en demanda de la salud* mural, 92–93, 94–95, 96–98; and indigenous health care, 180–82; lack of as defining element of indigenous "primitivity," 13–14; in *Mecanización de la tierra* mural, 87, 88–90; mestizo caciques in El Indio's films, 111–12; and modernization, 12–14; monsters and the "Other," 145–46; in *Pan-American Unity* mural, 83–86, 85; and racial identity in modern Mexico, 22–25, 177–80, 188–90; technological and racial hybridity, 185; technological, racial, and cultural hybridity and modernization, 6; "technologies of the self," 18–19; in *Vaccination* mural, 90–92, 91. *See also* Cyborg identities
Technology: industrialization and technological advancement programs in Mexico, Russia, and Italy, 63; positive and negative uses of, 92; preoccupation with as uniting factor for diverse thinkers, 12–13; role of technology in Vasconcelian utopia, 50–56; spread of as symptom of decadent society, 4; technophilia and fascism in *El hombre en llamas*, 73
Técnicos, 148
Tenorio Vasconcelos, Germán, 180
"Textual revolution": lack of technological hybridity as defining element of indigenous "primitivity," 13–14; letrados and Amerindian assimilation, 9–10; officialist artists and diverse perceptions of mexicanidad, 10–11; racialized understandings of modernity, 11–12; technological hybridity and modernization, 12–14
Tibol, Raquel, 76
Tierney, Dolores: on Dolores del Río in *Maria Candelaria*, 107; on *Enamorada* (film), 129, 137–38; on mexicanidad in El Indio's films, 101, 187; on nude painting of María Candelaria, 116; on state support of El Indio's films, 146
Tlatelolco massacre, 12, 140–41
Toledo-Pereyra, Luis H., 90–91
The Torch (film), 102–3, 127–33
Townsend, Sarah J., 41, 45
Transhumanism, 25
Trujillo Muñoz, Gabriel, 162

Universidad Autónoma de Chapingo, 88
Urzaiz, Eduardo, 162–63
U.S. civil rights movement, 167

Vaccination mural, 90–92, 91, 97
Vasconcelos, José: "aesthetic" ideal of racial hybridity, 31, 38, 151–52; "aesthetic monism," 35; antipositivism battles, 34–36; El Ateneo de

Vasconcelos, José—*continued*
la Juventud, 34–35; funding for nationalist art, 11; muralist movement, 59–60; and postrevolutionary nationalism, 57–58; protohuman discourse and critique of Anglo-Saxon society, 26, 194n10; role of technology in Vasconcelian utopia, 50–56; Secretariat of Public Education, 31, 32, 35–37, 55, 59, 61; and theories of cyborg identity, 23. *See also The Cosmic Race* essay; *Prometeo vencedor* (play)
Villegas, Abelardo, 34
Virgin of Guadalupe, 107, 108, 110–11, 113, 117, 119, 125–26, 166, 199n12

Weil, Simone, 164–65
Williams, Gareth, 20, 141

Winant, Howard, 2
Women: depicted in *Catarsis* mural, 72; *estridentistas* (female "technified muses"), 17–18, 193n24; medicine and "modernization" of primitive bodies in El Indio's films, 101–2; "ugly women" in *Prometeo vencedor*, 40, 48, 49, 52, 54–55. *See also Cortés y la Malinche* mural

Zapatismo, 130–31
Zea, Leopoldo, 34
Zoê, 21, 120, 135
Zombies in *Santo contra los zombies* (film) and *Santo y Blue Demon contra el doctor Frankenstein* (film), 154–57
Zum Felde, Alberto, 36, 194n7
Zylinska, Joanna, 171

DAVID S. DALTON is associate professor of Spanish at the University of North Carolina at Charlotte.

Reframing Media, Technology, and Culture in Latin/o America

EDITED BY HÉCTOR FERNÁNDEZ L'HOESTE AND JUAN CARLOS RODRÍGUEZ

Reframing Media, Technology, and Culture in Latin/o America explores how Latin American and Latino audiovisual (film, television, digital), musical (radio, recordings, live performances, dancing), and graphic (comics, photography, advertising) cultural practices reframe and reconfigure social, economic, and political discourses at a local, national, and global level. In addition, it looks at how information networks reshape public and private policies, and the enactment of new identities in civil society. The series also covers how different technologies have allowed and continue to allow for the construction of new ethnic spaces. It not only contemplates the interaction between new and old technologies but also how the development of brand-new technologies redefines cultural production.

Telling Migrant Stories: Latin American Diaspora in Documentary Film, edited by Esteban E. Loustaunau and Lauren E. Shaw (2018; paperback edition, 2021)

Mestizo Modernity: Race, Technology, and the Body in Postrevolutionary Mexico, by David S. Dalton (2018; first paperback edition, 2021)

The Insubordination of Photography: Documentary Practices under Chile's Dictatorship, by Ángeles Donoso Macaya (2020)

Digital Humanities in Latin America, edited by Héctor Fernández L'Hoeste and Juan Carlos Rodríguez (2020)

Pablo Escobar and Colombian Narcoculture, by Aldona Bialowas Pobutsky (2020)

The New Brazilian Mediascape: Television Production in the Digital Streaming Age, by Eli Lee Carter (2020)

Univision, Telemundo, and the Rise of Spanish-Language Television in the United States, by Craig Allen (2020)

Cuba's Digital Revolution: Citizen Innovation and State Policy, edited by Ted A. Henken and Sara Garcia Santamaria (2021)

Afro-Latinx Digital Connections, edited by Eduard Arriaga and Andrés Villar (2021)

The Lost Cinema of Mexico: From Lucha Libre to Cine Familiar and Other Churros, edited by Olivia Cosentino and Brian Price (2022)

Neo-Authoritarian Masculinity in Brazilian Crime Film, by Jeremy Lehnen (2022)

www.ingramcontent.com/pod-product-compliance
Lightning Source LLC
Chambersburg PA
CBHW020228170426
43201CB00007B/354